EMC KEYBOARDING

AND APPLICATIONS

CONSULTANTS

Dr. Sharon Dorner Andelora
Computer Specialist
Woodcliff School
Woodcliff Lake, New Jersey

Jane P. Ansell
Business Computer Teacher
Walt Whitman High School
Huntington Station, New York

Betty L. Boyce
Curriculum Specialist
Business Education Center
California State Polytechnic University
Pomona, California

Faye Hansen
Computer Applications Teacher
Caruso Junior High School
Deerfield, Illinois

Diane P. Hogan
Program Specialist, Business Education
Orange County Public School
Orlando, Florida

Mary Ann Shea
Business Education Instructor
Elementary Keyboarding Coordinator
Amherst-Pelham Regional School District
Amherst, Massachusetts

Robert L. Zbikowski
Business Education Teacher
Oakmont Regional High School
South Ashburnham, Massachusetts

EMC KEYBOARDING

AND APPLICATIONS

by

Jo Ann E. Sherron, Ed.D.

Ronald H. Sherron, Ph.D.

EMC Publishing
Saint Paul, Minnesota 55101

Editor: Eileen Slater

Production Supervisor: Kathleen Oftedahl

Designer: The Nancekivell Group

Illustrator: Lynn Fellman

Cover Photographers: Robert Brenner/PhotoEdit (upper left)

   Rollerblade, Inc. (center)

   David Young-Wolff, PhotoEdit (lower left, upper right)

   Tom McCarthy, PhotoEdit (lower right)

Interior Photographer: Mike Woodside Photography

Special appreciation to editor, Eileen Slater, for her guidance and her assistance in the preparation of this manuscript. Her diligence, patience, and support made the preparation of this project a pleasure. Also, special appreciation to Marsha Hubbard, Katherine Small, and Patricia Johnson, who served as consultants to the authors. Special thanks to family members LeAnn, Andy, Pam, and Sherry for their support during a very hectic and stressful time.

ISBN 0-8219-1011-6

Published by EMC Publishing
875 Montreal Way
St. Paul, Minnesota 55102

Printed in the United States of America
   5 6 7 8 9 10 XXX 99 98

TABLE OF CONTENTS

INTRODUCTION

Computers not only play a major role in business, but many people use computers at home as well.

Purpose of Program

The computer can be one of the most useful tools you will ever have. Computers play important roles in many school classes and most jobs today. The increased use of the computer for writing makes having touch keyboarding skills very important. If you are unable to keyboard effectively, you will find it difficult to enjoy all the benefits of a computer.

This text will help you develop your keyboarding skills using the computer. It also can help you if you are using a typewriter.

Objectives

Upon successfully completing this program, you will be able to:

1. Key straight-copy alphabetic material using proper touch techniques at 30 words a minute for two minutes.
2. Key copy with top-row numbers and selected symbols by touch.
3. Format documents used in personal, business, and professional writing.
4. Use the computer as a writing tool utilizing the steps in the writing process.
5. Acquire computer literacy knowledge through the use of the microcomputer system and the keying of computer literacy terminology.
6. Improve language arts skills through the completion of proofreading, punctuation, word usage, and other grammar activities.
7. Use the ten-key numeric keypad to key numeric copy using correct touch techniques.

Organization

This 90-lesson text, based on a space theme, has five units and an extensive enrichment section. A friendly space helper, UKey2, will help you with your assignments.

Unit One includes 22 lessons that will show you how to key by touch all of the alphabetic keys. Lesson 1 covers the **home keys: a s d f j k l ;**. Each lesson after Lesson 1 introduces two new keys. Every fourth lesson is a review and skill-building lesson to build your keying skill. In this first unit, you also will work on simple composition activities to build a foundation for more advanced composition activities that will follow.

Unit Two has 11 lessons that teach the top-row numbers and symbols. You will still have the opportunity to work on building your speed and accuracy as well as composition skills.

Unit Three, which has 16 lessons, teaches you how to use the word processor that is included with the software. You will learn valuable skills that you can use in preparing reports for other classes. This unit covers making corrections to documents using the editing keys, changing margins and spacing, and making changes to documents containing proofreader's marks. In this unit, you also have a complete review of punctuation. Once you have completed this unit, you will realize how useful a tool your computer is. Schoolwork for other classes will go much quicker when you use the word processor.

Unit Four teaches you how to format personal and business documents. The unit includes reports, correspondence, and tables. The unit also stresses continued straight-copy skill building and using the computer to write a daily journal.

Unit Five covers using the computer for the writing process. You will learn the steps in the writing process to compose documents at the keyboard. Some activities in this unit utilize a team approach to problem solving. Continued work with drills on correct word usage will help to make you a better writer.

Lesson Organization

The following sections are included in the lessons:

1. **Mission Briefing**—When you are on a space journey, you need to know what you will be doing on that mission. This part of the lesson shows you the learning goals.

2. **Countdown—Get Ready for Blast-off**—In a space mission you would be prepared for blast-off. Don't take off on these missions without being ready by following correct keying posture and techniques.

3. **Launch Review**—Before you run a mission, you need to check yourself on all your equipment and warm up your skills. This part of your mission helps you reviews all keys previously learned.

4. Destination—Each new mission takes you to a new target. This section presents the new keys and new skills for the lesson.

5. Landing Practice—When you reach your destination, you will want to become familiar with it. This section of the lesson reviews and reinforces skills learned.

6. Skill Exploration—At your destination, you will want to explore and use your new skills. This portion of the program lets you challenge the computer and run different space races. This exercise will tell you your keying speed.

7. Mission Assessment—At the end of a mission, your keying progress will be measured. Scores are recorded in your teacher's gradebook.

8. *Galaxy Gazette*—Put your keyboarding and word-processing skills to work to develop composition, editing, and grammar skills by working on the *Galaxy Gazette*, an interplanetary newspaper. Start as a Comet Reporter and work your way up to being a Universal Editor-in-Chief. The computer will check articles keyed in *Galaxy Gazette*. Scores are recorded in your teacher's gradebook.

9. Mission Report—This section helps you learn new skills in composition and formatting.

10. Open Screen Word Processor—This portion of the software lets you use the computer to write and key your own documents.

11. Reentry—When your mission is completed, you can follow the proper steps to either quit for the day or to proceed to the next lesson.

Start-Up Procedures—Computers

Look at the photographs on the next pages. If you are using a computer in this class, find the computer that looks most like yours. Study the parts of that computer.

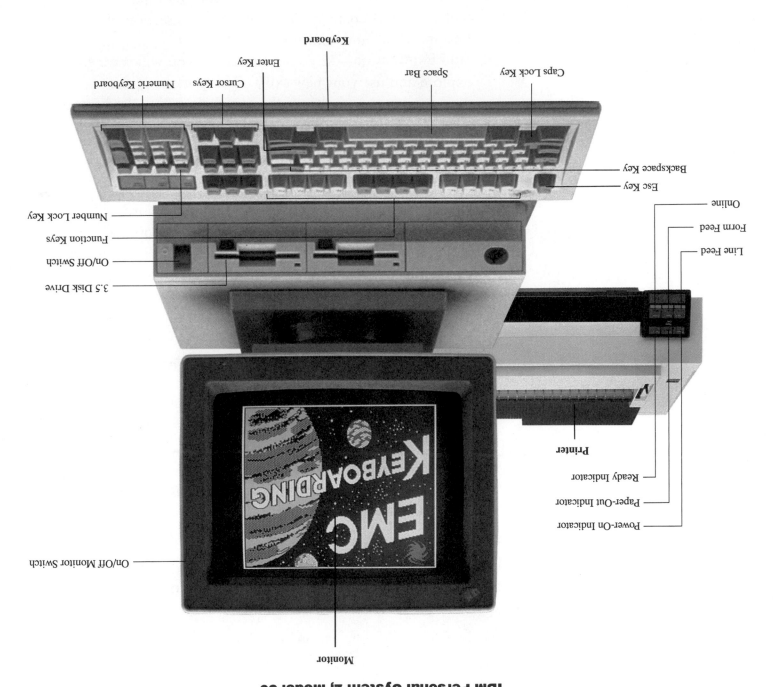

IBM Personal System 2, Model 30

Macintosh LCII

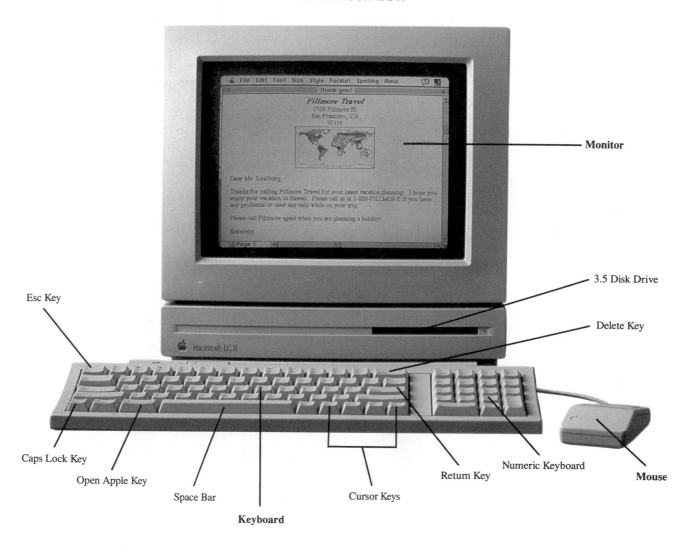

Monitor

3.5 Disk Drive

Delete Key

Esc Key

Caps Lock Key

Open Apple Key

Space Bar

Keyboard

Cursor Keys

Return Key

Numeric Keyboard

Mouse

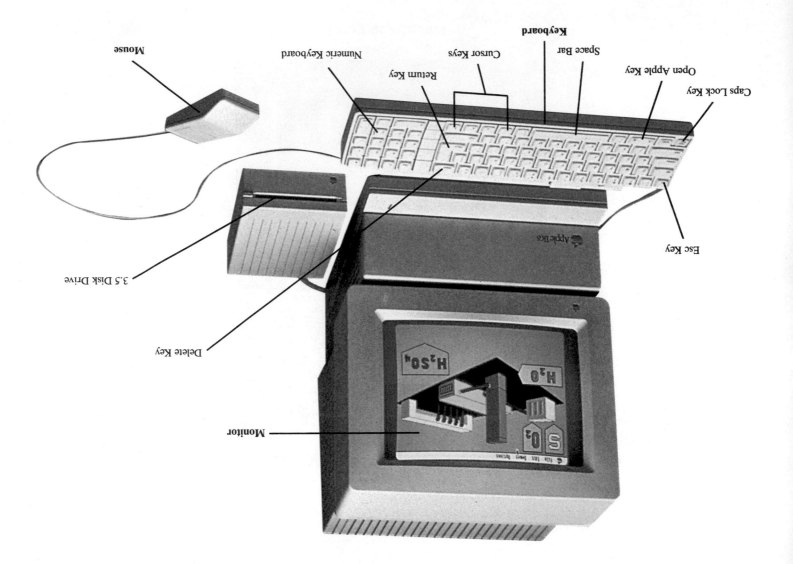

Mouse

Numeric Keyboard

Keyboard

Cursor Keys

Space Bar

Return Key

Open Apple Key

Caps Lock Key

Esc Key

3.5 Disk Drive

Delete Key

Monitor

Apple IIGS

Computer Keyboarding Glossary

active The drive in the computer that currently is in use.

alphanumeric Letters of the alphabet, numbers, and/or symbols. Used to refer to the keyboard, as in *alphanumeric keys*.

applications software A set of instructions that enable the computer to perform a specific function. Word-processing programs are a type of applications software.

arrow A key on some computers that you use to move the cursor back or to erase something you have keyed. Arrows can move the cursor backward, forward, up, or down.

author The person who writes a document.

backspace A key on some computers that moves the cursor back one space to the left and erases keyed characters at the same time.

boot To load all the instructions that your computer needs to start and run a specific program.

bug A mistake or error in a computer program or in the design of a computer.

catalog A command to the computer to list all the fields stored in a software source.

central processing unit The "brain" of the computer. Often referred to by the initials CPU.

character A symbol, letter, or number on the keyboard.

command An order that the computer processes.

cursor A small line or square light that appears on the screen to indicate where the next keystroke will appear. The cursor can be moved around the screen with the arrow keys.

data The information, numbers, letters, and symbols that you input into the computer for processing.

data processing The work the computer does to input material into a specific program.

default The settings the computer uses unless it receives instructions from the user. In word processing, default setting, usually control margins and tab settings.

delete In word processing, a key that tells the computer to remove data that has been input.

disk operating system The software that has the programs and instructions that run a computer. This software is usually referred to by its initials: DOS.

diskette Thin plastic disks that are used to store information to be used in the computer. Storing data to disk is like writing information on paper. The information is kept there for reference. Diskettes come in two sizes: 3½ inches and 5¼ inches.

document The text or information the author creates.

DOS prompt On some computers when the system is booted, a message that appears to tell the user which drive is active. For example, on IBM and compatible computers with a hard drive, when the computer is turned on the DOS prompt will read C:>.

Enter The key that sends a message from the keyboard to the central processing unit. Also, in word processing, after keying a line of text, pressing Enter will return the cursor the beginning of the next line. On some keyboards, Return and Enter have the same functions.

file A set of records stored under a specific name or label.

floppy disks Thin plastic disks that are used to store computer data. Floppy disks are inserted into the computer disk drive. The 5¼-inch disks are usually called floppy disks.

formatting In word processing, putting text into the proper arrangement for a letter, report, reference list, etc.

graphics The artwork, diagrams, pictures, charts, and graphs that are displayed on the screen or by the printer.

hard copy The paper copy of information stored in a computer or a document.

hard disk Permanent storage disk located inside the computer.

hardware All the parts of the computer system except the software programs. Hardware includes the CPU, the keyboard, the monitor, and the printer.

input Adding data into the computer. Can be done from the keyboard or from a disk.

keyboard The input device for word processing. It has the alphanumeric, symbol, and function keys.

load To place data from a file into the active memory of the computer.

memory The area in a computer in which data is stored for processing.

menu A listing in a software that gives you choices of what you can do or parts of the program with which you can work.

microdisks Plastic disks that are used to store computer data. This term refers to the 3½-inch diskette.

modem A device that connects one computer to another at a different location. Works through the phone lines.

monitor The part of the computer that looks like a television screen and shows information as it is entered.

mouse A handheld device used to move the cursor around the screen without using the keyboard.

move In word processing, a key or process that moves data from one spot in a document to another.

network A communications system that links computers so they can share information, software, and equipment. A device called a file server has the master files and programs on a disk.

output The data displayed, printed, or stored as the result of a specified process.

printer The computer hardware that makes hard copy from output.

prompt A cue that appears on the monitor and asks the user to give the computer new instructions.

retrieve To bring a document in word processing back onto the screen.

save In word processing, a function that keeps the document the user has created for later use.

software The programs and instructions that run the computer and allow the user to perform different functions.

space bar A key on the computer that moves the cursor forward one space at a time and leaves a blank space. Used between words. (In some specific software programs, the space bar is used to advance to the next screen.)

store To hold data on a disk, in memory, or on a tape for future use.

word processing Creating, editing, and formatting text.

wordwrap A feature of most word processing programs that moves a word that does not fit within the right margin to the beginning of the next line.

Start-Up Procedures—Software

Care of Diskettes

Software refers to the instructions and commands that make a computer work. A **software program** is a group of instructions that tells the computer how to do a special type of work. For example, your textbook has a software program that will help you learn how to keyboard.

The software for a microcomputer system is contained on magnetic disks. Disks come in two sizes: 3½ inches and 5¼ inches. Disks require proper use and storage. If a disk is damaged, you could lose all the information stored on it. Handle disks carefully. Do not force a disk when inserting it into a disk drive. Insert the disk slowly and gently. When handling disks, follow these precautions:

1. Do not fold or bend.
2. Do not touch the exposed surface.
3. Do not expose to extreme temperature or moisture.
4. Do not insert or remove the disk from the computer when the red "in use" light of a disk drive is on.
5. After use, store 5¼-inch disks in their protective sleeves. The 3½-inch disks are already in a protective cover. Keep disks in a vertical position in a disk holder or file.
6. Do not place disks near any magnetic or electrical fields such as monitors, telephones, or magnets.
7. Do not write on the protective cover of a disk with a pencil or a ballpoint pen. Write on the label provided and then attach it to the disk. You can use a felt-tip pen to write on a disk, but do not press too hard.

Do not bend or fold.

Never touch.

50°F ← 125°F

Insert carefully.

Protect.

Never place near magnetic fields.

Loading the Software

There are several different ways you can use the EMC *Keyboarding and Applications* software. Ask your teacher which of the following systems is like yours and then read the instructions.

DOS Computers

For IBM and IBM-compatible microcomputers to operate with software programs, the Disk Operating System (DOS) must be loaded. This is called "booting" the system. The DOS diskette is provided with the microcomputer and once loaded gives the computer instructions on running other programs.

Single or Dual Disk Computers

1. Insert the DOS disk in disk drive A.
2. Turn on the computer and the monitor.
3. When the date prompt appears, press Enter to accept the date shown or enter the new date.
4. When the time prompt appears, press Enter to accept the time shown or enter the new time.
5. An A> prompt should appear.
6. Remove the DOS disk and insert the *EMC Keyboarding and Applications* disk in drive A. Insert the disk label side up.
7. Key **EMC** and press Enter. This will start the program and the title screen will appear.
8. You will be asked to enter your name. Key in your name and press Enter.
9. The main menu will appear and you can start your lesson.

Press the Enter key with your little finger.

Hard Disk Drive Computers

1. Turn on the computer and monitor.
2. The computer will go through several steps to check that all systems are working. If everything is OK, DOS will be automatically loaded.
3. When the date prompt appears, press Enter to accept the date shown or enter the new date.
4. When the time prompt appears, press Enter to accept the time shown or enter the new time.
5. A C> prompt will appear.
6. Insert the *EMC Keyboarding and Applications* disk in the disk drive. Insert the disk label side up. Key **A:** at the C> prompt and press Enter.
7. You will see an A> prompt. Key **EMC** and press Enter. This starts the program and the title screen will appear.
8. You will be asked to enter your name. Key in your name and press Enter.
9. The main menu will appear and you can start your lesson.

Program Loaded onto Hard Disk Drive Computer

1. Your instructor may have previously loaded the *EMC Keyboarding and Applications* disk onto the hard drive and created a subdirectory (C:\EMC>).
2. If so, turn on the computer and monitor.
3. The computer will go through several steps to check that all of its systems are working. If everything is OK, DOS will be automatically loaded.

4. When the date prompt appears, press Enter to accept the date shown or enter the new date.

5. When the time prompt appears, press Enter to accept the time shown or enter the new time.

6. The C> prompt will appear. Change to the EMC directory by keying cd EMC. At the C:\EMC prompt, key EMC. The program will start and the title screen will appear.

7. You will be asked to enter your name. Key in your name and press Enter.

8. The main menu will appear and you can start your lesson.

Apple IIE and GS

1. Open the disk drive door. If you have more than one disk drive, use drive A. Insert the diskette with the label side up and close the door.

2. Turn on the computer. The diskette will boot automatically. There will be a short delay as the diskette loads your program. The red light on the disk drive will come on. Remember, do not remove the disk while the red light is on.

3. The program will start and the title screen will appear.

4. You will be asked to enter your name. Key in your name and press Return.

5. The main menu will appear and you can start your lesson.

Macintosh

1. Turn on the computer and the monitor.

2. Using the mouse, move the cursor to the keyboarding icon.

3. Double click on the icon by pressing the mouse button twice.

4. The program will start and the title screen will appear.

5. You will be asked to enter your name and then press Return.

6. The main menu will appear and you can start your lesson.

Network Systems

1. Your instructor may have previously loaded the EMC Keyboarding and Applications disk onto a network system.

2. If so, turn on the computer and the monitor.

3. The computer will go through several steps to check that all of its systems are working. If everything is OK, you will see a prompt.

4. Your teacher will have created a directory for this software, so find out how to switch to that directory. Then key EMC. The program will start and the title screen will appear.

5. Key in your name and press Enter.

6. The main menu will appear and you can start your lesson.

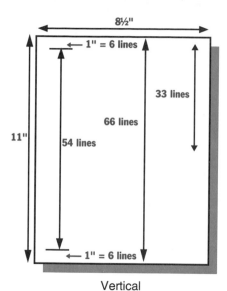

Vertical

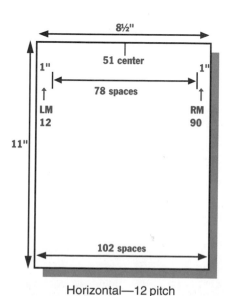

Horizontal—10 pitch

Vertical and Horizontal Spacing

Study the following information. You need to know this information to key documents in this text.

Vertical Spacing Based on Standard Paper Size

Each vertical inch has 6 lines. On 8½ x 11-inch paper there are 66 lines (6 x 11). There are 33 lines on a half sheet.

Most software programs are preset to allow for one-inch top and bottom margins. This leaves 54 lines for text: 2 x 6 = 12 and 66 - 12 = 54.

Horizontal Spacing Based on Standard Paper Size

The horizontal spacing used in a document must match the print wheel used on the printer or typewriter. This is measured in characters per inch and is called **pitch**. Standard sizes are 10 pitch and 12 pitch. Some typewriters use *pica* to refer to 10 pitch and *elite* for 12 pitch. Pitch refers to the number of characters that can be printed in one inch. Thus, 10 pitch means 10 characters can be printed in one inch, and 12 pitch means 12 characters can be printed in one inch. That means 10 pitch type is larger than 12 pitch type.

> 10 pitch = 10 characters per inch
> 12 pitch = 12 characters per inch

`This copy is 10 pitch type—10 spaces to an inch.`

`This copy is 12 pitch type—12 spaces to an inch.`
Study the illustrations.

Compute Margin Settings

Blank space on the left and right side of a document is controlled by the margin settings. Documents usually are keyed with equal left and right margins. Most software programs have preset margins called **default margins**. The defaults margins usually are one inch. You can change these margins in word-processing software to fit the document being keyed. On a typewriter, you also control the margin sets.

To determine the setting for margins, follow these steps:
1. Decide on the desired number of inches for the side margins.
2. **Left Margin:** Multiply the number of inches by the pitch (characters per inch) of your machine to determine the left margin (LM) setting.

Horizontal—12 pitch

For example:

1-inch side margin	10 pitch (1 x 10) = LM 10
1-inch side margin	12 pitch (1 x 12) = LM 12
2-inch side margin	10 pitch (2 x 10) = LM 20
2-inch side margin	12 pitch (2 x 12) = LM 24

3. **Right Margin: Computers**—In most word-processing programs, you set the right margin the way you do the left margin. In the *EMC Keyboarding and Applications Software,* you set margins by character count. In some word-processing software, you set margins by the inch (or fractions of an inch).

Right Margin: Typewriters—To make the right margin equal to the left, determine the right margin (RM) by subtracting the left margin setting from the total spaces across the page.

For example:

1-inch side margins
10 pitch: 85 characters per page - 10 = RM 75

1-inch side margins
12 pitch: 102 characters per page - 12 = RM 90

Reference Section—Typewriters

Study the illustration on the next page to help you know the various parts of a typewriter.

Insert Paper—Electric

1. Align the paper guide with zero on the line-of-writing scale.
2. Turn on the typewriter.
3. Pull the paper bail lever forward. Place the paper against the paper guide behind the platen.
4. Turn the right platen knob or strike the index key until paper is about one inch above the alignment scale.
5. If the paper is not straight, pull the paper release lever forward, straighten the paper, and then push back the paper release.
6. Adjust the paper bail rolls to divide the paper into thirds.

Insert Paper—Electronic

1. Align the paper with zero on the paper guide scale.
2. Turn on the typewriter.
3. Place the paper against the paper guide and insert the paper into the platen.
4. Strike the paper insert key. The paper will be inserted to the preset top margin.
5. If the paper is not straight, pull the paper release lever forward, straighten the paper, and push back the paper release lever.
6. Adjust the paper bail rolls to divide paper into thirds.

IBM Wheelwriter 10 / Series II

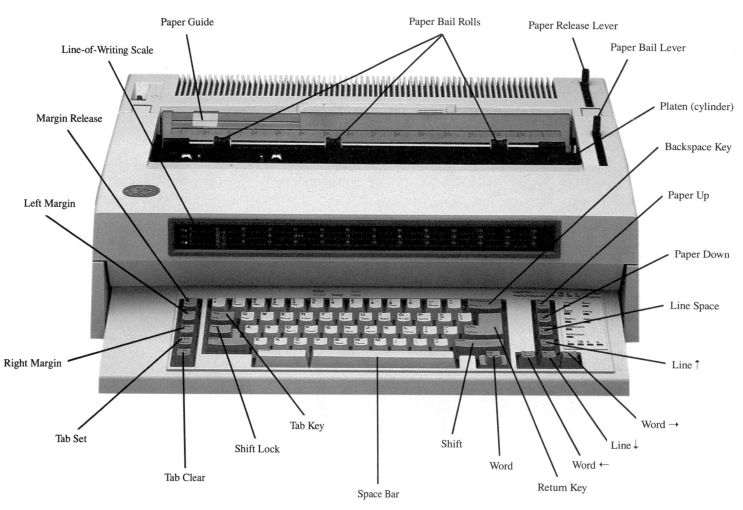

Paper Guide

Paper Bail Rolls

Paper Release Lever

Line-of-Writing Scale

Paper Bail Lever

Margin Release

Platen (cylinder)

Backspace Key

Left Margin

Paper Up

Paper Down

Line Space

Right Margin

Line ↑

Tab Key

Word →

Tab Set

Shift

Line ↓

Shift Lock

Word

Word ←

Tab Clear

Return Key

Space Bar

Credit:
Lexmark International
IBM and Wheelwriter are registered trademarks of International Business Machines Corporation in the United States and/or other countries and used under license.

Set Line Spacing and Select Pitch

Most typewriters are equipped with a line-space select key and at least two type sizes (pitch). If your machine has these features, make the appropriate adjustments.

1. Move the line-space select key to set single- or double-spacing.
2. Move the pitch selector to select the desired pitch. The material in the textbook should be keyed in 10 pitch or 12 pitch type. (Illustrations are shown in 10 pitch type.)

Set Margins

Set the typewriter margins as indicated at the beginning of the lessons. Refer to the margin chart below on how to compute margins. The procedure for setting margins varies with the model of equipment being used. Consult the manufacturer's operating booklet and your instructor for proper procedures.

Margin Chart for Typewriters				
	10 pitch		12 pitch	
	LM	RM	LM	RM
1 inch	10	75	12	90
1¼ inches	15	70	18	84
2 inches	20	65	24	78
2½ inches	25	60	30	72

Set Tabs

Tabs are used to indent paragraphs and to align columns. The tabulator key (tab key) moves the keying point to preset positions called tab stops. Use this procedure to clear and set tab stops:

Clear all present tab stops.

1. Locate the tab clear key.
2. Tab to each tab stop, and strike the tab clear key.
3. Repeat the procedure until all tab stops are cleared.

Set tab stops.

1. Locate the tab set key.
2. Move the carrier to the place you want a tab; strike the tab set key.
3. Repeat the procedure until all tab stops are set.

Tabulate.

1. Locate the tab key.
2. Tap the key lightly using the left little finger.
3. After the carrier has moved to the desired position, return your finger to the home position. Repeat for each tab.

This copy is keyed in
double-spacing.

Microcomputer Keyboarding
Writing on a Computer Can Be Easy and Fun
It's Easy to Compose with a Computer

This copy is keyed in
single-spacing.

Microcomputer Keyboarding
Writing on a Computer Can Be Easy and Fun
It's Easy to Compose with a Computer

Manual Horizontal Centering on Typewriters.

See Lesson 65, for the table discussed here.

   Here's how to compute the horizontal spacing and set tabs for the columns.

1. Clear all present tab stops.
2. Begin by determining the **key line**. The key line is the longest line of text in each column and the number of spaces between columns. For the example in Lesson 65, leave eight spaces between columns. Therefore, the key line for this table is

   Class Representative(8spaces)June Strickland

3. Space to the center of the line (42 for 10 pitch or 51 for 12 pitch).
4. Backspace once for every two spaces required by the key line. Ignore a single leftover character. The longest line in the left column is *Class Representative*. The longest line in the right column is *June Strickland*. Backspace once for every two letters and spaces as follows:
   Cl/as/s space/re/pr/es/en/ta/ti/ve/ju/ne/space s/tr/ic/kl/an/ (ignore d)
5. Continue to backspace once for every two spaces between columns (8 : 2 = 4), so backspace four times for the space between columns. If you backspaced properly, you should be at column 21 in 10 pitch (using 42 for center) or column 30 in 12 pitch (using 51 for center). If you did not backspace properly, try again.
6. This will be the tab setting for the first column. Make a note of it. Do not key anything at this time.
7. Space forward from the first column setting (21 or 30) for each letter or space in *Class Representative* plus the eight spaces between the columns. You should be at column 49 for 10 pitch or column 58 for 12 pitch. If not, try again. This will be the setting for the second column. Make a note of it. Do not key anything at this time.
8. Set a tab at position 21 or 30 for the first column, depending on the pitch, and position 49 or 58 for the second column.
9. The heading will be centered in all capitals on line 26. The table should be double-spaced.
10. To key the body of the table, press tab and key the first item in column one. Press tab and key the item in column two. Press Enter/Return. Go to the next line. Complete the document and compare it with the model. If it is not centered vertically and horizontally, key it again.

Compute Keying Speed on Skill Explorations and Mission Assessments

If you are using EMC software with this text, it will automatically compute your keying speed. If you are using a typewriter, however, you must manually compute your keying speed.

In computing keying speed, every five strokes (including spaces and punctuation marks) is counted as a word. Keying speed is measured in words keyed in one minute, which is abbreviated as **wam**. Each Skill Exploration and Mission Assessment in your lessons will have a word count scale printed under the last line of the drill. Use this word count scale to compute your keying speed.

Example:
Assume you took a one-minute timing on lines 1-3 below. Your speed would be computed as follows:

```
1 a faded elf; ask a sad seal; as it asks

2 ten sad teens; did last tests; fan sits

3 a tan teak desk; send dad a little task
  |   1   |   2   |   3   |   4   |   5   |   6 |   7   |   8   |
```

1. If you keyed line 1 and part of line 2 stopping after the word *teens,* your speed is 11 words a minute (wam).

2. If you keyed the first two lines stopping in line 3 after the word *desk,* your speed is 19 wam.

3. If you completed the drill one time, started over, and got to *tests* in line 2, your keying speed is 38.

To compute the speed for times longer than one minute, divide the total words keyed by the number of minutes in the timing.

Example:
1. If you keyed a total of 24 words in two minutes, your wam would be figured as 24 ÷ 2 = 12 wam.

2. If you keyed a total of 36 words in three minutes, your wam is 12 wam. Can you use the formula to check that figure? Some timings may be for less than one minute. Use this chart to convert your timing speed to wam:

If you keyed for	Multiply
10 seconds	number of words keyed x 6 = wam
15 seconds	number of words keyed x 4 = wam
30 seconds	number of words keyed x 2 = wam

Organize your work station by moving the keyboard to the edge of your computer stand or desk. Adjust the monitor so there is no glare on it. Place your *EMC Keyboarding and Applications* textbook to the side of the computer.

Sit up straight with your back supported by the chair.

Countdown—Organize Your Work Station

Before you begin to keyboard, you should arrange your work station in a manner that allows for efficient skill building. Having your work station properly arranged enables you to key copy accurately and quickly. Therefore, at the beginning of each lesson, you should arrange your working area as follows:

1. Move the keyboard even with the front edge of your desk and center it so that the J key is in the center of your body.
2. If you are using a computer, center the monitor at eye level and adjust it to eliminate glare. Adjust the contrast and brightness controls for ease of viewing.
3. Place your *EMC Keyboarding and Applications* textbook at the side of your computer, so it can be clearly seen and read.
4. Sit up straight, with your back supported by the chair.
5. Adjust the height of the chair so that your feet rest flat on the floor with one slightly in front of the other.
6. Sit the correct distance from the keyboard. To judge the distance, drop your arms straight down by your sides and then place your fingers on the keys. If you are in the correct position, your elbows will be straight down by your sides. You will be one hand span from the keyboard. If you are the correct distance you will be one hand span from the keyboard.

One hand span

Adjust the height of your chair so that your feet are flat on the floor. (Far left)

Adjust the height of the desk and sit the correct distance from the keyboard so that when your fingers rest on the keyboard your arms form an approximate 45 degree angle. (Left)

Assume Correct Finger Position

Proper finger position is essential in preventing keying errors and fatigue. When striking the keys, be sure you:

1. Place your fingers on the keys in a curved, upright position.
2. Slant your forearms at the same angle as the keyboard.
3. Keep your wrists low, *but do not rest them on the keyboard.*
4. Strike the keys with a firm, quick stroke as if they were hot.

Do not push the keys!

When You Have Completed a Mission

You can repeat each mission. If you are using a computer, follow Mission Control's instructions. If you are finished for the day:

1. Select Quit from the Mission Menu.
2. Remove the disk(s) from the computer.
3. Turn off the computer and monitor.

If you are using a typewriter, you have the following choices:

1. Repeat the mission.
2. Go to the next mission.
3. Quit for the day by removing your paper and turning off the power switch.

Good luck to you as you complete your study of EMC *Keyboarding and Applications.* If you continue to use your newly developed skills, you will have a skill that will benefit you for the rest of your life.

Place your fingers on the home keys—
a s d f j k l ; — in a curved position.

Slant your forearms at the same angle
as the keyboard.

Keep your wrists low, but make sure they
are not resting on the keyboard.

UNIT 1

LEARNING THE ALPHABETIC KEYBOARD

Welcome to the study of *EMC Keyboarding and Applications.* You are starting on an exciting journey that will benefit you the rest of your life. Keyboarding skills are essential for any career that you choose and are certainly important for success in school and your personal life.

This text and accompanying software will teach you to operate a keyboard by touch. Once you master touch keyboarding, you will save valuable time in completing school assignments. This new skill also will assist you in your college or work career.

The primary purpose of Unit 1 is to teach you to operate the alphabetic keyboard by touch. When you complete this unit, you will be able to key paragraph copy using all of the alphabet and punctuation keys at a minimum rate of 16 words a minute. With practice, you may, of course, achieve a much higher rate.

In this unit, you will complete exercises that will enable you to use the keyboard as a writing tool. By completing these simple composition activities, you will begin to build a foundation for writing at the keyboard.

You will be guided through your program by our space helper UKey2. UKey2 will provide you with valuable assistance in learning to keyboard. Follow UKey2's advice and you will experience great success. Have fun!

LESSON

mission
BRIEFING

In this mission, you will:
1. Demonstrate proper keyboarding position.
2. Key copy using the home keys, Enter/Return key, and space bar.

Computers—use default margins for all drills unless otherwise indicated.
Typewriters—use these margins unless otherwise indicated: 10 Pitch 2", 12 pitch 2½".
Single-spacing unless otherwise indicated.

Countdown—Get Ready for Blast-off

Sit up straight.

Keep feet flat on the floor.

Sit the correct distance from the keyboard.

Place fingers on the home keys in curved position.

Slant forearms at the same angle as the keyboard.

Keep wrists low, but not resting on the keyboard.

Destination—The Home Keys

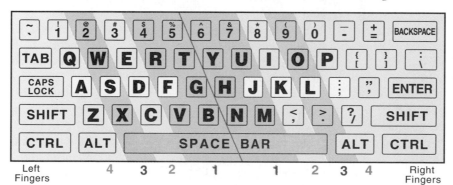

Here are the **home keys—A S D F J K L Semicolon (;)**. Place your fingers on them lightly. With your fingers in proper position, practice striking the keys several times. If you are using a computer, you can look at the screen while you key the exercise. If you prefer, you can keep your eyes on your text.

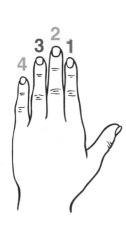

This is your first mission, good luck!

```
1  asdfjkl;asdfjkl;asdfjkl;asdfjkl;asdfjkl;

2  asdfjkl;asdfjkl;asdfjkl;asdfjkl;asdfjkl;
```

Your new destination is the
Enter/Return key. Mastery
of this key is essential for
all future missions.

Destination—The Enter/Return Key

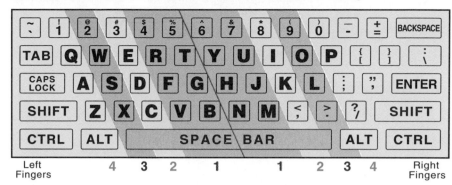

Left
Fingers

Right
Fingers

4   3   2   1   1   2   3   4

When you reach the end of a line, the Enter/Return key is used to return to the beginning of a new line. Key the Enter/Return key with your right little finger.

1. Here is the Enter/Return key.
2. Keep your fingers in the home key position and strike the Enter/Return key with your right little finger.
3. Be sure to keep your other fingers over the home keys so that you don't lose your place. (Keep as many of your right-hand fingers over the home keys as possible. If your fingers are too short and you cannot make the reach to the Enter/Return, be sure to at least keep your J finger in place.)
4. Strike the Enter/Return key quickly and immediately return your little finger to the semicolon key. (The Enter/Return key will be called the Enter key in the remainder of the text.)

Remember, do not rest
your wrists on the
keyboard.

Practice this reach several times. Press semicolon and then Enter.

```
1  ;Enter
2  ;Enter

3  ;Enter
4  ;Enter
```

Key the following lines so that each one begins on a new line. Strike the Enter key quickly at the end of the line and immediately return your little finger to the semicolon.

```
1  asdfjkl;(Enter)
2  asdfjkl;(Enter)
```

Very good, now proceed to
this next task.

Destination—The Space Bar

To leave spaces between letters or words, use the space bar.
1. The space bar is controlled with your right thumb. (If you are left-handed, you may find it easier to use your left thumb.)
2. Strike the space bar with a down-and-in motion of your thumb.
3. Strike the space bar quickly. Do not pause when making the reach to the space bar.
4. Practice keying the following:

Bold	The help wanted ad was titled word processor.	The help wanted ad was titled **word processor.**
Run in	Effective studying will improve your grades.	Effective studying will improve your grades.
Single-space SS	Work hard in school. You SS will be rewarded.	Work hard in school. You will be rewarded.
Double-space DS	Do you enjoy sports? Which one is your favorite? DS	Do you enjoy sports? Which one is your favorite?

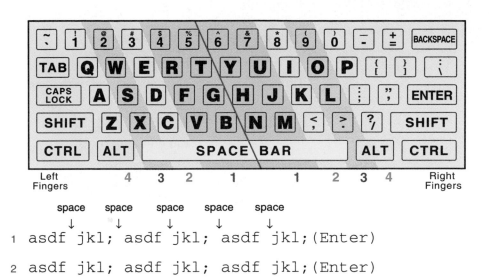

| Left Fingers | | 4 | 3 | 2 | 1 | | 1 | 2 | 3 | 4 | Right Fingers |

space ↓ space ↓ space ↓ space ↓ space ↓

```
1 asdf jkl; asdf jkl; asdf jkl;(Enter)

2 asdf jkl; asdf jkl; asdf jkl;(Enter)
```

Don't forget to assume proper body and finger position.

Landing Practice—The Home Keys, Enter, and Space Bar

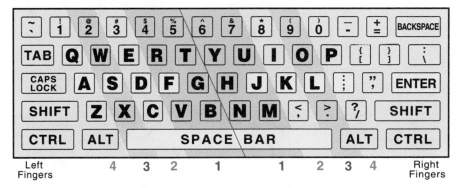

| Left Fingers | | 4 | 3 | 2 | 1 | | 1 | 2 | 3 | 4 | Right Fingers |

Practice the following lines. Strike the space bar between these letter groupings or words. When you see (Enter), strike the Enter key.

Be sure to use the little finger on Enter.

```
1 aa ss dd ff jj kk ll ;; asdf jkl; ajkl;(Enter)
2 aa ss dd ff jj kk ll ;; asdf jkl; ajkl;(Enter)
```

Space quickly.

```
3 aa ;; ss ll dd kk ff jj a;sl dkfj sl a;(Enter)
4 aa ;; ss ll dd kk ff jj a;sl dkfj sl a;(Enter)

5 fj dk sl a; fj dk sl a; a d ad sad fads(Enter)
6 fj dk sl a; fj dk sl a; a d ad sad fads(Enter)

7 a s as ads lad lads ask a l all f falls(Enter)
8 a s as ads lad lads ask a l all f falls(Enter)
```

Follow the proper reentry procedures you learned in the Introduction.

Mercury is the closest planet to the Sun. Temperatures range up to 806°F, hot enough to make a steel rod glow red in just minutes.

Proofreader's Marks

	Example	Revised Copy
Transpose	The outside layer of the Earth is called the crust. It is made of iron ore, gas, oil, water and other materials.	The outside layer of the Earth is called the crust. It is made of iron ore, oil, gas water, and other materials.
Move as shown	The middle layer, or mantle, is thicker than the crust.	The mantle, or middle layer, is thicker than the crust.
Insert	In the center is the core. of the Earth	In the center of the Earth is the core.
Close up space	Keyboar ding is fun.	Keyboarding is fun.
Add space	Good writing skills are necessary.	Good writing skills are necessary.
Delete	Word processors make writing very easy.	Word processors make writing easy.
Spell out	The U.S. is a wonderful place to live.	The United States is a wonderful place to live.
Lowercase	Writing on the Computer is fun.	Writing on the computer is fun.
Uppercase	come to the game after school.	Come to the game after school.
Move left	Playing sports is great fun.	Playing sports is great fun.
Move right	Homework is easier if you have a system.	Homework is easier if you have a system.
Let stand	What kind of new computer did you buy?	What kind of new computer did you buy?
New paragraph	Proofreader's marks will help you edit copy.	Proofreader's marks will help you edit copy.
Underline	Have you read <u>Tom Sawyer</u>?	Have you read <u>Tom Sawyer</u>?

LESSON

 **2** **Learning the E and N Keys**

Computers—use default margins for all drills unless otherwise indicated.
Typewriters—use these margins unless otherwise indicated: 10 Pitch 2", 12 pitch 2½".
Single-spacing unless otherwise indicated.

Countdown—Get Ready for Blast-off

 Sit up straight.

 Keep feet flat on the floor.

 Sit the correct distance from the keyboard.

 Place fingers on the home keys in curved position.

 Slant forearms at the same angle as the keyboard.

 Keep wrists low, but not resting on the keyboard.

Stand by for a new mission. In this lesson you will:
1. Review home keys, Enter, and space bar.
2. Key copy using the E and N keys.
3. Improve keyboarding techniques.
4. Improve keyboarding skill.

Let's review the previous mission before we blast off on a new one.

Launch Review

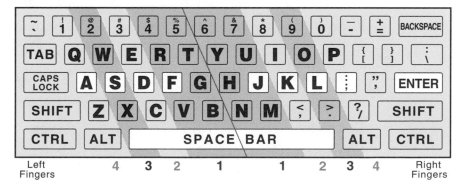

Strike the keys quickly as if they were hot.

Key the following lines.

```
1 asdf jkl; aa ;; ss ll dd kk ff jj fd ak
2 asdf jkl; aa ;; ss ll dd kk ff jj fd ak

3 lads all fall; all dads fall; ask a dad
4 lads all fall; all dads fall; ask a dad
```

APPENDIX

U.S. Post Office Two-Letter Abbreviations for States and Territories

Alabama	AL	Montana	MT
Alaska	AK	Nebraska	NE
Arizona	AZ	Nevada	NV
Arkansas	AR	New Hampshire	NH
California	CA	New Jersey	NJ
Colorado	CO	New Mexico	NM
Connecticut	CT	New York	NY
Delaware	DE	North Carolina	NC
Dist. of Columbia	DC	North Dakota	ND
Florida	FL	Ohio	OH
Georgia	GA	Oklahoma	OK
Guam	GU	Oregon	OR
Hawaii	HI	Pennsylvania	PA
Idaho	ID	Puerto Rico	PR
Illinois	IL	Rhode Island	RI
Indiana	IN	South Carolina	SC
Iowa	IA	South Dakota	SD
Kansas	KS	Tennessee	TN
Kentucky	KY	Texas	TX
Louisiana	LA	Utah	UT
Maine	ME	Vermont	VT
Maryland	MD	Virginia	VA
Massachusetts	MA	Virgin Islands	VI
Michigan	MI	Washington	WA
Minnesota	MN	West Virginia	WV
Mississippi	MS	Wisconsin	WI
Missouri	MO	Wyoming	WY

Silently say each key as
you strike it.

Key the following lines.

```
5 add fad lads; all lads; add a fad; lass
6 add fad lads; all lads; add a fad; lass

7 a lass adds; ask a lad; a sad lad falls
8 a lass adds; ask a lad; a sad lad falls
```

Destination—The E Key

To begin this destination,
you must learn the E key.

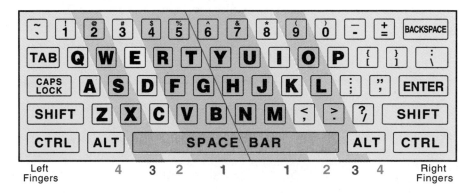

Left
Fingers   4   3   2   1   1   2   3   4   Right
Fingers

Here is the E key. It is keyed with your D finger. Place your fingers in a
curved, upright position on the home keys. Look at your D finger and
practice the reach to E. Keep your other fingers resting lightly on the
home keys.

```
ded ded ded ded ded ded ded ded ded ded
```

Now look away from the keyboard and practice. Look at your text, not
the keyboard.

```
ded ded ded ded ded ded ded ded ded ded
```

Key the following lines.

```
1 ded ded dede deed deeds dell dells dead
2 ded ded dede deed deeds dell dells dead

3 ded deal dele desk desks deaf deal deja
4 ded deal dele desk desks deaf deal deja

5 see leaf seed feed sale; sea seals flee
6 see leaf seed feed sale; sea seals flee
```

Strike the Enter key with
your little finger.

```
7 a deed; a fake; a sled; a jade; as ease
8 a deed; a fake; a sled; a jade; as ease
```

3

A chameleon is a type of lizard that lives in several countries. The chameleon has bulging eyes that operate separately. One eye may be looking at an insect while the other is following a blowing leaf. Chameleons are one of the few lizards that have grasping tails. Most lizards cling to branches with their sharp claws.

The chameleon may be slow moving on its feet but can catch an insect using its tongue like a streak of lightening. Its tongue is sticky and is about as long as the entire body of the lizard. It is controlled by powerful throat muscles. As the tongue swiftly shoots out, the sticky tip swells out and traps the prey.

Chameleons have the unusual ability of changing their skin color to blend in with their surroundings. Research has established that temperature, lighting, and the lizard's feelings may control these changes.

| 1 | 2 | 3 | 4 | 5 | 6 | 7 | 8 |

The next destination is to the N key.

Destination—The N Key

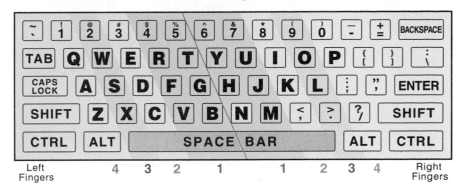

Left Fingers   4 3 2 1   1 2 3 4   Right Fingers

Here is the N key. It is keyed with your J finger. Place your fingers in a curved, upright position on the home keys. Look at your J finger and practice the reach to N. Keep your other fingers resting lightly on the home keys.

Strike the keys quickly as if they were hot.

jnj jnj jnj jnj jnj jnj jnj jnj jnj jnj

Now look away from the keyboard and practice. Look at your text, not the keyboard.

jnj jnj jnj jnj jnj jnj jnj jnj jnj jnj

Key the following lines silently saying each key as you strike it.

1 send lend a sad land dead end lake sand
2 send lend a sad land dead end lake sand

3 lend and send lean fans; land end deals
4 lend and send lean fans; land end deals

Remember, little finger on Enter at the end of each line.

5 faded jeans; sand and land; a fake jade
6 faded jeans; sand and land; a fake jade

7 flake lane sank a fan; defend sane fake
8 flake lane sank a fan; defend sane fake

REENTRY BRIEFING

You have completed this mission! Great job! If you are using a computer, follow Mission Control's instructions. You can repeat the lesson if you wish. If you are finished for the day:
1. Select quit from the Mission Menu.
2. Remove the disks from the computer.
3. Turn off the computer and monitor.

If you are using a typewriter, you have the following choices:
1. Repeat the mission.
2. Go to the next mission.
3. Quit for the day by removing your paper and turning off the power switch.

2

Cooking can be great fun. Good cooking today means using healthy, low calorie, and low cholesterol food. Start by selecting quality food and follow up by using the using the stove and oven. Get rid of your microwave and bring out your pots and pans.

You can use a steamer, either iron or bamboo, to cook vegetables or seafood. Bring water to a boil on the stove top and place the steamer over it. Steaming vegetqables will keep them crisp and colorful. You also can cook vegetables over a fire, such as on the grill. This is a great way to prepare corn on the cob. Wash the corn, place it on aluminum foil, sprinkle the corn with water, and close the foil so the corn can steam.

Meats should have the skin removed and fat cut off to reduce calorie and cholesterol intake. Oven baking, broiling, or grilling are healthy cooking choices. Enhance the flavor of your food by using seasonings. Garlic, onions, peppers, and herbs are great sources of flavor.

| 1 | 2 | 3 | 4 | 5 | 6 | 7 | 8 |

LESSON

 **Learning the T and I Keys**

Computers—use default margins for all drills unless otherwise indicated.
Typewriters—use these margins unless otherwise indicated: 10 Pitch 2", 12 pitch 2½".
Single-spacing unless otherwise indicated.

Countdown—Get Ready for Blast-off

Sit up straight.

Keep feet flat on the floor.

Sit the correct distance from the keyboard.

Place fingers on the home keys in curved position.

Slant forearms at the same angle as the keyboard.

Keep wrists low, but not resting on the keyboard.

BRIEFING

During this mission, you will learn:
1. Review home keys, Enter, space bar, E and N keys.
2. Key copy using the T and I keys.
3. Improve keyboarding techniques.
4. Improve keyboarding skill.

Launch Review

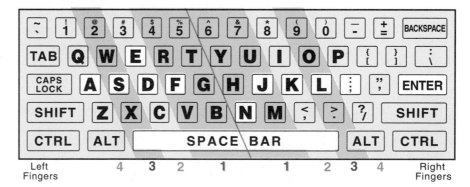

Left Fingers   4   3   2   1   1   2   3   4   Right Fingers

Remember, little finger on the Enter key.

As you review the previous missions, you will make better progress if you silently say each key as you strike it. Key each of these lines twice.

```
1  asdf jkl; aaa ;;; sss lll ddd kkk ff ff
2  asdf jkl; aaa ;;; sss lll ddd kkk ff ff

3  asdf jkl; jjj nnn jjj ddd eee ddd le nd
4  asdf jkl; jjj nnn jjj ddd eee ddd le nd
```

Extra Timed Writings

If you would like additional practice in speed building, key the following exercises using the timed screen of the word processor.

1

1 The Bahamas consist of 700 islands

2 scattered over 100,000 square miles.

3 The closest point to the United States

4 is only 55 miles from the coast of Palm

5 Beach, Florida. The islands offer

6 white sandy beaches, clear glistening

7 waters, and warm hospitality.

8 Temperatures average 80 to 90 degrees

9 during midsummer months and rarely drop

10 below 60 degrees on winter nights.

11 The islands are rich with ethnic

12 and cultural heritage. Visitors can

13 participate in a variety of watersports

14 such as sailing, scuba diving, and

15 snorkeling. While snorkeling below the

16 ocean's surface you can see an array of

17 neon-colored fish, shells, and coral.

| 1 | 2 | 3 | 4 | 5 | 6 | 7 | 8 |

5 a deed; a sale; an elf; a flake; a need
6 a deed; a sale; an elf; a flake; a need

7 an end; fall and fan; sad and fad; fend
8 an end; fall and fan; sad and fad; fend

This mission is to the T key.

Destination—The T Key

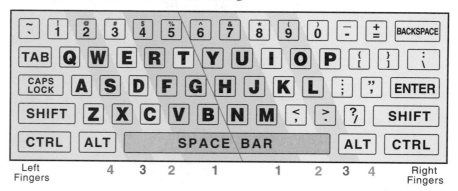

Here is the T key. It is keyed with your F finger. Place your fingers in a curved, upright position on the home keys. Lift your wrists slightly. Look at your F finger and practice the reach to T. Keep your other fingers resting lightly on the home keys.

ftf ftf ftf ftf ftf ftf ftf ftf ftf ftf

Now look away from the keyboard and practice. Keep your eyes on your text, not the keyboard.

ftf ftf ftf ftf ftf ftf ftf ftf ftf ftf

Key the following lines silently saying each key as you strike it.

1 ftf ftf fat tad tea ten sat ate net let
2 ftf ftf fat tad tea ten sat ate net let

3 tend tall tell tent nets take teak nest
4 tend tall tell tent nets take teak nest

Lift your wrists slightly off the keyboard.

5 at a nest; takes a test; lend ten tanks
6 at a nest; takes a test; lend ten tanks

7 dent a tent; a last fat ant; tell tales
8 dent a tent; a last fat ant; tell tales

```
320    PRINT "ENTER WIN OR LOSS"
330    INPUT X
340    PRINT
350    ON CP GOTO 400
360    FOR T = 1 TO 10
370    NEXT T
380    RETURN
390    REM TEAM STANDING
400    HOME
410    PRINT "WEEK # ";N;" : TEAM STANDING=";BA
420    GOSUB 459
440    PRINT :GOSUB 580
450    PRINT "DO YOU WISH A PLOT?"
460    PRINT "1-YES 0-NO"
470    INPUT T
480    IF A = 1 THEN 370
490    END
```

Destination—The I Key

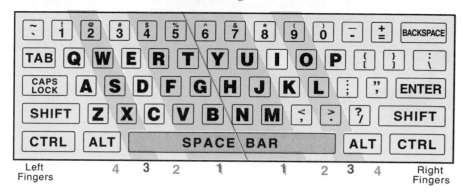

Here is the I key. It is keyed with your K finger. Place your fingers in a curved, upright position on the home keys. Lift your wrists slightly. Look at your K finger and practice the reach to I. Keep your other fingers resting lightly on the home keys.

```
kik kik kik kik kik kik kik kik kik kik
```

Now look away from your keyboard and practice. Look at your text, not the keyboard.

```
kik kik kik kik kik kik kik kik kik kik
```

Key the following lines silently saying each key as you strike it.

```
1 kik kik kik kit kid sit fit aid did lie
2 kik kik kik kit kid sit fit aid did lie

3 kite site slid sift list fine line dine
4 kite site slid sift list fine line dine

5 a list; a tail; a line; a task; a slide
6 a list; a tail; a line; a task; a slide

7 sift tin; fast kite tail; did last task
8 sift tin; fast kite tail; did last task
```

You have completed this mission and are making excellent progress!
If you are using a computer, follow Mission Control's instructions. You can repeat the lesson if you wish. If you are finished for the day:
1. Select quit from the Mission Menu.
2. Remove the disks from the computer.
3. Turn off the computer and monitor.

If you are using a typewriter, you have the following choices:
1. Repeat the mission.
2. Go to the next mission.
3. Quit for the day by removing your paper and turning off the power switch.

VENUS

On Venus, pressure from the atmosphere is 100 times greater than Earth's. You would have to wear a pressure suit so you wouldn't be crushed by the air.

Format a BASIC Program

In order to make computers perform certain functions, they must be programmed. People use programming languages to teach computers tasks. Just as people in other countries use different languages, computers have their own language, too. Once computers are programmed, people can communicate with them without using a special language.

The following computer program is written in BASIC, which is a popular programming language for writing instructions or programs for the microcomputer. This program tells a computer how to save and compare softball scores and batting averages.

Exercise

1. Using the word processor, key the following program indenting the lines as shown. Use default side margins.
2. After you finish keying the letter, proofread your document on the screen. Correct any keying errors with the error correction keys.
3. Select Alt-P (⌘-P) to print your document. Select Alt-N (⌘-N) to save it. Name it "Lang." Proof your printed copy and make any necessary corrections. Save your document again and print a final copy. Exit the word processor.

```
10    HOME: PRINT "PRACTICE"
20    PRINT "COPYRIGHT (C)"
30    PRINT "EMC"
40    PRINT
45    PRINT "THIS PROGRAM LETS YOU KEEP"
50    PRINT "SOFTBALL RECORDS"
60    PRINT "YOU CAN LIST ALL OF YOUR GAMES,"
100   PRINT "WINS OR LOSSES, AND THE"
210   PRINT "BATTING AVERAGE FOR EACH PLAYER."
220   GOSUB 410
230   IF CP = 5 THEN CM = 225
240   IF CP = 3 THEN CM = 18
250   IF CP = 1 THEN CM = 6
270   IF CP <1 OR CP >5 THEN 190
280   PRINT "ENTER THE GAME DATE"
300   INPUT P
```

LESSON

4 Review and Skill Building

Computers—use default margins for all drills unless otherwise indicated.
Typewriters—use these margins unless otherwise indicated: 10 Pitch 2", 12 pitch 2½".
Single-spacing unless otherwise indicated.

mission BRIEFING

There are no new destinations in today's mission. During this flight review, you will:

1. Review all keys learned.
2. Improve keyboarding techniques.
3. Improve keyboarding skill.

Countdown—Get Ready for Blast-off

Sit up straight.

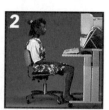
Keep feet flat on the floor.

Sit the correct distance from the keyboard.

Place fingers on the home keys in curved position.

Slant forearms at the same angle as the keyboard.

Keep wrists low, but not resting on the keyboard.

Launch Review

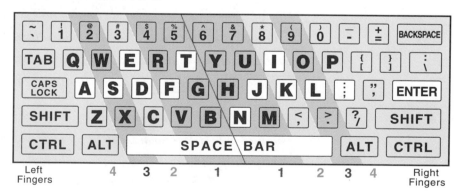

Key the following lines.

```
1 asdf jkl; aaa ;;; sss lll ddd kkk ff ff
2 asdf jkl; aaa ;;; sss lll ddd kkk ff ff

3 jjj ded ded jnj jnj ftf ftf kik kik tif
4 jjj ded ded jnj jnj ftf ftf kik kik tif
```

Use proper finger techniques.

Format Personal Business Letter
in Modified Block Style
from Edited Copy

1. Using the word processor, key the following personal business letter in modified block style with indented paragraphs. Clear all tabs and set tabs five spaces from the left margin and at center. Indent all paragraphs five spaces.
2. After you finish keying the letter, proofread your document on the screen. Correct any keying errors with the error correction keys.
3. Output a copy of your letter and mark any uncorrected errors.
4. Select Alt-P (⌘-P) to print your document. Select Alt-N (⌘-N) to save it. Name it "Modbus2." Proof your printed copy and make any necessary corrections. Save your document again and print a final copy. Exit the word processor.

1645 Mountain View
Madison, VA 22727
October 15, 19xx

Colonial Williamsburg, Inc.
932 Parkway Drive
Williamsburg, VA 23185

Ladies and gentlemen:

The Oakgrove Middle School has voted for its annual field trip to go to Colonial Williamsburg. The student council has requested that I contact you and get all the information available concerning your various tours, presentations, exhibits, and facilities available for school groups.

We are very interested in historical exhibits and demonstrations of colonial crafts, candlemaking, weaving, and cooking. It will be very helpful if cost figures and schedules for the activities are included.

We thank you for sending this information to help us plan our trip, and we look forward to our visit which is planned for April.

Sincerely yours,

Jason T. Palmer
Class Representative

```
5 tan lads; add dead eels; fast fine kids
6 tan lads; add dead eels; fast fine kids

7 dial ask an elf; dine late; a fake desk
8 dial ask an elf; dine late; a fake desk
```

Landing Practice—Review All Keys

Key each of the following lines.

```
1 as at ad an te na if is le ad an ne end
2 as at ad an te na if is le ad an ne end

3 aif fad ask dad jak dak sad alf lad net
4 aif fad ask dad jak dak sad alf lad net

5 fade jade tend lend dent tent kale sale
6 fade jade tend lend dent tent kale sale

7 ill jilt; tilt sill; fast fat flat feet
8 ill jilt; tilt sill; fast fat flat feet
```

Strike each key quickly and sharply. Snap your finger toward your palm after each stroke. As you repeat each line, try to increase your keying speed.

Skill Exploration

Take two 30-second timings on each of the following lines. Try to reach a new speed goal. Do not worry about errors. Try to increase your speed.

```
1 a tin tent; send it fast; ten fat kites
2 take an elf; need a desk; flat sea land
3 flake lake; tan lads talk; it is a leek
  | 1 | 2 | 3 | 4 | 5 | 6 | 7 | 8 |
```

This Skill Exploration will enable you to attempt to beat the computer as you build new skill levels. Good luck!

Mission Assessment

In computing keyboarding speed, every five strokes (including spaces and punctuation marks) count as a word. Keyboarding speed is measured in words keyed in one minute, which is abbreviated as wam. Each Mission Assessment gives a minimum words-a-minute (wam) goal. Try to reach or exceed that minimum goal. You can adjust the goal if necessary.

Take two 1-minute timings on the following lines. Following the copy in your book, key the lines on the computer or your typewriter. The computer will compute the speed. If you are working on a typewriter, you can figure out your speed using the formula you learned in the Introduction .

```
1 a faded elf; ask a sad seal; as it asks
2 ten sad teens; did last tests; fan sits
3 a tan teak desk; send dad a little task
  | 1 | 2 | 3 | 4 | 5 | 6 | 7 | 8 |
```

Minimum goal: 8 wam

In this Mission Assessment, your readiness for future destinations will be determined. Do your best! Key quickly. Do not worry about errors for now.

REENTRY BRIEFING

Follow the proper reentry procedures you learned in the Introduction.

2"
↓

center
↓

9481 West Prairie Drive
Omaha, NE 68121
September 25, 19xx

Middleburg Bakery, Inc.
1482 South Poe Street
Omaha, NE 68121

double-space

Ladies and Gentlemen:

double-space

Our class has decided to conduct a project to raise
money for two needy families. One suggested project
was to sell several types of cakes during the holiday
season. We would like to offer two or three types of
seasonal cakes in decorated cans.

double-space

Please send us information on the types of cakes and
containers that you could supply. It would be most
helpful if various price options could be included
with the discounts available for different quantity
purchases.

double-space

We need to make a decision at our next meeting and
look forward to receiving your price quotes as soon
as possible.

double-space

Sincerely yours,

Quon Lee Suni
Class Representative

1"→   ←1"

↑
1"

LESSON

5 Learning the H and Right Shift Keys

Computers—use default margins for all drills unless otherwise indicated.
Typewriters—use these margins unless otherwise indicated: 10 Pitch 2", 12 pitch 2½".
Single-spacing unless otherwise indicated.

Countdown—Get Ready for Blast-off

Sit up straight.

Keep feet flat on the floor.

Sit the correct distance from the keyboard.

Place fingers on the home keys in curved position.

Slant forearms at the same angle as the keyboard.

Keep wrists low, but not resting on the keyboard.

BRIEFING

You are now ready for new destinations. This mission will enable you to:
1. Review all keys learned.
2. Key copy using the H and right shift keys.
3. Improve keyboarding techniques.
4. Improve keyboarding skill.

Launch Review

TOP-NOTCH TRAINING TIP

Key each line **two times** before moving on to the next line. As you repeat the line, try to increase your speed.

Silently say each key as you strike it.

```
1 asdf jkl; aa ;; ss ll dd kk ff jj de ed
2 de ed jnj jnj ftf ftf kik kik asdf jkl;

3 ask daff lads and a lass; ten tan tents
4 it fits fine; sad den; a fat kite sails
```

Learning Modified Block Personal Business Letters

Personal business letters may be keyed in modified block style. Study the model personal business letter in modified block style on the following page. Look carefully at the formatting directions and how the document is arranged on the page. Paragraphs in the modified block style may be indented or not based on the writer's preference.

Exercise

1. Using the word processor, key the model personal business letter on page 333 in modified block style. Use default side margins. Begin the return address leaving two inches blank at the top of the page. Clear all tabs and set a tab at the center. Begin the return address, date, and closing lines at the center of the line.

2. After you finish keying the letter, proofread your document on the screen. Correct any keying errors with the error correction keys.

3. Select Alt-P (⌂-P) to print your document. Select Alt-N (⌂-N) to save it. Name it "Modbus1." Proof your printed copy and make any necessary corrections. Save your document again and print a final copy.

Destination—The H Key

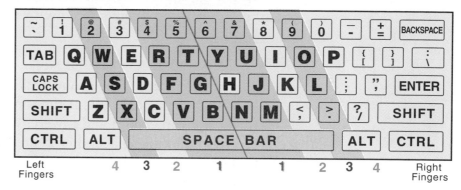

Left Fingers	4	3	2	1		1	2	3	4	Right Fingers

The first destination in this mission is to the H key.

Here is the H key. It is keyed with your J finger. Place your fingers in a curved, upright position on the home keys. Look at your J finger and practice the reach to H. Keep your other fingers resting on the home keys.

jhj jhj jhj jhj jhj jhj jhj jhj jhj jhj

Now look away from the keyboard and practice. Look at your text, not the keyboard.

jhj jhj jhj jhj jhj jhj jhj jhj jhj jhj

Key the following lines silently saying each key as you strike it. Key each line two times before moving on to the next line. Try to increase your speed on the second try.

1 jhj jhj jhj has she hid his hat she has

2 the lash; the hats; the hens; the shell

3 the hen had the hats; dash the head hit

4 thin fish at a leash; need to heal hate

Remember, key each line two times.

Destination—The Right Shift Key

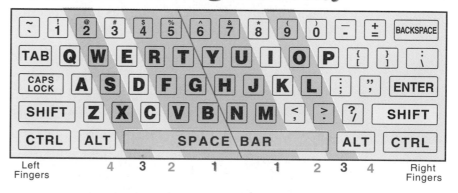

Left Fingers	4	3	2	1		1	2	3	4	Right Fingers

To make capital letters, you must use the shift keys. To capitalize letters keyed with the left hand, use the right shift key. Here is the right shift key.

When you use the right shift key, it is a three-step process:

1. Depress the right shift key with your right little finger and hold it down. (Keep your J and K fingers on the home keys.)
2. Strike the letter you want capitalized with your left-hand finger.
3. Release the shift key and return your finger to the semicolon key.

Remember, capital letters are used at the beginning of sentences and for the first letter in proper nouns.

Follow the report format when keying minutes of meetings except minutes are usually single-spaced with double-spacing between paragraphs.

To key the minutes of a meeting you:

1. Center the name of the group and/or meeting in all capital letters leaving two inches blank at the top of the page. Double-space; then center in capital and lowercase letters the date and time of the meeting. Double-space; then center the place where the meeting was held.

2. Key *Persons Present* and list those persons present. Key *Persons Absent* and list those absent.

3. Begin the first paragraph with a statement giving the exact time the meeting was called to order and by whom. Follow this statement with a discussion of the previous minutes.

4. List each announcement underneath a subhead *Announcements*.

5. Summarize each report under a subhead *Reports*.

6. Summarize old business under a a subhead *Old Business*.

7. Summarize new business under a subhead *New Business*.

8. The exact wording of all motions must be given in the minutes along with the person making and seconding the motion. Indicate whether the motion was passed, defeated, or tabled. Indicate the number of votes for yes and no and abstentions for each motion.

9. Indicate the time the meeting adjourned and the date of the next meeting.

10. End the minutes with the complimentary closing *Respectfully submitted*. Leave three blank lines and key the signature of the preparer's name. Begin the closing at the center or at the left margin.

Exercise

Compose a set of minutes for a meeting of your student council using the following notes:

1. The president of your school's student council called an emergency meeting for next Thursday afternoon at 1:00 in the auditorium.

2. Several parents have asked that students under age 16 not be allowed to travel in private cars to sporting events and that school activity buses or private buses be provided for all students who wish to attend sporting events.

3. The student council president (your school's president) and eight council members were present. (List eight students you know.) Four members were absent. (List four students you know.)

4. Minutes were distributed.

5. Fill in other information as needed.

Remember:
1. Depress the right shift key.
2. Strike the key with your left-hand finger.
3. Release the shift key and return to home position.

Look at your hands and practice the following reach:

```
Al; Al; Al; Al; Al; Al; Al; Al; Al; Al;
```

Now look away from the keyboard and practice. Look at your text, not the keyboard.

```
Al; Al; Al; Al; Al; Al; Al; Al; Al; Al;
```

Key each line two times before moving on to the next line. Try to increase your speed on the second try.

```
1  Fae Alf Eli Dan Ele Ada Edna Alan Eddie

2  Elsa Edna Ella Tadd Dale Elsi Tiki Elle

3  Dan asks Tina; Take a teal kite; Ask it

4  Did the sail fit; Sit and talk; Talk is
```

Skill Exploration

Take two 30-second timings on each of the following lines. Try to reach a new speed goal. Do not worry about errors now. Work to increase your speed. Try to beat the computer.

If you are using a typewriter, you can figure out your speed by using the formula in the Introduction.

```
1  Ask Tilli; Dale had a fat hen; Take ten

2  a seal tail; tent site; a fat jail fine

3  seek leak desk sale dead ants nest ease
   |  1  |  2  |  3  |  4  |  5  |  6  |  7  |  8  |
```

Mission Assessment

Take two 1-minute timings on the following lines. Following the copy in your book, key the lines on the computer or your typewriter. The computer will compute the speed. If you are using a typewriter, you can figure out your speed using the formula you learned in the Introduction.

Minimum goal: 8 wam

Key quickly. Do not worry about errors for now!

```
1  As it has flaked; Edna lent Elsa a tent

2  Tie the tail; She sat in the shade; Sis

3  Tell Dean a tale; Tiki said she is safe
   |  1  |  2  |  3  |  4  |  5  |  6  |  7  |  8  |
```

REENTRY BRIEFING

You have completed this mission! Proceed to the next task.

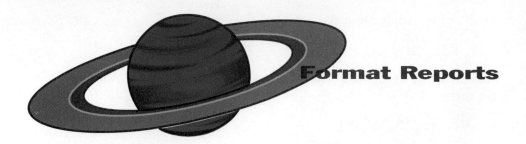

Format Reports

Book Report

A book report is a type of summary report in which you briefly describe what a book is about and your reactions or opinions. In a book report, you give an idea of the situation, the main characters, and the important ideas or incidents that occur in the book. The last part of the report should present your reactions to and opinions about the book. Value judgments about the content can be presented along with your recommendations to future readers of the book.

Exercise

Compose a short book summary on a book you have read recently. Compose this draft copy directly on the keyboard. Use the following guidelines:

1. Use the report format.
2. State the title and author(s) of the book.
3. Summarize the main ideas and information presented in the book.
4. Describe very simply and with examples what your reactions were to the book and what you learned from reading the book.
5. Edit the copy.
6. Output a final copy.

Minutes of Meetings

Minutes of a meeting represent another type of summary report. Minutes of meetings provide a written record of all the major business conducted by a group. Minutes vary in length and are usually written by the secretary of an organized group. Minutes should include:

1. Name of group.
2. Date, time, and place of meeting.
3. Names of persons present and, if needed, names of persons absent.
4. Actions taken on previous minutes.
5. Announcements.
6. Any subcommittee reports.
7. Old business.
8. New business.
9. Time the meeting adjourned and time and date of next meeting.
10. Name and signature of person submitting minutes.

LESSON 6 — Learning the O and R Keys

MISSION BRIEFING

This mission includes two new destinations. If you are successful, you will be able to:
1. Review all keys learned.
2. Key copy using the O and R keys.
3. Improve keyboarding techniques.
4. Improve keyboarding skill.

Computers—use default margins for all drills unless otherwise indicated.
Typewriters—use these margins unless otherwise indicated: 10 Pitch 2", 12 pitch 2½".
Single-spacing unless otherwise indicated.

Countdown—Get Ready for Blast-off

Sit up straight.

Keep feet flat on the floor.

Sit the correct distance from the keyboard.

Place fingers on the home keys in curved position.

Slant forearms at the same angle as the keyboard.

Keep wrists low, but not resting on the keyboard.

Launch Review

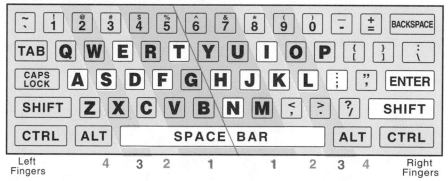

Key each line two times before moving on to the next line.

Strike the keys quickly as if they were hot. Try to increase your keying speed each time you repeat a line.

1 asdf jkl; aa ;; ss ll dd kk ff jj de ed

2 ded jnj jnj ftf ftf jhj jhj kik kik kik

3 Set a date; fish seek the sea and lakes

4 Ted lends Ella a fake title at his land

EXTRA PRACTICE EXERCISES

This section provides additional activities to further your keyboarding skills. You can learn how to format different types of reports and modified block personal business letters, and you will have the chance to try extra speed-building exercises.

Destination—The O Key

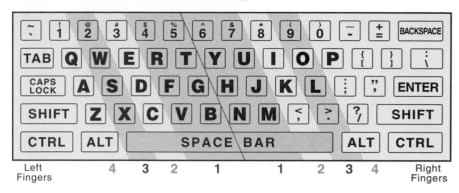

Left Fingers	4	3	2	1		1	2	3	4	Right Fingers

Here is the O key. It is keyed with your L finger. Place your fingers in a curved, upright position on the home keys. Look at your L finger and practice the reach to O. Keep your J and K fingers resting lightly on the home keys. Your semicolon finger may lift slightly if necessary.

```
lol lol lol lol lol lol lol lol lol lol
```

Now look away from the keyboard and practice. Look at your text, not the keyboard.

```
lol lol lol lol lol lol lol lol lol lol
```

Key each line two times before moving on to the next line.

```
1  lol lol too off ton tod son sod oak one

2  not one dot to the tot old oak oil soil

3  fool told old jokes; look one foal sold

4  Don Solons is the host of the toad hold

5  Those old tools; The tot and doll floss
```

Destination—The R Key

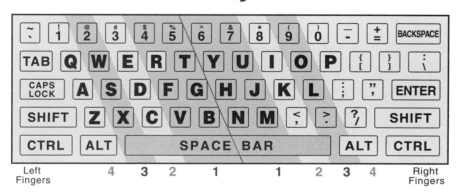

Left Fingers	4	3	2	1		1	2	3	4	Right Fingers

Here is the R key. It is keyed with your F finger. Place your fingers in a curved, upright position on the home keys. Look at your F finger and practice the reach to R. Keep your other fingers resting lightly on the home keys.

```
frf frf frf frf frf frf frf frf frf frf
```

Strike the space bar quickly. Do not pause between words.

Keep your fingers curved and upright.

1	555	5.50	.05	0.66	6.6
2	0.50	4.50	.01	1.02	7.8
3	5.6	.04	1.04	2.04	.7
4	40.7	9.2	8.04	3.04	.05
5	3.01	5.0	5.90	3.04	.94
6	87.06	233.9	20.10	100.1	20.10
7	104.0	11.33	45.12	231.1	978.1
8	40.03	761.2	.6112	1.798	.0050
9	1.001	2.123	54.12	6.058	1.035

Review All Reaches

Practice keying these drills until you can key them by touch. Remember to apply the number-reading principles to these drills.

Key the following numbers across the rows. Press tab between the number groups. Press Enter at the end of each row.

1	4110	3690	7901	10987
2	3042	8135	2001	87674
3	0246	1059	8346	76438
4	4321	4279	6947	78938
5	6420	1324	7805	43210
6	5893	4903	8402	32109
7	6420	7593	8403	23106
8	3902	8948	3420	30950
9	3032	2083	2091	39038
10	3109	3902	3934	00932

Now look away from the keyboard and practice. Look at your text, not the keyboard.

```
frf frf frf frf frf frf frf frf frf frf
```

Key each line two times before moving on to the next line.

Remember to keep your fingers resting lightly on the home keys.

1 sir era rid fir red roar dark risk rain

2 road rake dear fair dare tree area rear

3 There are other reasons for their tears

4 Ron rakes rare red roses after the rain

5 These letters are rare; Toss her a rose

Skill Exploration

Take two 30-second timings on the each of the following lines. Try to reach a new speed goal. Do not worry about errors for now. Try to beat the computer. If you are using a typewriter, you can figure out your speed using the formula in the Introduction.

Try to beat the computer!

1 Sarah told her a tale; she is there too

2 The final order is in; Toss the jar lid

3 The flat train is here; Ron sent theirs
```
| 1 | 2 | 3 | 4 | 5 | 6 | 7 | 8 |
```

Mission Assessment

Take two 1-minute timings on the following lines. Following the copy in your book, key the lines on the computer or your typewriter. The computer will compute the speed. If you are using a typewriter, you can figure out your speed using the formula you learned in the Introduction.

Minimum goal: 8 wam

Key quickly. Do not worry about errors for now.

1 Tell Andrea to send a tire for the Ford

2 Send Rhet tools and a rake for his soil

3 Their data and files are stored on disk
```
| 1 | 2 | 3 | 4 | 5 | 6 | 7 | 8 |
```

Galaxy Gazette

Welcome to the office of the *Galaxy Gazette*. All during your keyboarding program, you will be working for the *Gazette*. You will begin as a Comet Reporter. As you improve in skill, you will be promoted to Star Reporter, Supernova Editor, and finally Universal Editor-In-Chief. You must make continuous improvement in your skill to reach Universal Editor-in-Chief.

In *Galaxy Gazette,* you will complete activities designed to help you be a better writer at the keyboard. These activities will include composition, editing, and grammar drills—all essential skills for a good editor. You also will learn to format documents. This first activity will help you to learn to compose at the keyboard. This is a skill that all editors need.

6	215	326	469	158	321	986
7	641	231	151	462	137	218
8	736	692	581	478	363	762
9	831	329	682	346	732	586
10	324	156	241	312	458	216

Learning the Numeric Keypad—
0 and the Decimal Point

In this mission, you will:
1. Review the other numeric keys.
2. Learn the 0 and the decimal point keys using the numeric keypad.

Destination—The 0 Key

The location of the 0 key may vary on different keyboards. Use the appropriate finger for the location of the key on your keyboard. (If the 0 is located beneath the 1, it is keyed with the thumb.)

Look at your fingers as you make the initial reaches. Then practice until you can key these drills by touch. Key across the rows. Press tab between the number groups. Press Enter at the end of each row.

1	44	410	203	120	050	950
2	11	203	590	780	003	304
3	00	305	210	780	590	309
4	40	390	302	406	780	230
5	10	400	680	520	100	320
6	04	500	580	390	204	420
7	01	340	201	806	604	890
8	00	403	903	780	310	203

Destination—The Decimal Point Key

The location of the decimal point (.) key to be used with the numeric keypad may vary on different keyboards. Use the appropriate finger for the location of the key on your keyboard.

Look at your fingers as you make the initial reaches. Then practice until you can key these drills by touch. Key across the rows. Press tab between the numbers. Press Enter at the end of each row.

Select Mission Report from the main menu, and then select *Galaxy Gazette*. From the list of the words below, choose the word that best matches the thought in 1 through 10. Key the words in proper order in one column key one word per line.

```
tent          fin

shell         fish

shirt         rose

desk          doll

dark          tire
```

1. A toy.
2. Found on the sea shore.
3. Used for camping.
4. Lives in the sea.
5. Found in a classroom.
6. An article of clothing.
7. The opposite of light.
8. A flower.
9. Found on a fish.
10. Found on a car.

When you are finished, press F1 (⌘-?) to have Ukey2 check your work. Move the highlight bar to *Galaxy Gazette* Score and press Enter. After you read your score, press Enter to save your document and select yes to print it. Press Esc to exit the *Galaxy Gazette*.

REENTRY
BRIEFING

You have completed this mission and are ready to go to the next one! Keep up the good work!
If you are using a computer, follow Mission Control's instructions. You can repeat the lesson if you wish. If you are finished for the day:
1. Select quit from the mission menu.
2. Remove the disks from the computer.
3. Turn off the computer and monitor.

If you are using a typewriter, you have the following choices:
1. Repeat the mission.
2. Go to the next mission.
3. Quit for the day by removing your paper and turning off the power switch.

| 8 | 495 | 748 | 864 | 759 | 546 | 465 |
| 9 | 956 | 748 | 857 | 946 | 589 | 498 |

Learning the Numeric Keypad— 1, 2, and 3

In this mission, you will:
1. Review the 4, 5, 6, 7, 8, and 9 keys.
2. Learn the 1, 2, and 3 keys using the numeric keypad.

Destination—The 1, 2, and 3 Keys

The 1, 2, and 3 keys are located in the row below the 4, 5, and 6 keys. With your fingers resting on the 4, 5, and 6 keys, practice the drills until you can key them by touch. Remember to read the numbers in groups.

Look at your fingers as you make the initial reaches. Then practice until you can key these drills by touch. Key across the rows. Press tab between the number groups. Press Enter at the end of each row.

1	44	444	55	555	66	631
2	11	111	22	222	33	321
3	41	144	52	247	63	623
4	14	511	24	622	36	123
5	44	714	55	541	66	743
6	11	651	22	125	33	392
7	41	981	25	218	63	153
8	14	174	52	712	36	134
9	11	146	22	146	33	321

Review All Reaches

Key the following numbers. Key across the rows. Press tab between the number groups. Press Enter at the end of each row.

1	111	876	328	478	641	721
2	222	123	873	982	873	187
3	333	789	782	871	832	167
4	453	214	298	476	892	427
5	313	647	423	721	224	168

LESSON

7 Learning the C and M Keys

MISSION BRIEFING

When you complete this mission, you will be able to:
1. Review all keys learned.
2. Key copy using the C and M keys.
3. Improve keyboarding techniques.
4. Improve keyboarding skill.

Countdown—Get Ready for Blast-off

Sit up straight.

Keep feet flat on the floor.

Sit the correct distance from the keyboard.

Place fingers on the home keys in curved position.

Slant forearms at the same angle as the keyboard.

Keep wrists low, but not resting on the keyboard.

Launch Review

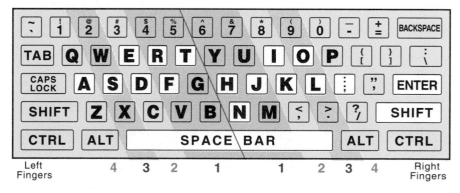

Strike the keys quickly as if they were hot. Try to increase your keying speed each time you repeat a line.

Key each line two times before moving on to the next line.

```
1 asdf jkl; ded ded jnj jnj ftf ftft jhjh

2 jhj kik kik lol lol frf frf Ron and Ann

3 one steer horn; torn their oar; this is

4 after dark dare; dear order stern roses

5 A load of ore for a tired and old train
```

Learning the Numeric Keypad— 7, 8, and 9

BRIEFING

In this mission, you will:
1. Review the 4, 5, and 6 keys.
2. Learn the 7, 8, and 9 keys using the numeric keypad.

Destination—The 7, 8, and 9 Keys

The 7, 8, and 9 keys are located in the row above the 4, 5, and 6 keys. Keep your fingers resting on the home keys and practice the new reaches.

Look at your fingers as you make the initial reaches. Then practice until you can key these drills by touch. Key across the rows. Press tab between the number groups. Press Enter at the end of each row.

1	44	444	55	555	66	666
2	47	777	58	888	69	999
3	77	776	88	857	99	649
4	44	475	55	846	66	549
5	77	575	88	648	96	468
6	74	747	85	568	69	895
7	47	574	58	478	99	479
8	77	746	88	748	66	689
9	44	757	55	857	96	879

Review All Reaches

Key the following numbers. Key across the rows. Press tab between the number groups. Press Enter at the end of each row.

1	486	658	849	575	645	787
2	556	699	878	456	985	677
3	989	875	678	556	794	478
4	654	659	748	698	745	467
5	598	675	976	649	847	746
6	987	846	458	987	859	648
7	546	469	769	846	978	699

Destination—The C Key

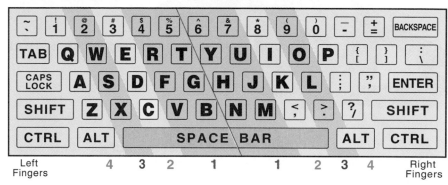

| Left Fingers | 4 | 3 | 2 | 1 | | 1 | 2 | 3 | 4 | Right Fingers |

Here is the C key. It is keyed with your D finger. Place your fingers in a curved, upright position on the home keys. Look at your D finger and practice the reach to C. Keep your other fingers resting lightly on the home keys.

Space quickly.

dcd dcd dcd dcd dcd dcd dcd dcd dcd dcd

Now look away from the keyboard and practice. Look at your text, not the keyboard.

dcd dcd dcd dcd dcd dcd dcd dcd dcd dcd

Key each line two times before moving on to the next line.

Silently say each key as you strike it.

1 dcd dcd dcd can cat call care cads code

2 calf clock face the cook cools the cake

3 cast cash dice can; sick card corn case

4 coin scales jack cost class office cane

5 Cal called the office; cool clock ticks

Destination—The M Key

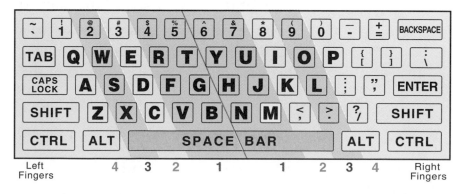

| Left Fingers | 4 | 3 | 2 | 1 | | 1 | 2 | 3 | 4 | Right Fingers |

Here is the M key. It is keyed with your J finger. Place your fingers in a curved, upright position on the home keys. Look at your J finger and practice the reach to M. Keep your other fingers curved and resting lightly on the home keys.

jmj jmj jmj jmj jmj jmj jmj jmj jmj jmj

Learning the Numeric Keypad— 4, 5, and 6

MISSION BRIEFING

In this mission, you will:
1. Learn the 4, 5, and 6 using the numeric keypad.

On many microcomputers, the numeric keypad is located to the right of the alphabetic keyboard. Other microcomputers may have a different location for the numeric keypad, but the arrangement of the keys is basically the same. The key arrangement is also the same on electronic calculators. Locate the numeric keyboard on your computer.

To activate the numeric keypad on a computer, press the Num Lock key. Always activate the Num Lock key before entering data using the numeric keypad. Press the Num Lock again after keying data to resume regular keyboarding functions.

Destination—The 4, 5, and 6 Keys

The home keys on the numeric keypad are the 4, 5, and 6. Place the J, K, L fingers on the 4, 5, and 6 keys.

When operating the numeric keypad, use the correct finger position:
1. Rest your fingers lightly over the home keys: 4, 5, and 6.
2. Keep your fingers curved and upright.
3. Use quick, snappy strokes.

The Enter key is used when inputing numbers the same as it is in word processing: to move the cursor down to the next line. Locate the Enter key that is closest to the numeric keypad. If it is located to the left of the 4 key, use the 4 finger on the Enter key. If it is located to the right of the 6 key, use the little finger on the Enter key.

Look at your fingers as you make the initial reaches. Then practice until you can key these drills by touch. Key across the rows. Press tab between the groups. Press Enter at the end of each row.

1 44	55	44	444	444	444
2 44	54	55	555	555	555
3 44	44	66	666	666	666
4 55	45	65	644	646	456
5 55	44	64	656	456	654
6 55	55	56	465	466	455
7 66	66	46	466	545	654

Now look away from the keyboard and practice. Look at your text, not the keyboard.

jmj jmj jmj jmj jmj jmj jmj jmj jmj jmj

Key each line two times before moving on to the next line.

Do not rest your wrists on the keyboard.

1 jmj jmj jmj me ma mi mo men mat ham met

2 men miss momma; mad Sam made lame meals

3 metal smile almost melted the iced malt

4 meet me at the mall for ice cream Elida

5 Fame comes to most homes; make the time

Landing Practice—Space Bar and Enter

Key the following. Strike the space bar quickly after each word. Do not hesitate. Strike the Enter key quickly at the end of the line.

1 As it is;

2 See all the cars;

3 She can ride the train;

4 The cat eats at all of the docks;

5 let all the rats catch a fat old toad;

Key the lines again. Try to key them in less time.

Mission Assessment

Take two 1-minute timings on the following lines. Following the copy in your book, key the lines on the computer or your typewriter. The computer will compute the speed. If you are using a typewriter, you can figure out your speed using the formula you learned in the Introduction.

Minimum goal: 9 wam

Key quickly!

1 Calico cat ate the rat at the main mill

2 Take the cash card and the credit cards

3 Tell Cam and Fae and Carl to call Carol

| 1 | 2 | 3 | 4 | 5 | 6 | 7 | 8 |

ENRICHMENT ACTIVITIES

Most microcomputers have a numeric keypad that is used to input documents that have a lot of numbers. Numeric data can be entered faster with the numeric keypad than with the top-row number keys.

In this section you will have the opportunity to develop your skills using the numeric keypad.

Galaxy Gazette

Select Mission Report from the main menu and then choose *Galaxy Gazette*. From the list of words below, choose the word that best matches the thoughts in 1 through 10. Key the words in one column in the proper order. Key one word per line. Do not key the numbers.

```
office          melt

catch           cool

chance          meat

mall            camel

elm             mimic
```

1. To grab a ball.
2. A shopping area.
3. A place where people work.
4. A type of tree.
5. To turn from ice to liquid.
6. A possibility.
7. To imitate.
8. A type of food.
9. The opposite of warm.
10. A desert animal.

When you are finished, press F1 (⌘-?) to have Ukey2 check your work. Move the highlight bar to *Galaxy Gazette* Score and press Enter. After you read your score, press Enter to save your document and select yes to print it. Press Esc to exit the *Galaxy Gazette*.

You have completed this mission! Keep up the good work. You are doing great!

As a shortcut, you can press Alt-G (⌘-G) to have Ukey2 check your work.

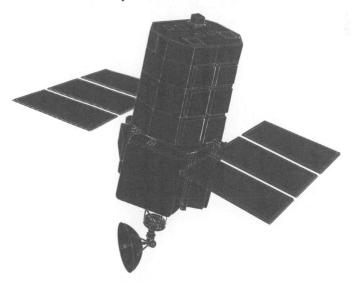

SOLAR MAXIMUM MISSION SATELLITE

Mission Report—Learn to Compose Summary Reports

In your work for the *Galaxy Gazette*, you will need to write reports and summaries of chapters, books, activities, important events, meetings, and research projects. The ability to compose these writing tasks directly on the keyboard will save time and greatly enhance your personal achievements.

One of the most common and useful reports is a summary. The summary report provides a short report, which is usually no longer than 20 to 30 percent of the original article. Steps in creating a summary are as follows:

1. When you review an article, try to identify the main ideas.
2. In your own words you then briefly key the main ideas. The purpose of a summary is to convey the main ideas with a minimum of descriptive details.
3. Using the main ideas, you compose your draft directly on the keyboard. Remember, while you are composing do not worry about errors just get your thoughts down.
4. Output a copy of your draft. Proofread the draft copy. Mark any changes and make the corrections. Output a final copy.

Exercise

With these steps in mind, retrieve your movie review document, in the word processor "Movie," and summarize it. Print and save a copy of your summary. Name it "Moviesum."

BRIEFING

Your final mission is complete. You have finished your work on the space station. The shuttle will pick you up for your return to Earth. Congratulations!

LESSON

MISSION BRIEFING

This is a flight review. You will review all previous destinations to build a foundation for future space voyages. During this lesson, you will:
1. Review all keys learned.
2. Improve keyboarding techniques.
3. Improve keyboarding skill.

8 Review and Skill Building

Computers—use default margins for all drills unless otherwise indicated.
Typewriters—use these margins unless otherwise indicated: 10 Pitch 2", 12 pitch 2½".
Single-spacing unless otherwise indicated.

Countdown—Get Ready for Blast-off

Sit up straight.

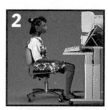

Keep feet flat on the floor.

Sit the correct distance from the keyboard.

Place fingers on the home keys in curved position.

Slant forearms at the same angle as the keyboard.

Keep wrists low, but not resting on the keyboard.

Launch Review

Strike the keys quickly as if they were hot. Try to increase your keying speed each time you repeat a line.

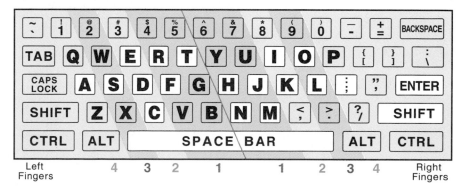

Key each line two times before moving on to key the next line.

1 ded ded jnj jnj ftf ftf jhj jhj kik kik

2 kik lol lol frf frf jmj jmj dcd dcd cam

3 time cash deck face cast dock calk cane

4 case tick tock coil cord nick card lock

5 call the stars to make dreams seem real

Minimum speed goal:
30 wam
Maximum errors allowed:
4

Mission Assessment

Take two 2-minute timings on the following paragraphs. Study the material; then following the copy in your book, key the lines on the computer or your typewriter.

1   Your writing skills have improved

2   a great deal since you began this

3   writing unit. You should now find it

4   much easier to write articles using

5   your keyboard. Continue to practice

6   these skills, and you will see how

7   much easier writing can be.

8   Now that you can write and edit

9   documents with ease, you can think

10 about the final presentation of your

11 articles. By using desktop publishing

12 software, you will be able to add

13 artwork to your writing. Some desktop

14 publishing software has graphics that

15 you can use. You simply pick the

16 topic and then look at the graphics

17 available on that subject.

18   The software will bring the

19 graphics into your document. You can

20 place them wherever you want on the

21 page. Your final report will look

22 very professional when you use this

23 new software.

| | 1 | | 2 | | 3 | | 4 | | 5 | | 6 | | 7 | | 8 | |

Landing Practice—Review All Keys

Key each line two times. Try to increase your keying speed as you repeat each line.

1 if it is of to no on an or ha hi he nil

2 can the tea cat and add tin tar for oar

3 fan net not car ran tin ten sat set jet

4 aced rode risk rest torn cord cast care

5 Dona sold one clock; she sells tan sand

Skill Exploration

Take two 30-second timings on each of the following lines. Try to reach a new speed goal. Do not worry about errors now. Try to beat the computer.

1 Sal told Rosa to notice all of the cars

2 Those folks stood to stare at the stars

3 The credit classes are also for Ranella
| 1 | 2 | 3 | 4 | 5 | 6 | 7 | 8 |

If you are using a typewriter, figure out your speed using the formula in the Introduction.

Minimum goal: 9 wam

Do not worry about errors for now. Key quickly.

Mission Assessment

Take two 1-minute timings on the following lines. Following the copy in your book, key the lines on the computer or your typewriter. The computer will compute the speed. If you are using a typewriter, you can figure out your speed using the formula you learned in the Introduction.

1 at first art lesson sales soared for me

2 Dan said that local ore comes from here

3 The Feds hated to lease the trash areas
| 1 | 2 | 3 | 4 | 5 | 6 | 7 | 8 |

EARTH

The planet Earth is called the water planet. It is the only planet known to have water on its surface and the only planet known to have life on it.

TOP-NOTCH TRAINING TIP

Galaxy Gazette—Build Word-Processing Skills

Word Comparisons

Their, There, They're

Their is the possessive form of *they*. *There* means at a particular point or location. *They're* is the contraction of they are.

From the main menu, select Mission Report and *Galaxy Gazette*. Study and key each sentence.

1 That is their Game Kid game, and they use it every day.

2 There are a lot of video games at Silver Skateworld.

3 They're also going to King's Kingdom.

Key each sentence with the correct choice of word.

1 His father likes to skydive, and (there, their, they're) family goes out to watch him on Sunday afternoons.

2 Look over (there, their, they're) behind the garage, and you will see my new bicycle.

3 Nelson is taking flying lessons at the Bird Airport, and (there, their, they're) costing his family $50 per hour.

4 At the new Super Hamburger South, (there, their, they're) are ten choices of items you can put on your hamburger.

1. When you are finished, proofread your text on the screen and then press Alt-P (⌂-P) to print a copy. Press Alt-S (⌂-S) to save a copy and name it "Lesson90."
2. Proofread your printed copy and then make any needed corrections on the computer.
3. When you are satisfied with your work, press Alt-G (⌂-G) to have UKey2 check your work. Press Enter to save your work and select yes to print a final copy. Press Esc to exit the *Galaxy Gazette*.

Galaxy Gazette

Select Mission Report from the main menu and then choose *Galaxy Gazette*. From the list of words shown here, choose the word that best completes the sentences 1 through 10. Key only the words in a column in proper order. Key one word per line. Do not key the numbers.

```
deck          concern

moat          cord

dock          foam

mice          clock

cooked        smiled
```

1. The situation caused considerable _____.
2. They pulled the boat up to the _____.
3. Do you have a _____ of cards?
4. Do you have an alarm _____?
5. The balloon was attached with a strong _____.
6. Most _____ like to eat cheese.
7. Miecha _____ dinner last night.
8. The _____ on the root beer float tickled my nose.
9. She _____ for the camera.
10. The castle was surrounded by a _____ filled with water.

When you are finished, press Alt-G (⌘-G) to have Ukey2 check your work. After reading your score, press Enter to save your document and select yes to print it. Press Esc to exit the *Galaxy Gazette*.

You have completed this mission! You are making great progress!

Mission Report—Practice the Writing Process

1. Retrieve "Movlist" that you created in Lesson 88. Think about which type of paragraph would best fit your article: a narrative paragraph, a descriptive paragraph, or an expository paragraph. Remember: You may use a combination of more than one type.
2. Using your printed list as a guide, key for ten minutes without stopping. Write about your thoughts on the movie. Do not worry about correctness of copy at this point. Just attempt to get all your ideas down.
3. Print and save a copy. Name it "Movie."
4. Read the copy for content, order, and how well it will fit your readers. Using proofreader's marks, indicate any changes to the copy.
5. Retrieve the draft copy, then make content changes to it. Print a copy. Replace "Movie." Carefully edit the copy for grammar, spelling, and punctuation.
6. Make the final changes to the document. Process the document with the writing team.
7. Prepare the final copy for presentation.

BRIEFING

You are doing great.

90 The Writing Process— Compose Summary Reports

Computers—use default margins for all drills unless otherwise indicated.
Typewriters—use these margins unless otherwise indicated: 10 Pitch 2", 12 pitch 2½".
Single-spacing unless otherwise indicated.

Countdown—Get Ready for Blast-off

Review the countdown procedures.

Launch Review

Key each line two times.

1 The total for the 149 items was $87.63.

2 Zebras are small, fast African equines.

3 Pat Smyth-Medo wants to move to Dallas.

4 Will all of you be glad about vacation?

BRIEFING

In this mission, you will:
1. **Review word comparisons.**
2. **Write a summary report.**

Strike the keys quickly.

Keep your eyes on the copy.

LESSON

9 Learning the Period, Left Shift, and Caps Lock Keys

Computers—use default margins for all drills unless otherwise indicated.
Typewriters—use these margins unless otherwise indicated: 10 Pitch 2", 12 pitch 2½".
Single-spacing unless otherwise indicated.

MISSION BRIEFING

Your flight review was a success. You are ready for the next mission. You will:

1. Review all keys learned.
2. Key copy using the period, left shift, and caps lock keys.
3. Improve keyboarding techniques.
4. Improve keyboarding skill.

Countdown—Get Ready to Blast-off

Review the countdown procedures.

Launch Review

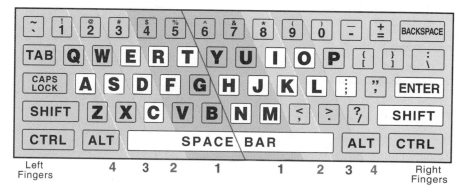

Key each line two times before moving on to key the next line.

1 ded ded jnj jnj ftf ftf jhj jhj kik kik

2 kik lol lol frf frf jmj jmj dcd dcd Fae

3 A jar from the trash landed on the dock

4 Ask Allen and Todd and Elaine to see me

Destination—The Period Key

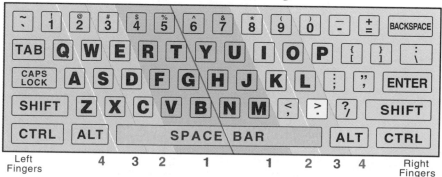

Very soon you will know all the punctuation marks.

Here is the period key. It is keyed with your L finger. Look at your L finger and practice the reach to the period key. Keep your other fingers curved and resting lightly on the home keys. Your semicolon finger may lift slightly.

1.1 1.1 1.1 1.1 1.1 1.1 1.1 1.1 1.1 1.1

4 Last week, I won a contest at my favorite radio
station, and they gave me the opportunity to (sit,
set) in the announcer's box at the baseball game.

1. When you are finished, proofread your text on the screen and then press Alt-P (⌘-P) to print a copy. Press Alt-S (⌘-S) to save a copy and name it "Lesson89."
2. Proofread your printed copy and then make any needed corrections.
3. When you are satisfied with your work, press Alt-G (⌘-G) to have UKey2 check your work. Press Enter to save your work and select yes to print a final copy. Press Esc to exit the *Galaxy Gazette*.

Mission Assessment

Take two 2-minute timings on the following paragraphs. Study the material; then following the copy in your book, key the lines on the computer or your typewriter.

Minimum speed goal:
30 wam
Maximum errors allowed:
4

1   Camping is a great source of

2 recreation and fun for many people.

3 Camping may be as simple as pitching a

4 tent in your backyard. It also could

5 mean packing your supplies and

6 backpacking into the woods.

7   When you go on a camping trip, it

8 is important to take equipment and

9 supplies with you. Planning to sleep

10 in a tent is a good idea, especially

11 if it starts to rain.

12   You'll also need waterproof

13 matches, a flashlight, a first-aid

14 kit, and the right clothes. If it

15 will be cold, take a warm jacket.

16 Good food to cook over the campfire

17 will make the trip an enjoyable

18 experience. Remember, be prepared.

| 1 | 2 | 3 | 4 | 5 | 6 | 7 | 8 |

Now look away from the keyboard and practice. Look at your text, not the keyboard.

`1.1 1.1 1.1 1.1 1.1 1.1 1.1 1.1 1.1 1.1`

Space twice after a period at the end of a sentence. Space once after a period following a personal initial or abbreviation. (For example, James J. Lamm, Ph.D., C.O.D., M.D., U.S.) Some abbreviations such as wam and ml are usually keyed without internal punctuation, caps, or internal spaces. Other abbreviations such as AMA, NASA, MPH, RPM, MPG, and IBM are usually keyed in all caps without internal spacing. (Check a reference manual or dictionary when in doubt.)

Key each line two times before moving on to key the next line.

Strike the keys quickly as if they were hot. Try to increase your keying speed each time you repeat a line.

1 `1.1 1.1 1.1 Sid is.  Call Ann.  Ask Al.`

2 `Eli is late for dinner.  Danni is here.`

3 `Carlos is to join the A.F.S. in France.`

4 `Tilli landed that jet on the racetrack.`

5 `Erin is not ill.  She has not seen Dan.`

Destination—The Left Shift Key

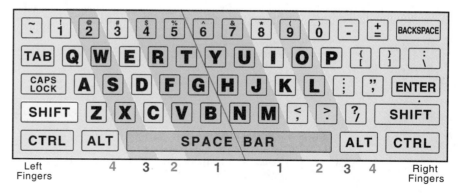

Left Fingers   4   3   2   1   1   2   3   4   Right Fingers

To capitalize letters keyed with the right hand, you must use the left shift key. Here is the left shift key. It is keyed with your A finger.

When you use the left shift key, it is a three-step process:

1. Depress the left shift key with your left little finger and hold it down. (Keep your F and D fingers on the home keys.)
2. Strike the letter you want capitalized with your right-hand finger.
3. Release the shift key and return your finger immediately to the A key.

Look at your hands and practice the following reach.

`Ja Ja Ja Ja Ja Ja Ja Ja Ja Ja Ja Ja Jac`

Now look away from the keyboard and practice. Look at your text, not the keyboard.

`Ja Ja Ja Ja Ja Ja Ja Ja Ja Ja Ja Ja Jac`

LESSON

89 Review the Writing Process

MISSION BRIEFING

In this mission, you will:
1. **Review word comparisons.**
2. **Review the writing process.**

Strike the keys quickly.

Keep your eyes on the copy.

TOP-NOTCH TRAINING TIP

Computers—use default margins for all drills unless otherwise indicated.
Typewriters—use these margins unless otherwise indicated: 10 Pitch 2", 12 pitch 2½".
Single-spacing unless otherwise indicated.

Countdown—Get Ready for Blast-off

Review the countdown procedures.

Launch Review

Key each line two times.

1 Fawzia sold 9 concert tickets @ $25.50.

2 Di had a quaint, quiet way with quotes.

3 Did you find Maria Scone's lost wallet?

4 When may we see what she fixed for her?

Galaxy Gazette—Build Word-Processing Skills

Word Comparisons

Set, Sit

Set means to place, position, or organize. *Sit* means to be seated or to take a seat.

From the main menu, select Mission Report and *Galaxy Gazette*. Study and key each sentence.

1 I set my favorite CD on the table in the den.

2 My friend Seth wants to sit down after he does

karate.

Key each sentence with the correct choice of word.

1 One of my duties for Thanksgiving was to (sit, set)

the table.

2 Our two dogs, Fifi and Bongo, like to (sit, set) on

my parent's bed.

3 After she finished her French cooking class, she

(sit, set) her main dish on the counter.

Remember—

1. Depress the left shift key.
2. Strike key with right-hand finger.
3. Release shift key and return to home position.

Space twice after a colon when it is used as punctuation.

Key each line two times before moving on to key the next line.

1 Ja Ja Ja Jan Kal Hal Mike Kea Les Kitti

2 Cari asked Leslie to come to the dance.

3 Hank sells chains and jackets and cots.

4 Ken and Jeff and Nate and Jan are here.

5 No one can find time to race for Conni.

The colon is the shift of the semicolon. A colon is used as punctuation after a complete thought that introduces a listing of items. Key this line twice.

Order these: coins and chains and jam.

Destination—The Caps Lock Key

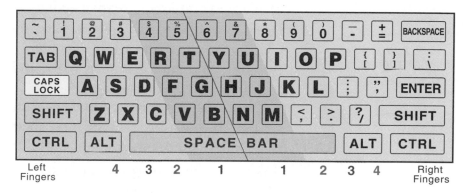

To key a series of letters or words in all capital letters, use the caps lock key. Here is the caps lock key. It is located on the left side of the keyboard and is keyed with your A finger.

Follow these steps when keying words or sentences in all caps:
1. Depress the caps lock key with your A finger.
2. Enter the letters to be capitalized.
3. When you are finished keying the capitalized words, depress the caps lock key again. This releases the caps lock key so the next words will not be in all caps.

NASA NASA NASA NASA NASA NASA NASA NASA

Now look away from your keyboard and practice. Look at your text, not the keyboard.

NASA NASA NASA NASA NASA NASA NASA NASA

Key each line two times before moving on to key the next line.

1 KARI and LANI and CHRIS and CINDA left.

2 Carl has the order for the SANDS CONDO.

1. When you are finished, proofread your text on the screen and then press Alt-P (⌘-P) to print a copy. Press Alt-S (⌘-S) to save a copy and name it "Lesson88."
2. Proofread your printed copy and then make any needed corrections on the computer.
3. When you are satisfied with your work, press Alt-G (⌘-G) to have UKey2 check your work. Press Enter to save your work and select yes to print a final copy. Press Esc to exit the *Galaxy Gazette*.

Destination—Practice the Writing Process

This activity will review the writing process. You will develop a topic and complete all parts of the writing process through the final presentation.

Have you ever painted a picture, baked a cake, or built a doghouse? These are examples of creative activities that make something. The process is similar for all creative activities, including writing.

- First, you get your tools together. For example, you would get the paint, cake mix, hammer, nails, and so forth. This gets rid of things you do not need.
- Next, you organize the materials and use them in the right order. You follow a logical sequence, such as a recipe used to bake a cake.
- Finally, you paint, bake, or build until the product is complete.

Likewise, the writing process is used to create a finished product, such as an essay, a book report, a letter, or a research paper. It is necessary to follow the steps in the process.

Exercise

For this activity you will prepare a movie review.

1. Key at the top of the page the title of the last movie you saw. Then, as you think about the movie, list everything that comes to mind. At this point, don't leave out anything. For example, you may remember that it was raining the night you saw this movie. Include in your list whatever details about the rain you recall. Was it a downpour or a light sprinkle? Make your list as complete as possible. After you've listed as many details as you can, read over your list. Print and save this list. Name it "Movlist."
2. Now remove items from your list that do not relate to the movie itself. Use proofreader's marks. Remember: The finished product will be a movie review. You only want those "tools" or ideas that will add to the final product. Do you need to add anything? If so, write in the ideas. Note the order in which you would like to discuss each item on the list.
3. Retrieve the document to the screen. Use the editing keys to correct the list. Print the correct list. Save it. Replace "Movlist."

Fantastic progress!

Mission Assessment

Take two 1-minute timings on the following lines. Following the copy in your book, key the lines on the computer or on your typewriter. The computer will figure out the speed. If you are using a typewriter, you can compute your speed using the formula you learned in the Introduction.

1 The cane rakes that Jo has are ancient.

2 I can feel that cold air if I sit here.

3 Katie read Thomas all the final scores.

4 James feeds his lame cat the fish dish.

| 1 | 2 | 3 | 4 | 5 | 6 | 7 | 8 |

REENTRY BRIEFING

You have completed this mission! You are doing great!

LESSON

10 Learning the Comma and B Keys

MISSION BRIEFING

Enjoy this mission. You will:
1. Review all keys learned.
2. Key copy using the comma and B keys.
3. Improve keyboarding techniques.
4. Improve keyboarding skill.

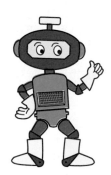

Computers—use default margins for all drills unless otherwise indicated.
Typewriters—use these margins unless otherwise indicated: 10 Pitch 2", 12 pitch 2½".
Single-spacing unless otherwise indicated.

Countdown—Get Ready for Blast-off

Review the countdown procedures.

Launch Review

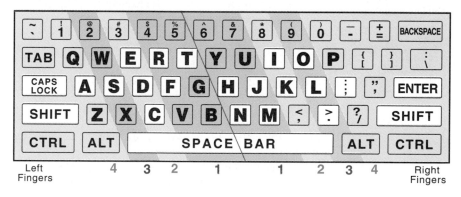

Key each line two times before moving on to key the next line.

1 corn cook face chalk credit chase scale

2 The soot and smoke concerned the chief.

3 Ask Kit or Jo or Leah to lease the car.

4 Joni can access the CAD class for Karl.

5 I can cook these foods: ham and cakes.

LESSON

88 Practice the Writing Process

MISSION
BRIEFING

In this mission, you will:
1. **Review word comparisons.**
2. **Review the writing process.**

Strike the keys quickly.

Keep your eyes on the copy.

TOP-NOTCH TRAINING TIP

Computers—use default margins for all drills unless otherwise indicated.
Typewriters—use these margins unless otherwise indicated: 10 Pitch 2", 12 pitch 2½".
Single-spacing unless otherwise indicated.

Countdown—Get Ready for Blast-off

Review the countdown procedures.

Launch Review

Key each line two times.

1 The bill listed 7 @ $.25 and 8 @ $1.37.

2 Zebras zip with dizzy zest and buzz Ed.

3 Say what you mean; I will get the idea.

4 Do you like to use the new French book?

Galaxy Gazette—Build Word-Processing Skills

Word Comparisons

Stationary, Stationery

Stationary means not movable. *Stationery* means writing material.

From the main menu, select Mission Report and *Galaxy Gazette*. Study and key each sentence.

1 She wrote me a note on lavender stationery.

2 The table in the restaurant is bolted to the wall

and is in a stationary position.

Key each sentence with the correct choice of word.

1 That (stationery, stationary) is recycled paper.

2 I rode the (stationery, stationary) bicycle today.

3 The exercise equipment in the studio has been placed

in a (stationery, stationary) position.

4 Office Objects carries a large variety of

(stationery, stationary) for thank-you notes.

Destination—The Comma Key

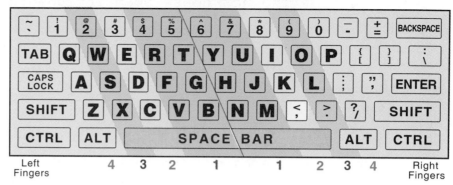

Here is the comma key. It is keyed with your K finger. Place your fingers in a curved, upright position on the home keys. Look at your K finger and practice the reach to the comma key. Keep your other fingers resting lightly on the home keys.

Don't forget proper body and finger position.

k,k k,k k,k k,k k,k k,k k,k k,k k,k k,k k,k

Now look away from the keyboard and practice. Look at your text, not the keyboard.

k,k k,k k,k k,k k,k k,k k,k k,k k,k k,k k,k

Key each line two times before moving on to key the next line.

Strike the keys quickly as if they were hot. Try to increase your keying speed each time you repeat a line.

1 real, drain, rode, rakes, these, there,

2 The list has daisies, trees, and roses.

3 Send Shan a letter, a file, and a list.

4 Take Sal, Cill, and Ann to the red car.

5 Dear Meicha, Dear Carol, Dear Catherine

Destination—The B Key

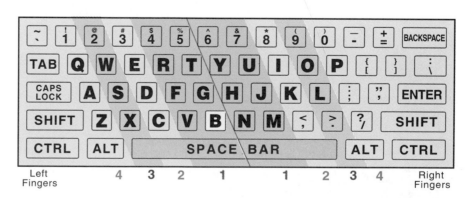

Here is the B key. It is keyed with your F finger. Place your fingers in a curved, upright position on the home keys. Look at your F finger and practice the reach to B. Keep your other fingers curved and resting lightly on the home keys.

fbf fbf fbf fbf fbf fbf fbf fbf fbf fbf

3 The new house loan included a (principal,

principle) of $85,000.

4 Earning enough money to buy a Korvan sports car was

the (principal, principle) reason I studied hard

while I was in college.

1. When you are finished, proofread your text on the screen and then press Alt-P (⌘-P) to print a copy. Press Alt-S (⌘-S) to save a copy and name it "Lesson87."
2. Proofread your printed copy and then make any needed corrections on the computer.
3. When you are satisfied with your work, press Alt-G (⌘-G) to have UKey2 check your work. Press Enter to save your work and select yes to print a final copy. Press Esc to exit the *Galaxy Gazette*.

Mission Report—Preparing a Table from Survey Data

1. Meet with your writing team to select a topic to survey your class. This topic can be anything of interest to your group. Some suggestions: What kind of pet do you have? Who is your favorite musical group? What is the most important social issue today? You are not restricted to these, but clear your topic with your instructor.
2. Design your survey form. You can use the example here as a guide. Since you will report the results of your survey in table format, you can save yourself time by designing an easy-to-use form. Survey your class or several classes to collect your data.
3. Tally your data and design a table to report the results.
4. Use the steps in the writing process to prepare the table for presentation.

FAVORITE PETS

Do you have a pet? Check (x) the ones you do.

Dog _____

Cat _____

Bird_____

Fish_____

None_____

Other (please specify) _____

Nice job.

Now look away from the keyboard and practice. Look at your text, not the keyboard.

`fbf fbf fbf fbf fbf fbf fbf fbf fbf fbf`

Key each line two times before moving on to key the next line.

1 `best bid dab mob ban bell ball bit barb`

2 `best bare bear bone; beef back; fib bib`

3 `fiber object bender; debit border block`

4 `Bob bakes the best breakfasts for Barb.`

5 `Both boats block the sand bar at Boden.`

Skill Exploration

Take two 30-second timings on each of the following lines. Try to reach a new speed goal. Do not worry about errors for now. Work to beat the computer. If you are using a typewriter, you can figure out your speed using the formula in the Introduction.

1 `Christine talks to her calm black lamb.`

2 `Catch a cab to take the bid books back.`

3 `Better ballet dancers dream of careers.`

| 1 | 2 | 3 | 4 | 5 | 6 | 7 | 8 |

Mission Assessment

Take two 1-minute timings on the following lines. Following the copy in your book, key the lines on the computer or your typewriter. The computer will compute the speed. If you are using a typewriter, you can figure out your score using the formula you learned in the Introduction.

1 `Send the cab bill to the border branch.`

2 `Abbie left for Bons, France, on a boat.`

3 `Kareem barters his best baseball cards.`

4 `Kirbie barked at the drab, lone robber.`

| 1 | 2 | 3 | 4 | 5 | 6 | 7 | 8 |

Space quickly.

Minimum goal: 10 wam

BRIEFING

You have completed this mission!

LESSON

87 The Writing Process—Create a Table from Survey Data

MISSION BRIEFING

In this mission, you will:
1. Review word comparisons.
2. Format a table from survey data.

Strike the keys quickly.

Keep your eyes on the copy.

TOP-NOTCH TRAINING TIP

Computers—use default margins for all drills unless otherwise indicated.
Typewriters—use these margins unless otherwise indicated: 10 Pitch 2", 12 pitch 2½".
Single-spacing unless otherwise indicated.

Countdown—Get Ready for Blast-off

Review the countdown procedures.

Launch Review

Key each line two times.

1 Please send Keiko 25 new bathing suits.

2 A music shop had a sale on new zithers.

3 Leontine, I think you know what I mean!

4 Let us all go to the beach this summer.

Galaxy Gazette—Build Word-Processing Skills

Word Comparisons

Principal, Principle

Principal is used as a noun and means either a capital sum or a school official. *Principal* is also used as an adjective and means highest in importance. *Principle* is used as a noun and means a general or basic truth.

From the main menu, select Mission Report and Galaxy *Gazette*. Study and key each sentence.

1 The principal on the loan was $15,000.

2 A principal is in charge of your school.

3 The rules concerning debits and credits are
  examples of principles of accounting.

Key each sentence with the correct choice of word.

1 Being honest is an important (principal, principle)
  for life.

2 Learning is the (principal, principle) reason for
  attending school.

11 Learning the W and U Keys

This mission involves two very important destinations. When you complete this mission, you will be able to:

1. **Review all keys learned.**
2. **Key copy using the W and U keys.**
3. **Improve keyboarding techniques.**
4. **Improve keyboarding skill.**

Computers—use default margins for all drills unless otherwise indicated.
Typewriters—use these margins unless otherwise indicated: 10 Pitch 2", 12 pitch 2½".
Single-spacing unless otherwise indicated.

Countdown—Get Ready for Blast-off

Review the countdown procedures.

Launch Review

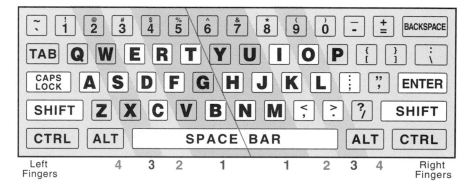

Key each line two times before moving on to key the next line.

1 kik kik lol lol frf frf dcd dcd l.l l.l

2 jmj jmj fbf fbf met mob job bee bat bar

3 Ed is able to take all the mobile mail.

4 Amber melts mints amid makeshift moats.

5 Most catchers belt a baseball. Hit it.

Destination—The W Key

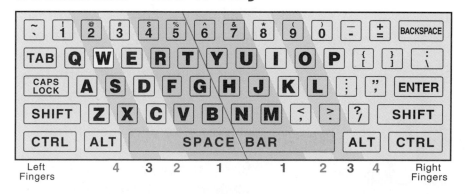

Here is the W key. It is keyed with your S finger. Place your fingers in a curved, upright position on the home keys. Look at your S finger and practice the reach to W. Your A finger may lift slightly, but keep your other

From the main menu, select Mission Report and *Galaxy Gazette*. Study and key each sentence.

1 The cat passed the dog with ease.

2 Janet has lived here for the past 15 years.

Key each sentence with the correct choice of word.

1 I have had Fluff for the (past, passed) 15 years.

2 During the (past, passed) 11 years, we have visited

several states including Washington and California.

3 The truck (past, passed) us on the interstate

highway and cracked our windshield with a stone.

4 There was a lady at the grocery store who (past,

passed) me in one of the aisles in a big rush.

1. When you are finished, proofread your text on the screen and then press Alt-P (⌘-P) to print a copy. Press Alt-S (⌘-S) to save a copy and name it "Lesson86."
2. Proofread your printed copy and then make any needed corrections.
3. When you are satisfied with your work, press Alt-G (⌘-G) to have UKey2 check your work. Press Enter to save your work and select yes to print a final copy. Press Esc to exit the *Galaxy Gazette*.

Mission Report—Composing Personal Business Letters

Your Mission Control Task Force has been assigned to rescue a satellite that is falling from its proper orbit. Your team will take a spacecraft to rescue it. You will need to retrieve the satellite from space, bring it back to your spacecraft, and attach a booster rocket. The rocket will then be fired to project the spacecraft back into proper orbit.

1. Using the word processor, write a letter to Mission Control. In this letter explain the problem to them and ask them for their help solving the mathematical problems you have had. Divide into your writing teams and brainstorm to come up with the list of questions. For example, if the satellite, which is 10 miles in space, is falling at 100 feet an hour, how soon will it hit the planet's atmosphere?
2. Each team member should draft a letter to Mission Control. Name it "Rescue."
3. Meet with your writing team to use the steps in the writing process to prepare a final copy. Present your final copy in business letter format. Print and save a final copy of "Rescue."

REENTRY
BRIEFING

Message received.

fingers curved and resting lightly on the home keys.

Space quickly.

sws sws sws sws sws sws sws sws sws sws

Now look away from the keyboard and practice. Look at your text, not the keyboard.

sws sws sws sws sws sws sws sws sws sws

Key each line two times before moving on to key the next line.

Strike the keys quickly. Try to increase your keying speed each time you repeat a line.

1 wet new now won web few two law win jaw

2 raw snow down with walk twin west drawl

3 The water follows the flow of the snow.

4 Will works with Walt. Win wants a cow.

5 Waltham wished he knew where to wander.

Destination—The U Key

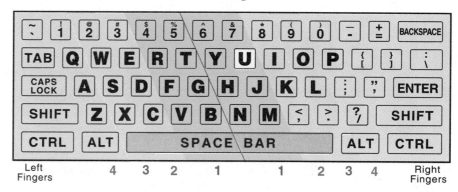

Here is the U key. It is keyed with your J finger. Place your fingers in a curved, upright position on the home keys. Look at your at your J finger and practice the reach to U. Keep your other fingers curved and resting lightly on the home keys.

juj juj juj juj juj juj juj juj juj juj

Now look away from the keyboard and practice. Look at your text, not the keyboard.

juj juj juj juj juj juj juj juj juj juj

Key each line two times before moving on to key the next line.

Press the keys quickly as if they were hot.

1 us sun fun mud but cut rub sue due suds

2 but bulb hunt dour just turn fuel clubs

3 endure manuals about actual build fruit

4 Our annual Run for Fun was held in sun.

5 Urie uses actual manuals to build huts.

had as the basis for your dialogue. Make up names for these characters.

Setting: Teacher's classroom, after school.

Situation: Student has received a low grade on a math test and feels the test was unfair. Student has an appointment with the math teacher to discuss the grade.

Characters: Teacher (Insert Name)

                 Student (Insert Name)

2. Write the dialogue and have the characters work through the problem. Remember, start a new line each time the speaker changes. After each character has spoken three times, you may use initials or short names for each one.

3. Prepare a draft copy of the script using the word processor. Print and save a copy. Name it "Script."

Extended Activities

4. Meet with your writing team to work on your script.

5. Make corrections and print a final copy. Replace "Script."

REENTRY BRIEFING

Keep up the good work.

LESSON

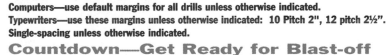

86 The Writing Process— Personal Business Letters

Computers—use default margins for all drills unless otherwise indicated.
Typewriters—use these margins unless otherwise indicated: 10 Pitch 2", 12 pitch 2½".
Single-spacing unless otherwise indicated.

Countdown—Get Ready for Blast-off

Review the countdown procedures.

Launch Review

Key each line two times.

```
1 My hat was $5.95; on sale it was $2.50.

2 Zack quickly buzzed quiet, watchful Ny.

3 Bob, Charles, and Cynthia went to York.

4 Chi hopes that we are able to go today.
```

Galaxy Gazette—Build Word-Processing Skills

Word Comparisons

Passed, Past

Passed is used as a verb which means to go by. *Past* is used as a noun or adjective and means time gone by or ended.

MISSION BRIEFING

In this mission, you will:
1. **Review word comparisons.**
2. **Compose personal business letters.**

Strike the keys quickly.

Keep your eyes on the copy.

TOP-NOTCH TRAINING TIP

Skill Exploration

Take two 30-second timings on each of the following lines. Try to reach a new speed goal. Do not worry about errors for now. Work to beat the computer. If you are using a typewriter, you can figure out your speed using the formula in the Introduction.

1 The woman walked the route with Winnie.

2 Ms. Watt rushed for a junk bond refund.

3 Wil wants to use the old, rundown auto.

| 1 | 2 | 3 | 4 | 5 | 6 | 7 | 8 |

Mission Assessment

Take two 1-minute timings on the following lines. Following the copy in your book, key the lines on the computer or your typewriter. The computer will figure out the speed. If you are using a typewriter, you can compute your speed using the formula you learned in the Introduction.

1 It is much warmer there after it snows.

2 Our swim team waits for the last score.

3 Wend thinks football is a hard workout.

4 A nurse uses a manual to figure it out.

| 1 | 2 | 3 | 4 | 5 | 6 | 7 | 8 |

Mission Report

From the main menu, select Mission Report and then choose the open screen option. You have learned most of the alphabetic keys. You can already key most words. Here are the keys you know: a s d f j k l ; e n t h i o r c m . b , w u. Construct as many words as you can building on each of the letters shown. Use only those keys that you have already learned.

Example: a

                  an

                  and

                  band

                  bands

a   e   i   o   u

When you are finished, press Alt-P (⌘-P) to print your work. Press Alt-N (⌘-N) to save your document. Name it "Lesson11." Press Alt-Q (⌘-Q) to quit.

From the main menu, select Mission Report and *Galaxy Gazette*. Study and key each sentence.

1 I don't mean to be personal but are you upset?

2 Please report to the personnel department to receive your assignment.

Key each sentence with the correct choice of word.

1 Kong is a (personal, personnel) friend of mine.

2 Olean is employed in the (personal, personnel) department.

3 The (personal, personnel) at the local computer center are friendly and helpful.

4 Where you choose to take your vacation is a (personal, personnel) decision.

1. When you are finished, proofread your text on the screen and then press Alt-P (⌂-P) to print a copy. Press Alt-S (⌂-S) to save a copy and name it "Lesson85."
2. Proofread your printed copy and then make any needed corrections on the computer.
3. When you are satisfied with your work, press Alt-G (⌂-G) to have UKey2 check your work. Press Enter to save your work and select yes to print a final copy. Press Esc to exit the *Galaxy Gazette*.

Mission Report—Writing Skits and Plays

Dialogue is a conversation between two or more characters. **Script** is the written direction for a play including descriptions of the characters, where they are, what is taking place, and which character is speaking. An example of the script form of dialogue is as follows:

John: Please open the door!
Mary: You open it. I am busy!

In keying a script, observe the following:
1. Key the name of the character.
2. Key a colon (:) then press tab.
3. Key the spoken words. Press Enter to start a new line for each character.

Exercise

1. Think about the following situation and write a brief dialogue that seems natural for what is taking place and the people involved. You may want to use people you know or experiences you have

LESSON

12 Review and Skill Building

Countdown—Get Ready for Blast-off

Review the countdown procedures.

Launch Review

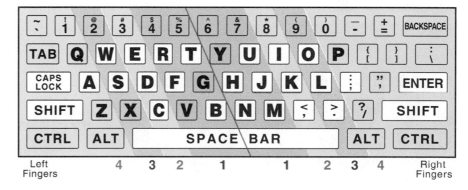

Key each line two times before moving on to key the next line.

1 kik kik lol lol frf frf k,k k,k dcd dcd

2 l.l l.l jmj jmj fbf fbf sws sws juj juj

3 We had fun because the route was short.

4 Boats are nice. Mine is safe but fast.

5 We rush the fruit to the usual account.

Landing Practice—Review All Keys

Key each line two times before moving on to key the next line. Try to increase your keying speed as you repeat each line.

1 two few won drab raw; bees use mob balm

2 Fault finds fault; rumors endure truth.

3 Adults better brush under fruit fibers.

4 Ed knows words flow west and will swim.

5 Ask Bill. Call Barrie. Sara is swell.

If time permits, attempt to key each line with no more than two incorrect words.

MISSION BRIEFING

You do not have any new destinations during this mission. Prepare flight plans for the next destinations as you:
1. Review all keys learned.
2. Improve keyboarding techniques.
3. Improve keyboarding skill.

Strike the keys quickly. Try to increase your keying speed each time you repeat a line. Do not pause between words.

Write a story about your visit. Be creative and make your writing as interesting as possible. Be detailed in describing your visit. You probably will want to talk about the sizes of objects found there and the difficulty you had moving around. What did you eat while you were there? How did you talk to the people? You may want to mention their weight, the size of their homes, and the size of other objects you saw during your visit.

Exercise

1. Using the word processor, brainstorm and prepare your draft copy. Name it "Smalpeop."
2. Process your draft with your writing team.
3. Make revisions.
4. Prepare the story for presentation. You may want to include drawings to illustrate your story.

BRIEFING

Good progress.

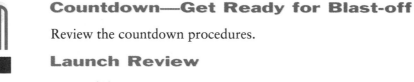

85 The Writing Process— Skits and Plays

BRIEFING

In this mission, you will:
1. **Review word comparisons.**
2. **Write a dialogue.**

Strike the keys quickly.

Keep your eyes on the copy.

Computers—use default margins for all drills unless otherwise indicated.
Typewriters—use these margins unless otherwise indicated: 10 Pitch 2", 12 pitch 2½".
Single-spacing unless otherwise indicated.

Countdown—Get Ready for Blast-off

Review the countdown procedures.

Launch Review

Key each line two times.

1 Please order items #7 and #9 for $7.86.

2 You yielded the yearly yodeling trophy.

3 Tracy and Ian will move from Baltimore.

4 Now is the time to voice your opinions.

Galaxy Gazette—Build Word-Processing Skills

Word Comparisons

Personal, Personnel

Personal means private or individual. *Personnel* refers to employees or employment.

TOP-NOTCH TRAINING TIP

Skill Exploration

Take two 30-second timings on each of the following lines. Try to reach a new speed goal. Do not worry about errors for now. Work to beat the computer. If you are using a typewriter, you can figure out your speed using the formula in the Introduction.

Remember to lift your
wrists slightly.

1 He was at fault if her bike was ruined.

2 All banks can insure the loan accounts.

3 The jaded man walked to the junk store.

| 1 | 2 | 3 | 4 | 5 | 6 | 7 | 8 |

Minimum goal: 11 wam

Mission Assessment

Take two 1-minute timings on the following lines. Following the copy in your book, key the lines on the computer or your typewriter. The computer will figure out the speed. If you are using a typewriter, you can compute your speed using the formula you learned in the Introduction.

Key quickly.

1 The clock has hands that will not work.

2 A wild team makes the swim meet no fun.

3 Bald William likes to wear cotton hats.

4 A nurse went to the hall for the shots.

| 1 | 2 | 3 | 4 | 5 | 6 | 7 | 8 |

Your flight preparation is complete. Proceed to the next destination!

Mission Report

From the main menu, choose Mission Report and then select open screen. In teams of two, construct as many sentences as you can using the keys you have learned. Take turns keying them directly on the computer. Do not worry about errors. Use the keys you have learned: a s d f j k l ; e n t h i o r c m . b , w u.

When you are finished, press Alt-P (⌘-P) to print your work. Press Alt-N (⌘-N) to save your document. Name it "Lesson 12." Press Alt-Q (⌘-Q) to quit.

Mars has the largest volcano in the solar system. It is named Olympus Mons and juts up 15 miles from the planet's surface.

4 Mary Elisabeth is a very (quite, quiet) and calm

baby.

1. When you are finished, proofread your text on the screen and then press Alt-P (⌂-P) to print a copy. Press Alt-S (⌂-S) to save a copy and name it "Lesson84."
2. Proofread your printed copy and then make any needed corrections on the computer.
3. When you are satisfied with your work, press Alt-G (⌂-G) to have UKey2 check your work. Press Enter to save your work and select yes to print a final copy. Press Esc to exit the *Galaxy Gazette*.

Mission Assessment

Take two 2-minute timings on the following paragraphs. Study the material; then following the copy in your book, key the lines on the computer or your typewriter.

1   The narrative paragraph begins

2 with an interest-grabbing statement.

3 Supporting ideas are presented in

4 order of time. Vivid details are used

5 to hold interest and support the main

6 idea of the topic sentence.

7   These paragraphs are usually

8 written in first person if the writer

9 is involved, or in third person when

10 the writer is not part of the details.

11 Make your paragraphs as interesting as

12 possible for your reader. The words

13 you choose to describe your ideas will

14 help to do this.

| 1 | 2 | 3 | 4 | 5 | 6 | 7 | 8 |

Mission Report—Narrative Writing

Your Mission Control Task Force has just visited a planet where the people are very small. Most of them are only six inches tall. Because you are so much bigger, only three people from your team could actually land on the planet. You were one of the three who made the trip.

LESSON

13 Learning the P and G Keys

This mission takes you to two important destinations. Proceed with speed as you:
1. Review all keys learned.
2. Key copy using the P and G keys.
3. Improve keyboarding techniques.
4. Improve keyboarding skill.

Computers—use default margins for all drills unless otherwise indicated.
Typewriters—use these margins unless otherwise indicated: 10 Pitch 2", 12 pitch 2½".
Single-spacing unless otherwise indicated.

Countdown—Get Ready for Blast-off
Review the countdown procedures.

Launch Review

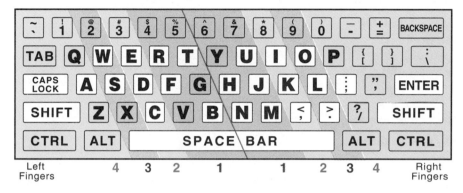

Key each line two times before moving on to key the next line.

1 jut jam saw sud use wash when with were

2 Here is where Warner and Bob ate cones.

3 She is with Marian, Connie, and Borren.

4 We are awkward when we walk on the ice.

Destination—The P Key

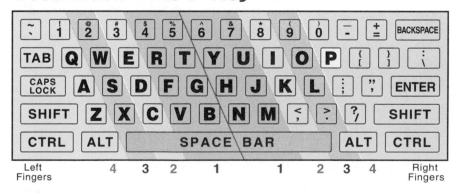

Here is the P key. It is keyed with your semicolon finger. Place your fingers in a curved, upright position on the home keys. Look at your semicolon finger and practice the reach to P. Keep your other fingers curved and resting lightly on the home keys.

;p; ;p; ;p; ;p; ;p; ;p; ;p; ;p; ;p; ;p;

LESSON

84 The Writing Process— Narrative Writing

Countdown—Get Ready for Blast-off

Review the countdown procedures.

Launch Review

Key each line two times.

1 Invoice #63 was $9.85 and #21 was $5.87.

2 Excise taxes exist for excellent X-rays.

3 Will Marci be able to win the next race?

4 If the car is stuck in the mud, push it.

Galaxy Gazette—Build Word-Processing Skills

Word Comparisons

Quiet, Quite

Quiet is a noun that means calm. *Quite* means completely or actually.

From the main menu, select Mission Report and *Galaxy Gazette*. Study and key each sentence.

1 While the ice skaters are competing, it is important to be very quiet.

2 A girl from our county was quite happy after she won the national spelling bee.

Key each sentence with the correct choice of word.

1 Peter had (quite, quiet) a good time jumping off the high diving board.

2 The haunted house was very (quite, quiet) and scary.

3 Yolanda is (quite, quiet) a good skier and came down the advanced slope very fast.

MISSION BRIEFING

In this mission, you will:
1. Review word comparisons.
2. Write a narrative article.

Strike the keys quickly.

Keep your eyes on the copy.

TOP-NOTCH TRAINING TIP

Now look away from the keyboard and practice. Look at your text, not the keyboard.

```
;p; ;p; ;p; ;p; ;p; ;p; ;p; ;p; ;p; ;p;
```

Key each line two times before moving on to key the next line.

Strike the keys quickly. Try to increase your keying speed each time you repeat a line.

1 cup pie pan pat pen tap lap put tip map

2 The prices to the pale, pink pier peak.

3 Special maps appear for posted project.

4 Price of the pen and pencil pair is up.

5 Philip placed an order for plaid pants.

Destination—The G Key

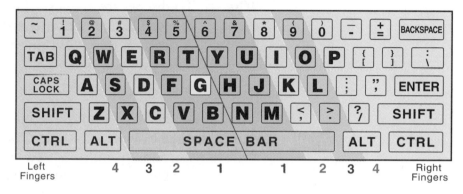

Left Fingers   4 3 2 1   1 2 3 4   Right Fingers

Here is the G key. It is keyed with your F finger. Place your fingers in a curved, upright position on the home keys. Look at your F finger and practice the reach to G. Keep your other fingers curved and resting lightly on the home keys.

Check your posture.

```
fgf fgf fgf fgf fgf fgf fgf fgf fgf fgf
```

Now look away from the keyboard and practice. Look at your text, not the keyboard.

```
fgf fgf fgf fgf fgf fgf fgf fgf fgf fgf
```

Key each line two times before moving on to key the next line.

Space quickly between words. Do not pause.

1 nag fog log sag nog good song high gear

2 Get the green gadget. Sign it, George.

3 Our college grad program is going well.

4 Grain growing budget figures were high.

5 Garrett signed up for the gear program.

Mission Report—What's Happening?

Articles in newspapers have expository paragraphs that give facts about a single topic. The familiar who, what, where, when, why, and how are often used as a guide. These are known as the 5W's and H.

Below is a newspaper fact sheet giving some of the basic information for a story. Now that you have proven your ability to write, your editor at the *Galaxy Gazette* wants you to do an article reporting the results of a recent starship council meeting.

Who Members of the starship council

What Held a meeting

Where In the Mars conference room

When Wednesday afternoon, October 15, after navigational checks were done

Why To discuss the request of crew members who want access to the main computer to make their own games

Result A decision that you think is fair about personal use of company equipment

Exercise

1. Using these facts and other information that you wish to add in the word processor, write an article describing the event. Use one of the brainstorming techniques you learned in previous lessons and draft the article directly on the keyboard. Print and save the draft. Name it "Council."
2. Work with your writing team to edit the article for content and proofread. Revise it. Print and save. Replace "Council."
3. Edit the article for grammar, spelling, and punctuation. Make changes in the word processor. Print and save. Replace "Council."

Extended Activity

4. Prepare it for presentation to your editor. (You may want to add photos or artwork to your article.)

REENTRY

BRIEFING

Nice job.

Mission Assessment

Take two 1-minute timings on the following lines. Following the copy in your book, key the lines on the computer or your typewriter. The computer will figure out the speed. If you are using a typewriter, you can compute your speed using the formula you learned in the Introduction.

Key quickly.

1 The dogs growled at large, green giants.

2 That path to product success is growing.

3 Paul wants to go golfing on the grounds.

4 Gil plans to plant a garden this spring.

| 1 | 2 | 3 | 4 | 5 | 6 | 7 | 8 |

Mission Report

From the main menu, select Mission Report and then choose the open screen option. Make each of these thoughts a complete sentence. Use words that contain only those keys you have learned. They are a s d f j k l ; e n t h i o r c m . b , w u p g. Do not key the entire sentence. Key only the words you need to complete the statements. Start each one on a new line.

1. My best sport _____.
2. I like friends who _____.
3. After I finish school, I would like _____.
4. After school, I sometimes _____.
5. My best school subject _____.
6. My favorite pastime is _____.
7. I wish _____.
8. This weekend I plan to _____.
9. My favorite meal is _____.
10. My favorite memory is _____.

When you are finished, press Alt-P (⌘-P) to print your work. Press Alt-N (⌘-N) to save your document. Name it "Lesson13." Press Alt-Q (⌘-Q) to quit.

REENTRY
BRIEFING

Your mission was successful. Keep up the good work!

1. When you are finished, proofread your text on the screen and then press Alt-P (⌘-P) to print a copy. Press Alt-S (⌘-S) to save a copy and name it "Lesson83."
2. Proofread your printed copy and then make any needed corrections on the computer.
3. When you are satisfied with your work, press Alt-G (⌘-G) to have UKey2 check your work. Press Enter to save your work and select yes to print a final copy. Press Esc to exit the *Galaxy Gazette*.

Mission Assessment

Take two 2-minute timings on the following paragraphs. Study the material; then following the copy in your book, key the lines on the computer on your typewriter.

Minimum speed goal:
30 wam
Maximum errors allowed:
4

1   Transitional words and phrases

2 are used to improve a paragraph.

3 Transitional means moving or changing.

4 Transitional words help the reader to

5 follow the order of the paragraph and

6 your ideas as they develop. They help

7 the reader understand the order in

8 which things happened and how one

9 thing relates to another. They also

10 link ideas between sentences.

11   The following are examples of

12 words that indicate order: soon, now,

13 first, formerly, and finally. Spatial

14 words might include inside, near,

15 above, below, behind, or ahead.

16 Linking words can be in addition,

17 however, therefore, as a result, and

18 in conclusion. Using these

19 transitional words will help your

20 thoughts flow more smoothly.

| 1 | 2 | 3 | 4 | 5 | 6 | 7 | 8 |

LESSON

14 Learning the X and Y Keys

Computers—use default margins for all drills unless otherwise indicated.
Typewriters—use these margins unless otherwise indicated: 10 Pitch 2", 12 pitch 2½".
Single-spacing unless otherwise indicated.

Countdown—Get Ready for Blast-off

Review the countdown procedures.

Launch Review

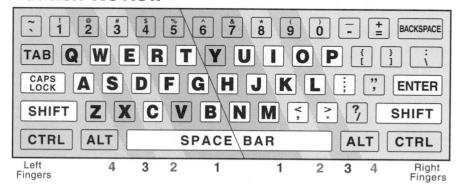

Key each line two times before moving on to key the next line.

1 jmj jmj fbf fbf sws sws juj juj ;p; ;p;

2 The good dog wags its tail at the kids.

3 She is glad about good goats and lambs.

4 Put the napkins and forks on the table.

5 Please bring Ari the pastel artist kit.

Destination—The X Key

Here is the X key. It is keyed with your S finger. Look at your S finger and practice the reach to X. Your A finger may lift slightly, but keep your other fingers curved and resting lightly on the home keys.

SXS SXS SXS SXS SXS SXS SXS SXS SXS SXS

LESSON

83 The Writing Process— Expository Writing

Computers—use default margins for all drills unless otherwise indicated.
Typewriters—use these margins unless otherwise indicated: 10 Pitch 2", 12 pitch 2½".
Single-spacing unless otherwise indicated.

MISSION BRIEFING

In this mission, you will:
1. Review word comparisons.
2. Write an expository article.

Countdown—Get Ready for Blast-off

Review the countdown procedures.

Launch Review

Key each line two times.

1 The trip charges were $87.95 and $95.35.

2 Walking is a wellness program she likes.

3 Writing with the word processor is easy.

4 Using zip codes speeds my mail delivery.

Galaxy Gazette—Build Word-Processing Skills

Word Comparisons

Loose, Lose

Loose is an adjective that means not fastened or secure. *Lose* is a verb that means to fail to keep or to misplace.

From the main menu, select Mission Report and *Galaxy Gazette*. Study and key each sentence.

1 The door hinges are loose; we need to repair them.

2 I hope I don't lose the tennis match with Selina.

Key each sentence with the correct choice of word.

1 If you follow the map closely on your drive to

  Baltimore, you will not (lose, loose) your way.

2 While I was riding my horse, Ieba, the saddle

  started to come (lose, loose).

3 Be sure not to (lose, loose) your computer diskette.

4 While I was sitting in a seat at the movie theater,

  the arm came (lose, loose) from the seat.

TOP-NOTCH TRAINING TIP

Now look away from your keyboard and practice.

sxs sxs sxs sxs sxs sxs sxs sxs sxs sxs

Key each line two times before moving on to key the next line.

Key each line two times.

1 fix lax taxes; foxes exit from the taxi

2 six exact oxen relax; toxic text exists

Remember to lift your wrists slightly.

3 An influx of toxins mixed in the annex.

4 Maxine examined the anxious foxes last.

5 Leni excels at taxes and complex exams.

6 Examine the waxed exits for extra axes.

Destination—The Y Key

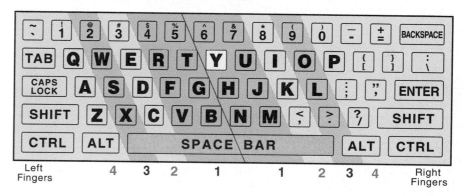

Here is the Y key. It is keyed with your J finger. Place your fingers in a curved, upright position on the home keys. Look at your J finger and practice the reach to Y. Keep your other fingers curved and resting lightly on the home keys.

jyj jyj jyj jyj jyj jyj jyj jyj jyj jyj

Now look away from the keyboard and practice. Look at your text, not the keyboard.

jyj jyj jyj jyj jyj jyj jyj jyj jyj jyj

Key each line two times before moving on to key the next line.

Strike the keys quickly.
Use a quick, firm touch.

1 may fry try yes day say type copy yawns

2 They pay easy money for my yellow yams.

3 Tamy types daily with rhythm and style.

4 The Yankees won the playoffs this year.

5 The daily hay supply is likely to stay.

6 The deluxe yellow yacht is from Yakima.

Mission Report—Expository Writing

Your assignment is to explain how to complete one of the activities listed below. Choose the activity that you wish to write about from the list.

Wash a dog.
Wax a car.
Brush your teeth.
Wash your clothes.
Clean a fish.
Hit a baseball.
Kick a football.
Do a handstand.
Bake a cake.
Cook breakfast.
Other (select your own).

Exercise

1. In the word processor, brainstorm in short phrases or sentences a list of the tasks that you would do in the activity. Name the document "Expolist." Print a copy.

2. Look at each task on your list and decide the proper order for the steps. For example, you do not place a cake in the oven before you mix the ingredients. Number your list in order from first task to last. Make any needed spelling corrections on your printed copy using proofreader's marks.

3. Retrieve the list in your word processor and use the move function keys and editing keys to get your list in proper sequence.

4. Change each item on the list to a complete sentence. Save your document. Replace "Expolist."

5. Change the sentences to paragraph copy. Print and save a copy. Replace "Expolist."

6. Proof your printed copy. Edit your copy to be sure that the steps are clearly explained and in order. Use proofreader's marks to note any changes.

7. Retrieve your document in the word processor, make any remaining changes, and print the final version. Save the copy. Replace "Expolist."

REENTRY
BRIEFING

Good job.

Skill Exploration

Take two 30-second timings on each of the following lines. Try to reach a new speed goal. Do not worry about errors for now. Work to beat the computer. If you are using a typewriter, you can figure out your speed using the formula in the Introduction.

1 An angry senator pledged a budget goal.

2 Tiny blue fish jump in the ocean swell.

3 People use computers for multiple jobs.

| 1 | 2 | 3 | 4 | 5 | 6 | 7 | 8 |

Maximum goal: 12 wam

Mission Assessment

Take two 1-minute timings on the following lines. Following the copy in your book, key the lines on the computer or your typewriter. The computer will figure out the speed. If you are using a typewriter, you can compute your speed using the formula you learned in the Introduction.

1 Public bids for extended exports exist.

2 Exact math exams are taxing to the boy.

3 Six oxen exist in boxed cages in Texas.

4 Deluxe yellow taxis exit from the yard.

5 Max excels in exact, rhythmic yodeling.

| 1 | 2 | 3 | 4 | 5 | 6 | 7 | 8 |

Key quickly. Try to set a new speed goal.

Galaxy Gazette

You must possess good grammar skills to be a good editor. Some of the writing assignments in the *Galaxy Gazette* will review grammar skills.

A **pronoun** is a word that takes the place of a noun. Pronouns help us to speak or write clearly and simply. Study the following sentences.

> Juan made a sandwich. Juan put mustard on the sandwich.
> Then Juan ate the sandwich.

These sentences could be simpler if pronouns were used in place of some of the nouns. For example:

> Juan made a sandwich. He put mustard on the sandwich.
> Then he ate it.

In this example, *he* takes the place of Juan in the second and third sentences. *It* takes the place of sandwich in the third sentence.

1. When you are finished, proofread your text on the screen and then press Alt-P (⌘-P) to print a copy. Press Alt-S (⌘-S) to save a copy and name it "Lesson82."
2. Proofread your printed copy and then make any needed corrections on the computer.
3. When you are satisfied with your work, press Alt-G (⌘-G) to have UKey2 check your work. Press Enter to save your work and select yes to print a final copy. Press Esc to exit the *Galaxy Gazette*.

Mission Assessment

Take two 2-minute timings on the following paragraphs. Study the material; then following the copy in your the book, key the lines on the computer or your typewriter.

1   The expository paragraph explains

2 what, when, where, why, and how

3 something happened. It presents

4 details about a single topic.

5 Explaining step-by-step how to do

6 something is an example of an

7 expository article. Also, articles

8 that give facts, such as news reports,

9 are examples of this type of writing.

10   The sentences in an expository

11 paragraph usually present facts or

12 reasons supporting the topic sentence.

13 The order of the sentences can follow

14 the time in which the events took

15 place, or a simple-to-complex order

16 can be used to present supporting

17 details. In summary, using the

18 correct type of paragraph for the form

20 of writing that you are doing will

21 improve your writing style. Paragraph

22 planning is essential for good writing.

| 1 | 2 | 3 | 4 | 5 | 6 | 7 | 8 |

From the main menu, select Mission Report and then choose *Galaxy Gazette*. Key the following sentences. Key one sentence on each line. Do not key the numbers. Replace the proper nouns with pronouns.

1. Max and Joe like to fish.
2. Gary prefers to play soccer.
3. Erica likes butter on pancakes.
4. Janet gave lunch to the twins.
5. Joni and Tim completed the assignment quickly.
6. Katie plans to play golf after work.
7. Sarah has a cat called Mousie.
8. Alex and James are publishing a book.
9. Chris is happy she won the lottery.
10. Christine had an eye exam and got new glasses.

REENTRY
BRIEFING

Good work!

When you are finished, press Alt-G (⌘-G) to have Ukey2 check your work. After reading your score, press Enter to save your document and select yes to print it. Press Esc to exit the *Galaxy Gazette*.

LESSON

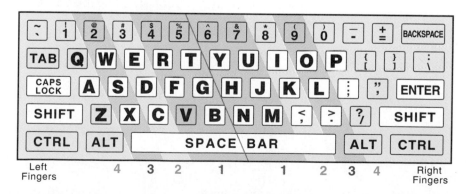

15 Learning the V and Z Keys

MISSION
BRIEFING

After completing this mission, you will be able to:
1. Review all keys learned.
2. Key copy using the V and Z keys.
3. Improve keyboarding techniques.
4. Improve keyboarding skill.

Computers—use default margins for all drills unless otherwise indicated.
Typewriters—use these margins unless otherwise indicated: 10 Pitch 2", 12 pitch 2½".
Single-spacing unless otherwise indicated.

Countdown—Get Ready for Blast-off

Review the countdown procedures.

Launch Review

LESSON

82 The Writing Process— Expository Writing

MISSION BRIEFING

In this lesson you will:
1. Review word comparisons.
2. Write an expository article.

Strike the keys quickly.

Keep your eyes on the copy.

TOP-NOTCH TRAINING TIP

Computers—use default margins for all drills unless otherwise indicated.
Typewriters—use these margins unless otherwise indicated: 10 Pitch 2", 12 pitch 2½".
Single-spacing unless otherwise indicated.

Countdown—Get Ready for Blast-off

Review the countdown procedures.

Launch Review

Key each line two times.

1 Sales fell six percent after the storm.

2 Voters vow to preserve valued wetlands.

3 A bald eagle soared over the mountains.

4 Robots were used to paint the machines.

Galaxy Gazette—Build Word-Processing Skills

Word Comparisons

Complement, Compliment

Complement means that which is needed to make something complete.
Compliment means to praise or flatter.

From the main menu, select Mission Report and *Galaxy Gazette*. Study and key each sentence.

1 The roses on the table complemented the painting.

2 The dentist complimented me on my good habits.

Key each sentence with the correct choice of word.

1 My teacher (complimented, complemented) my work.

2 The woven rug (compliments, complements) the chair.

3 In order to form a 90-degree angle, a 30-degree

angle and a 60-degree angle are (compliments,

complements) of each other.

4 The children who helped at the animal shelter were

(complimented, complemented) on their work.

Key each line two times before moving on to key the next line.

1 yes flax yarn excess say coy copy types

2 today study systems except policy money

3 examine company luxury yardage property

4 Take the extra mixes to the play today.

5 Many young people try new style trends.

Destination—The V Key

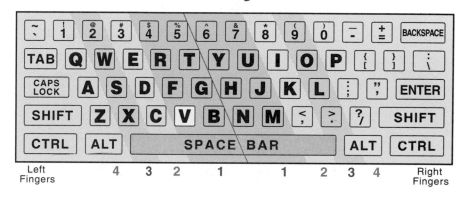

Here is the V key. It is keyed with your F finger. Place your fingers in a curved, upright position on the home keys. Look at your F finger and practice the reach to V. Keep your other fingers curved and resting lightly on the home keys.

fvf fvf fvf fvf fvf fvf fvf fvf fvf fvf

Now look away from the keyboard and practice. Look at your text, not the keyboard.

fvf fvf fvf fvf fvf fvf fvf fvf fvf fvf

Key each line two times before moving on to key the next line.

1 vet vex vat via vie vow van even travel

2 Vic and Eve have a vain view of Victor.

3 David and Vivian have seven live vines.

4 Average voters have proven value to Vi.

5 Get the vacation vaccine for the vault.

Strike the keys quickly. Try to increase your keying speed each time you repeat a line.

2. Proofread your printed copy and then make any needed corrections on the computer.

3. When you are satisfied with your work, press Alt-G (⌂-G) to have UKey2 check your work. Press Enter to save your work and select yes to print a final copy. Press Esc to exit the *Galaxy Gazette*.

Mission Report—Writing Rainbows

Color words are useful in writing descriptive paragraphs. There are many common color words that we use: blue skies, green pastures, bright future.

Exercise

1. Look at the questions below. Key two or three words or phrases in the word processor to answer each question. Do not worry about errors. Just key whatever comes to mind.
   - What looks blue?
   - What sounds pale?
   - What smells green?
   - What tastes yellow?
   - What feels bright?
   - What seems black?

2. Print and save the document. Name it "Colors."

3. Now use these words or phrases to compose a short poem of eight lines. Your poem may or may not rhyme. It's up to you. Do not worry about errors. Just key your thoughts. Print and save a copy. Name the poem "Colpoem."

4. Proofread your printed copy of the poem. Mark any suggested changes on the copy. Retrieve your poem in the word processor files. Make the needed changes. Print and save a final copy. Replace "Colpoem."

Extended Activity

5. Prepare your poem for display by finding artwork to go with it. Present your poem by reading it to the class, sending it to the school newspaper, or putting it on the classroom bulletin board.

Your mission was successful.

Destination—The Z Key

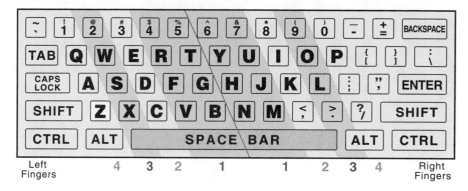

Here is the Z key. It is keyed with your A finger. Place your fingers in a curved, upright position on the home keys. Look at your A finger and practice the reach to Z. Keep your other fingers curved and resting lightly on the home keys.

`aza aza aza aza aza aza aza aza aza aza`

Now look away from the keyboard and practice. Look at your text, not the keyboard.

`aza aza aza aza aza aza aza aza aza aza`

Key each line two times before moving on to key the next line.

1 `zoo zip zig zag zen zeal whiz buzz zero`

2 `Seven zany lizards zip by the zoo zone.`

3 `The zeppelin zooms past a crazy bazaar.`

4 `Zelda analyzed the prizes for the game.`

5 `Ziggy played crazy jazz with zany zeal.`

Mission Assessment

Take two 1-minute timings on the following lines. Following the copy in your book, key the lines on the computer or your typewriter. The computer will figure out the speed. If you are using a typewriter, you can compute the speed using the formula you learned in the Introduction.

1 `Vickie and Vince play crazy card games.`

2 `Citizens seize my frozen ice cream van.`

3 `Itemize the dozen tax hazards, Suzanne.`

4 `Lazy, crazy zebra wins Bronx zoo prize.`

`| 1 | 2 | 3 | 4 | 5 | 6 | 7 | 8 |`

Minimum goal: 13 wam

LESSON

81 The Writing Process— Writing Rainbows

MISSION BRIEFING

In this mission, you will:
1. Review word comparisons.
2. Write a descriptive article.

Strike the keys quickly.

Keep your eyes on the copy.

TOP-NOTCH TRAINING TIP

Computers—use default margins for all drills unless otherwise indicated.
Typewriters—use these margins unless otherwise indicated: 10 Pitch 2", 12 pitch 2½".
Single-spacing unless otherwise indicated.

Countdown—Get Ready for Blast-off

Review the countdown procedures.

Launch Review

Key each line two times.

1 Order 920 reams of 8" x 11" bond paper.

2 Unions unite underpaid, unique umpires.

3 Tim tends to whistle tunes in 2/2 time.

4 Red squash is one of my favorite foods.

Galaxy Gazette—Build Word-Processing Skills

Word Comparisons

All Ready, Already

All ready is an adjectival term meaning completely prepared. *Already* is an adverb that means before now.

From the main menu, select Mission Report and *Galaxy Gazette*. Study and key each sentence.

1 I am all ready to go with you.

2 He has gone already.

Key each sentence with the correct choice of word.

1 Dinner is (all ready, already).

2 Robert has finished his speech (all ready, already).

3 The entire class was (all ready, already) for the

debate.

4 She had (all ready, already) left when I called.

1. When you are finished, proofread your text on the screen and then press Alt-P (⌘-P) to print a copy. Press Alt-S (⌘-S) to save a copy and name it "Lesson81."

Galaxy Gazette

A **possessive pronoun** is a pronoun that names who or what has something. Some possessive pronouns are:

my	our	mine	ours
your	your	yours	yours
his, her, its	their	his, hers	theirs

Here are some examples of how these pronouns are used.

I found my books.
The green book bag is hers.
Kathleen brought her lunch.
The gym suit is mine.

From the main menu, select Mission Report and then choose *Galaxy Gazette*. Key each of the following sentences. When you key the sentence, change the italicized words to a possessive pronoun.

1. Nadia lost *Nadia's* watch.
2. *Jason's* favorite sport is basketball.
3. That bag is *Rafael and Suzanne's* and *my* bag.
4. The homework is not *Alfredo's*.
5. The mistake was *Mrs. Smith's* fault.
6. Kirby autographed *Kirby's* baseball card for the young girl.
7. Jeff and Norine plan to get married at *Norine's* parents' house.
8. Salvadore saved *Salvadore's* money to buy a VCR.
9. Paul and Cathy rode *Paul and Cathy's* bicycles through the park.
10. Michael lost *Michael's* contact lenses while he was swimming.

When you are finished, press Alt-G (⌘-G) to have Ukey2 check your work. Press Enter to save your document and select yes to print it. Press Esc to exit the *Galaxy Gazette*.

Your mission was A-OK.
Keep up the good work.

Mission Report—Editing Previous Work

Many times it is helpful to have some time between when you write an article and when you edit it. With a little "distance" between you and your original creativity, you may find ways to make your article clearer or you may more easily catch errors in punctuation and grammar. For this exercise, retrieve your document "Friend."

Exercise

1. Read your copy and use proofreader's marks to make changes to content, grammar, and vocabulary.
2. Using the corrected copy as a guide, make corrections using the editing keys. Include a centered title: My Friend. Include subheads keyed at the left margin on lines by themselves. Your subheads could be Physical Characteristics, Dress, and Personality. Print and save the document. Replace "Friend."
3. Edit the copy for grammar, spelling, and punctuation. Underline your subheads. Print a final document. Replace "Friend."

Extended Activity

4. Process the document with your team writing group. Make final changes and prepare the document for presentation.

You're making good progress.

LESSON

16 Review and Skill Building

Computers—use default margins for all drills unless otherwise indicated.
Typewriters—use these margins unless otherwise indicated: 10 Pitch 2", 12 pitch 2½".
Single-spacing unless otherwise indicated.

Countdown—Get Ready for Blast-off

Review the countdown procedures.

Launch Review

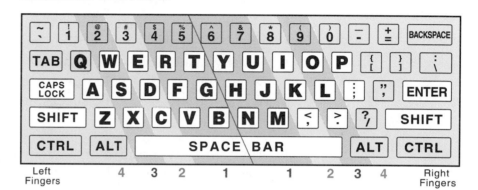

Left Fingers 4 3 2 1 1 2 3 4 Right Fingers

Key each line two times before moving on to key the next line.

1 six dogs got tags zany spy buys gas box

2 next axle vine exam flex even vain raze

3 The tax whiz will divide good fortunes.

4 Her zeal for practice amazed the crowd.

5 Geri will adjust the oxygen gas hazard.

Landing Practice—Review All Keys

Key each line two times before moving on to key the next line. Try to increase your speed as you repeat the line.

1 to if an as ox he in so or it at be bye

2 got for too big and but may gym cut pat

3 vat lot red tax win mail head take pale

4 wait raze move love rely true cook boys

5 is it, in it, as it, and to it, go for,

6 to go, to it, by my, and in, and it is,

MISSION BRIEFING

This mission is a flight review. In this review, you will:

1. Review all keys learned.
2. Improve keyboarding techniques.
3. Improve keyboarding skill.
4. Learn wordwrap on the computer.

Think and key each phrase.

1. When you are finished, proofread your text on the screen and then press Alt-P (⌘-P) to print a copy. Press Alt-S (⌘-S) to save a copy and name it "Lesson80."
2. Proofread your printed copy and then make any needed corrections on the computer.
3. When you are satisfied with your work, press Alt-G (⌘-G) to have UKey2 check your work. Press Enter to save your work and select yes to print a final copy. Press Esc to exit the *Galaxy Gazette*.

Mission Report—Descriptive Writing

Think of something you did recently. It could have been going to a party, ball game, picnic, field trip, or other social event. Think about how you reacted to the activity according to the following:

- How you felt — happy, funny, hurt, sick.
- How you acted — silly, serious, mad, sad.
- What you smelled — food, flowers, trees.
- What you tasted — cold, hot, bitter, sweet.
- What you saw — colors, shades, movement.

Exercise

1. Once you have decided on an activity, use the word processor to write several paragraphs describing your reactions. Write for five to eight minutes without stopping (depending on the time you are given). This activity is another type of brainstorming. Write anything that comes to mind. Do not worry about organizing or correcting the copy now. Leave a two-inch top margin. Double-space the copy.
2. Print a copy and save the document. Name it "React."
3. Review your "React" document. Check the content, grammar, and vocabulary. Note needed corrections with proofreader's marks.
4. Retrieve the document in the word processor. Use the editing keys to make the needed changes. Print and save the document. Replace "React."

Extended Activities

5. Process the document with your team writing group.
6. Make final changes to the document including grammar, spelling, and punctuation. Print and save the final copy. Give the document a new name, "Reactfnl," for *react final.* Prepare the document for presentation.

Automatic Wordwrap

Your keyboarding computer software is equipped with an automatic wordwrap feature. This allows automatic returns at the end of each line. Any word that does not fit within the right margin is automatically carried to the next line. When keying paragraph copy, you will not need to strike the Enter key at the end of each line. Continue to strike Enter at the end of drill lines, however. If you are using a typewriter, you will need to continue to strike the Return key at the end of each line.

From the main menu, select the Mission Report and choose the open screen option. Practice keying the following paragraph two times. Do not strike the Enter key at the end of the lines.

```
The invention of the computer has

caused our society to enter the

Computer Age.  There is hardly any

part of our lives that is not touched

by computers.  A person preparing to

be part of the Computer Age must have

basic skills in computer use.
```

When you are finished, press Alt-P (⌘-P) to print your work. Press Alt-Q (⌘-Q) to exit the word processor. Do not save your work.

Skill Exploration

Take two 30-second timings on each of the following lines. Try to reach a new speed goal. Do not worry about errors for now. Work to beat the computer. If you are using a typewriter, you can figure out your speed using the formula in the Introduction.

```
1 The girls were enjoying the spy novels.

2 Summer vacation is a good time to swim.

3 Her pets are a dog, hamster, and horse.
   |  1  |  2  |  3  |  4  |  5  |  6  |  7  |  8  |
```

Minimum goal: 13 wam

Mission Assessment

Take two 1-minute timings on the paragraph on the following page. Following the copy in your book, key the lines on the computer or your typewriter. If you are using a computer, do not press the Enter key. The wordwrap will take you to each new line. If you are using a typewriter, you will need to strike the Return key at the end of every line. The computer will compute your keying speed. If you are using a typewriter, you can figure out your speed using the formula you learned in the Introduction.

LESSON

80 The Writing Process— Descriptive Writing

Computers—use default margins for all drills unless otherwise indicated.
Typewriters—use these margins unless otherwise indicated: 10 Pitch 2", 12 pitch 2½".
Single-spacing unless otherwise indicated.

Countdown—Get Ready for Blast-off

Review the countdown procedures.

Launch Review

Key each line two times.

1 Does (12 + 3 + 5) x (14 - 2 + 3) = 650?

2 Sorry, sour salespeople seldom succeed.

3 Will teachers be taking talented teens?

4 Will you come with Kit today to see us?

Galaxy Gazette—Build Word-Processing Skills

Word Comparisons

Accept, Except

Accept is a verb that means to agree or approve. *Except* means excluded or only.

Study and key each sentence in the *Galaxy Gazette*.

1 They accept the terms and will sign the contract.

2 Our paper is delivered every day except Sunday.

3 All of the students went to the festival except

Euli who was not feeling well.

Key each sentence with the correct choice of word.

1 Please (accept, except) this payment for all of

your hard work.

2 I like all of the colors (accept, except) the

turquoise.

3 I would go there for vacation (accept, except) it's

too far.

TOP-NOTCH TRAINING TIP

1 One of the basic skills needed by

2 people who rely on a computer is the

3 ability to access programs easily.

4 People need to be able to input data

5 in a computer, too. A touch keying

6 skill is necessary for using a

7 computer. Students who have a touch

8 keying skill will have an advantage

9 over those who do not.

| 1 | 2 | 3 | 4 | 5 | 6 | 7 | 8 |

Galaxy Gazette

You use a capital letter to begin the first word of each sentence and to begin proper nouns and titles.

Examples:
1. Jose Garcia lives in Houston, Texas.
2. Mr. Steinmetz and I will attend the meeting on Monday, February 23.

From the main menu, select Mission Report and then choose *Galaxy Gazette*. Rekey the following paragraph. Use capital letters where necessary. Remember, with paragraph copy you do *not* need to press the Enter key.

when i was a child, i was always interested in

space travel. i spent many hours dreaming

about going to the moon. i read many books

dealing with space exploration. my favorite

one was about neil armstrong, the first man to

walk on the moon. because of my interest in

space travel, one summer i attended space camp

in huntsville, alabama. i have decided that i

want to be an astronaut when i get out of

college.

When you are finished, press Alt-G (⌘-G) to have Ukey2 check your work. After reading your score, press Enter to save your document and select yes to print it. Press Esc to exit the *Galaxy Gazette*.

Mission Control is pleased with your progress.

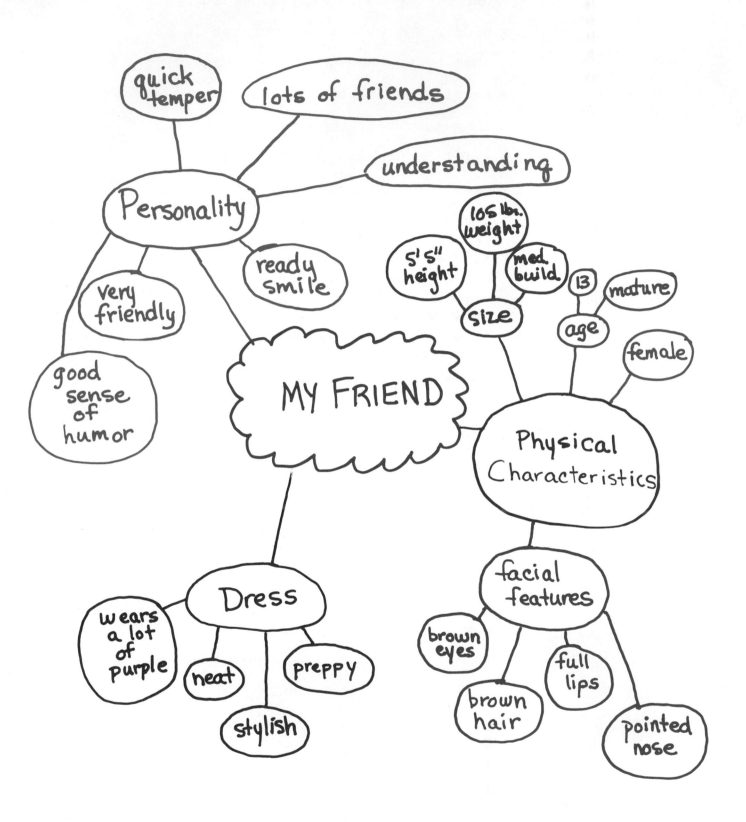

quick temper

lots of friends

understanding

Personality

very friendly

ready smile

good sense of humor

105 lbs. weight

5'5" height

med. build

13

mature

size

age

female

MY FRIEND

Physical Characteristics

Dress

wears a lot of purple

neat

preppy

stylish

facial features

brown eyes

full lips

brown hair

pointed nose

LESSON

17 Learning the Q, Question Mark, and Diagonal/ Slash Keys

Computers—use default margins for all drills unless otherwise indicated.
Typewriters—use these margins unless otherwise indicated: 10 Pitch 2", 12 pitch 2½".
Single-spacing unless otherwise indicated.

Countdown—Get Ready for Blast-off

Review the countdown procedures.

Launch Review

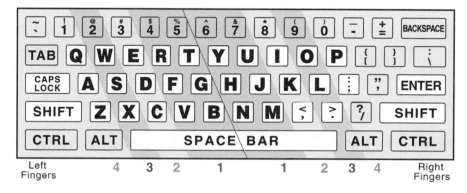

Key each line two times before moving on to key the next line.

1 sxs sxs jyj jyj fvf fvf aza zoom extras

2 excess zoo next flaxen year vapor seize

3 be amazed travel vault yawn maybe types

4 Maybe Nels would like to go to the zoo.

5 Ezra examines the texts for exact data.

Destination—The Q Key

Here is the Q key. It is keyed with your A finger. Place your fingers in a curved, upright position on the home keys. Look at your A finger and

MISSION BRIEFING

In this mission you will complete the destinations to the alphabetic keys. When you complete the mission, you will be able to key words containing all the alphabetic characters. In this mission, you will:

1. Review all keys learned.
2. Key copy using the Q, question mark, and diagonal/slash keys.
3. Improve keyboarding techniques.
4. Improve keyboarding skill.

Strike the keys quickly.

Mission Report—Descriptive Writing

Descriptive writing includes words that give the reader sensory information about feelings, activities, sights, smells, sounds, tastes, and touch. The opening sentence of a descriptive paragraph states what is to be described. The rest of the paragraph uses action verbs, adverbs, and adjectives that tell what is happening and the shape, size, and color of what is being described.

Exercise

1. Your assignment is to write an article in the word processor describing a friend. You do not need to give the name of your friend. You may use a mind map to generate ideas, or you may brainstorm a list of descriptive words. A mind map is a quick and easy way of putting together similar ideas. See the example on the next page. That why it's called a map. The map lets you see how your ideas are hooked together. In making a map, you use key words and phrases. You do not need to use complete sentences. A mind map for this exercise might look like this.

    A. **Physical Characteristics**
       Size — height, weight, build
       Age — youthful, mature, babyish
       Sex — male, female
       Facial features — lips, nose, eyes, hair
       Movement — calm, slow, quick, jerky

    B. **Dress**
       Style
       Neat or sloppy
       In fashion

    C. **Personality**
       Relationships with others
       Interpersonal skills
       Strengths and weaknesses
       Moods

2. Prepare a mind map to brainstorm the article describing your friend. With the mind map as a guide, write a draft copy of your article using the open screen of the word processor. Double-space the copy. Remember that in the draft copy you do not need to worry about correctness. Print and save the document. Name the document "Friend."

REENTRY
BRIEFING

Great job!

practice the reach to Q. Keep your other fingers curved and resting lightly on the home keys.

```
aqa aqa aqa aqa aqa aqa aqa aqa aqa aqa
```

Now look away from the keyboard and practice. Look at your text, not the keyboard.

```
aqa aqa aqa aqa aqa aqa aqa aqa aqa aqa
```

Key each line two times before moving on to key the next line.

1 aqua quit quota equal quiet quick quart

2 unique antique quilt equip equate quail

3 My question was a request to the Queen.

4 The unique antique is of equal quality.

5 Quint inquires about the quaint quilts.

6 The quiet quest for quotas was complex.

COMPUTER TIP

On computer keyboards, you also will find a backslash key (\). This key is used to create subdirectories when filing documents on computers. The backslash shows the connections between the subdirectories.

Destination—The Diagonal or Slash Key

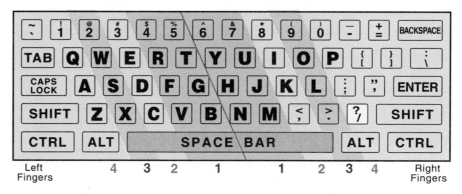

Left Fingers   4 3 2   1   1   2 3 4   Right Fingers

A **diagonal** or **slash** (/) is used between letters in some abbreviations, between the numbers in a fraction, and between certain interchangeable expressions. No space is left before or after a diagonal.

Here is the diagonal key. It is keyed with your semicolon finger. Place your fingers in a curved, upright position on the home keys. Look at your semicolon finger and practice the reach to the diagonal key. Keep your other fingers curved and resting lightly on the home keys.

```
;/; ;/; ;/; ;/; ;/; ;/; ;/; ;/; ;/; ;/;
```

Now look away from the keyboard and practice. Look at your text, not the keyboard.

```
;/; ;/; ;/; ;/; ;/; ;/; ;/; ;/; ;/; ;/;
```

TOP-NOTCH TRAINING TIP

1. When you are finished, proofread your text on the screen and then press Alt-P (⌘-P) to print a copy. Press Alt-S (⌘-S) to save a copy and name it "Lesson79."
2. Proofread your printed copy and then make any needed corrections.
3. When you are satisfied with your work, press Alt-G (⌘-G) to have UKey2 check your work. Press Enter to save your work and select yes to print a final copy. Press Esc to exit the *Galaxy Gazette*.

Mission Assessment

Take two 2-minute timings on the following paragraphs. Study the material; then following the copy in your book, key the lines on the computer or your typewriter.

> Minimum speed goal:
> 29 wam
> Maximum errors allowed:
> 4

1   A descriptive paragraph tells

2 about people and places using action

3 verbs, adverbs, and adjectives. These

4 words often appeal to the senses of

5 touch, smell, sight, sound, and taste.

6 Specific words describe color, shape,

7 and size in a lively way.

8   Well-written descriptive

9 paragraphs make the reader see and

10 feel the details so that they come

11 alive to the reader. The reader

12 actually seems to experience the

13 feeling and events described.

14   The following sentences are

15 examples of the types that would be

16 found in descriptive paragraphs. The

17 sparkling waves lapped softly at the

18 warm, sandy beach. The long-legged

19 sandpipers sprinted in all directions

20 as we chased them through the moonlit,

21 salty ocean mist.

| 1 | 2 | 3 | 4 | 5 | 6 | 7 | 8 |

Key each line two times before moving on to key the next line.

1 ;/; ;/; ;/; or/to his/her a/an yes/none

2 either/or; high/low; pass/fail; up/down

3 I/O means input/output computer device.

4 The pass/fail rule was unfair to Yamel.

5 Quail and/or turkeys inhabit the field.

Destination—The Question Mark Key

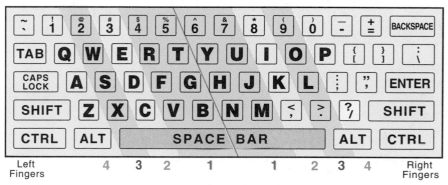

Here is the question mark key. It is keyed by holding down the left shift key and striking the question mark key with your semicolon finger. Place your fingers in a curved, upright position on the home keys. Look at your semicolon finger and practice the reach to the question mark. Keep your other fingers curved and resting lightly on the home keys.

;?; ;?; ;?; ;?; ;?; ;?; ;?; ;?; ;?; ;?;

Now look away from the keyboard and practice. Look at your text, not the keyboard.

;?; ;?; ;?; ;?; ;?; ;?; ;?; ;?; ;?; ;?;

Key each line two times before moving on to key the next line.

Space twice after a question mark at the end of a sentence.

1 ;?; ;?; ;?; Who me? Did Lonnie attend?

2 Have you seen Vicki? Why do they work?

3 Will they come? Has Kim called Carrie?

4 When will you go see the new hit movie?

5 How did you spend your summer vacation?

LESSON

79 The Writing Process— Descriptive Writing

Computers—use default margins for all drills unless otherwise indicated.
Typewriters—use these margins unless otherwise indicated: 10 Pitch 2", 12 pitch 2½".
Single-spacing unless otherwise indicated.

MISSION BRIEFING

In this mission, you will:
1. Review word comparisons.
2. Write a descriptive article.

Strike the keys quickly.

Keep your eyes on the copy.

TOP-NOTCH TRAINING TIP

Countdown—Get Ready for Blast-off

Review the countdown procedures.

Launch Review

Key each line two times.

1 There were 22 @ $8.10 totaling $178.20.

2 Ray rarely reads real rational reports.

3 Vans are not good for moving big bears.

4 They will go when the tickets are sold.

Galaxy Gazette—Build Word-Processing Skills

Word Comparisons

Good, Well

Good is an adjective that describes a noun or pronoun. *Well* is an adverb that describes a verb, an adjective, or another adverb. It is the correct word to choose when speaking of a person's health or well being.

From the main menu, select Mission Report and *Galaxy Gazette*. Study and key each sentence.

1 That shirt is a good color match.

2 Andrea has done well in her photography class.

Key each sentence with the correct choice of word.

1 Our youth group has many projects to do (good, well)

things for people in need.

2 Nita did not feel (good, well) today.

3 The minty medicine tastes (good, well).

4 Pizza tastes (good, well), and I eat it a lot.

5 I am not doing (good, well) in school this semester.

Mission Assessment

Take two 1-minute timings on the following paragraphs. Following the copy in your book, key the lines on the computer or your typewriter. The computer will figure out the speed. If you are using a typewriter, you can compute your speed using the formula you learned in the Introduction.

1 Most of the personal computers that

2 students use store data and programs on

3 disks. There are four types of disks

4 being used. Of the four types, the

5 floppy disk is used the most in schools.

6 These disks should be protected with

7 covers so they are not damaged.

| 1 | 2 | 3 | 4 | 5 | 6 | 7 | 8 |

Remember, for paragraph copy you do not need to press the Enter key on the computer.

Galaxy Gazette

From the main menu, select Mission Report and choose *Galaxy Gazette*. Rekey the following paragraph using capital letters where needed. Remember, with paragraph copy you do *not* need to press the Enter key on your computer. You will need to strike Return on your typewriter.

Hint: Remember the capitalization and punctuation rules you learned in Lesson 9.

i recently visited the nasa space center in florida. while i was there, i saw exhibits of all the old space ships and capsules that the astronauts used. our tour of the space center was conducted by captain michael everett. captain everett was a very knowledgeable guide and made the tour very interesting.

When you are finished, press Alt-G (⌂-G) to have Ukey2 check your work. After reading your score, press Enter to save your document and select yes to print it. Press Esc to exit the *Galaxy Gazette*.

REENTRY
BRIEFING

You have completed this mission. Congratulations!

2"
↓

HOW TO CREATE AND EDIT A DATABASE ← Center and all capitals

↓ tab   double-space document

tab → I. Define the Database Structure

        ↓ tab

        A. Identify Records

        B. Define and Name Fields

   tab C. Determine Field Type

        D. Determine Field Size

tab → II. Create Database Entry Forms

        A. Default Data Entry Screen

1" →   tab B. Fixed/Variable Length Fields   ← 1"

        C. Customize the Input Screen

tab → III. Enter Data

tab → IV. Save a Database File

tab → V. Edit a Database File

        A. Edit Fields

        B. Add Records

        C. Delete Records

↑
1"

LESSON

18 Learning the Apostrophe, Quotation Mark, and Hyphen Keys

Computers—use default margins for all drills unless otherwise indicated.
Typewriters—use these margins unless otherwise indicated: 10 Pitch 2", 12 pitch 2½".
Single-spacing unless otherwise indicated.

Countdown—Get Ready for Blast-off

Review the countdown procedures.

Launch Review

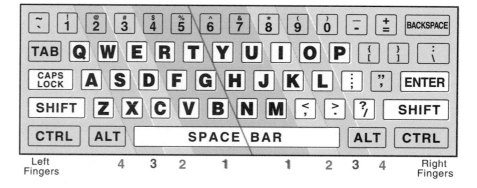

Key each line two times before moving on to key the next line.

1 ;/; ;/; ;?; ;?; aqua equals quiet quick

2 requires quantity up/down in/out yes/no

3 Is Will in? Does she require time out?

4 Did he get equal quotient? This is it?

5 Ask Quane to call Quint with the quest.

Destination—The Apostrophe and Quotation Mark Keys

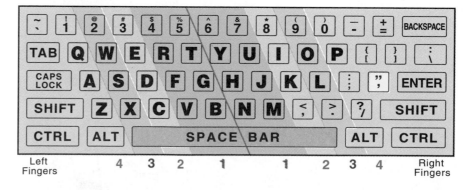

The **apostrophe** (') is used to show the possessive case of nouns as in *Dave's hat*, to show the omission of a letter or letters such as *don't you*, and to mark the omission of figures, such as the *class of '99*.

Top-Notch Training Tip ➡

Mission Report—Organizing Your Writing

1. Using the open screen of the word processor, key at the top of a page the heading "Things I Can Do to Stay Healthy."

2. Brainstorm as many ideas as possible, using the following prewriting method: Make an unarranged listing of everything that comes to mind about the subject.

3. Meet with your writing team and compare your lists. Working as a team, look for ideas from all the lists that could be grouped under subheads. For example, bike riding and swimming could be grouped under "Exercise," and eating fruit and avoiding fats could be grouped under "Nutrition."

4. Working with your team, identify the main headings that will be in the report and the list of items to be included under each subhead.

5. Prepare an outline following the one shown on page 291. To indent the subheadings, press the tab key. When creating an outline, it is important to be consistent. Decide if you will use the sentences or phrases and then stick with your choice. Also, if you want to include subentries (A, B, C, etc.), you must always use more than one. Save your outline. Name it "Outline."

6. Now using your outline as a guide, draft a copy of the article. Center the title in capitals, and double-space the copy. Key each subhead on a line by itself. Underline your subheads. Remember that during the draft stage you do not need to worry about correctness. Print and save the document. Name it "Health."

Extended Activities

6. Meet with your writing team to edit and proof the draft copies. Make the corrections needed.

7. Print and save the final copy. Replace "Health" with your final version.

Great mission.

Here is the apostrophe key. It is keyed with your semicolon finger. Place your fingers in a curved, upright position on the home keys. Look at your semicolon and practice the reach to the apostrophe. Keep your other fingers curved and resting lightly on the home keys.

```
;'; ;'; ;'; ;'; ;'; ;'; ;'; ;'; ;'; ;';
```

Now look away from the keyboard and practice. Look at your text, not the keyboard.

```
;'; ;'; ;'; ;'; ;'; ;'; ;'; ;'; ;'; ;';
```

Key each line two times before moving on to key the next line.

1 `;'; ;'; Is this Ali's?  I'll wait here.`

2 `Can't they visit the children's school?`

3 `What was this week's pay for work, Tim?`

4 `She'll match the companies' worth soon.`

Quotation marks are used to mark words that are spoken by someone else. For example:
   Maurice says, "Let's all go swimming."
   Quotation marks also mark words or passages that have been published in another book. For example:
   Webster's Dictionary defines "computer" as "a programmable device that can store, retrieve, and process data."
   Quotation marks also can be used in order to make a word stand out in a sentence so its meaning is clearer. Look again at the sentence about *Webster's Dictionary* and notice how computer is in quotation marks.
   On your keyboard, the quotation mark (") is the shift of the apostrophe. To make a quotation mark, hold down the left shift key and use the semicolon finger to strike the quotation mark key.

Look at your hands and practice the reach to the quotation mark.

```
;"; ;"; ;"; ;"; ;"; ;"; ;"; ;"; ;"; ;"; ;";
```

Now look away from your keyboard and practice. Look at your text, not the keyboard.

```
;"; ;"; ;"; ;"; ;"; ;"; ;"; ;"; ;"; ;"; ;";
```

Periods and commas always go inside the quotation mark. The question mark is placed inside the quotation mark when the question is part of the quoted material. Place the question mark outside the quotation mark when the question is not part of the quoted material. For example:
   Roger asked, "Are you ready to leave?"
   Have you noticed the ad "Fly for free"?

1. When you are finished, proofread your text on the screen and then press Alt-P (⌘-P) to print a copy. Press Alt-S (⌘-S) to save a copy and name it "Lesson78."
2. Proofread your printed copy and then make any needed corrections.
3. When you are satisfied with your work, press Alt-G (⌘-G) to have UKey2 check your work. Press Enter to save your work and select yes to print a final copy. Press Esc to exit the *Galaxy Gazette*.

Mission Assessment

Take two 2-minute timings on the following paragraphs. Study the material; then following the copy in your book, key the lines on the computer or your typewriter.

> Minimum speed goal:
> **29 wam**
> Maximum errors allowed:
> **4**

1   Prior to writing, you will find

2   it helpful to develop an outline. You

3   may choose from several options: a

4   mind map, a cluster, or a linear

5   outline. An outline has the major

6   headings and related ideas and

7   information you will include in your

8   story. The outline is a major

9   planning tool for writing a paper.

10   The line outline usually has four

11   outline levels. If desired, this can

12   be adjusted depending on the length

13   and detail of the ideas given. The

14   main ideas are indicated by Roman

15   numerals. The related ideas that

16   support the main ideas are indented

17   under the Roman numerals and labeled

18   with letters. Always prepare some

19   type of outline before you write your

20   report. You will find it is much

21   easier to organize your report.

| 1 | 2 | 3 | 4 | 5 | 6 | 7 | 8 |

Key each line two times before moving on to key the next line.

1 ;"; ;"; ;"; Quisa said, "See the snow."

2 "I am going skiing soon," said Raymond.

3 Did Jackie read "The Song of Hiawatha"?

4 Rita said, "Where is my blue book bag?"

Destination—The Hyphen Key

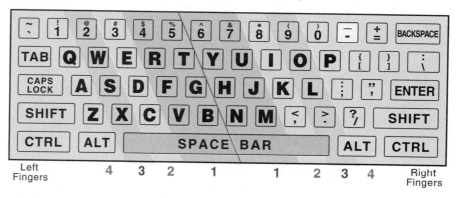

The **hyphen** (-) is used to join words to form compound words such as *Texas two-step* or to show that two adjectives are used as a unit modifier for a noun, such as the *small-shop owner.* A hyphen also is used to mark the syllables of a word such as *knowl-edge,* or in printed materials to show when part of a word is carried over to another line.

Here is the hyphen key. It is keyed with your semicolon finger. Place your fingers in a curved, upright position on the home keys. Look at your semicolon finger and practice the reach to the hyphen key. Keep your other fingers curved and resting lightly on the home keys.

;-; ;-; ;-; ;-; ;-; ;-; ;-; ;-; ;-; ;-;

Now look away from the keyboard and practice. Look at your text, not the keyboard.

;-; ;-; ;-; ;-; ;-; ;-; ;-; ;-; ;-; ;-;

Key each line two times before moving on to key the next line.

1 ;-; ;-; ;-; part-time self-concept ;-;-

2 Word-processing systems are productive.

3 That girl's self-concept was very high.

4 Judith Ann works for her mother-in-law.

A **dash** is two hyphens keyed without spaces. A dash is used to show a break in thought or to give emphasis to a phrase. For example, key the following:

1 His game--not mine--begins before noon.

2 Learn the concepts--and learn them well.

TOP-NOTCH TRAINING TIP

LESSON

78 The Writing Process— Organizing the Subject

MISSION BRIEFING

In this mission, you will:
1. Review word comparisons.
2. Improve composition skills.

Strike the keys quickly.

Keep your eyes on the copy.

Countdown—Get Ready for Blast-off

Review the countdown procedures.

Launch Review

Key each line two times.

1 They cost $3.55 per 10 or $6.75 per 20.

2 Quick, quiet quasars provoke questions.

3 Soccer players arrive early to warm up.

4 Will the staff handle all the problems?

Galaxy Gazette—Build Word-Processing Skills

Word Comparisons

Lay, Lie

Lay is a verb that means to put or place. Lay is used with an object. *Lie* is a verb that means to recline. Lie does not have an object.

Study and key each sentence in the *Galaxy Gazette.*

1 Please lay my wrist weights on the exercise bench.

2 Bill went to the clinic to lie down.

Key each sentence with the correct choice of word.

1 It is a good idea to (lie, lay) down and take a nap.

2 Anthony will (lie, lay) his keys on the dresser.

3 Willnette, are you going to (lie, lay) the bouquet of flowers by the front door?

4 The pink carpet looked so inviting that I thought I might (lie, lay) down and watch television.

5 When you get home, (lie, lay) your books on your desk rather than leaving them in the living room.

Mission Assessment

Take two 1-minute timings on the following paragraph. Following the copy in your book, key the lines on the computer or on your typewriter. The computer will figure out the speed. If you are using a typewriter, you can compute your speed using the formula you learned in the Introduction.

1 The United States has what is called a

2 "free enterprise system." Our laws

3 and traditions favor giving everyone

4 as much freedom as possible and

5 allowing them to run their own lives.

6 This system allows people the freedom

7 to start and run their own businesses.

| 1 | 2 | 3 | 4 | 5 | 6 | 7 | 8 |

You have successfully completed this mission!

LESSON

19 Learning the Exclamation Point and Parentheses

Computers—use default margins for all drills unless otherwise indicated.
Typewriters—use these margins unless otherwise indicated: 10 Pitch 2", 12 pitch 2½".
Single-spacing unless otherwise indicated.

Countdown for Blast-off

Review the countdown procedures.

Launch Review

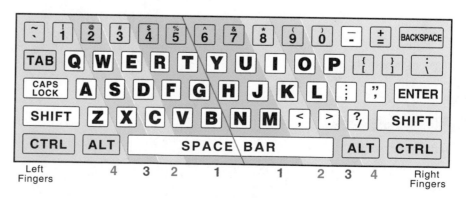

Are you ready for more punctuation destinations? In this mission you will:
1. Key copy using the exclamation point and parentheses keys.
2. Review all keys learned.
3. Improve keyboarding techniques.
4. Improve keyboarding skill.

Mission Report—Writing with a Purpose

Song lyrics are easy to remember because they are set to a beat or rhythm. Lyrics often rhyme but not always. Words that are arranged to form a definite rhythm, or beat, become poetry. Rap is a current form of poetry. Hammer is a well-known rapper. Rappers write about issues that concern them, such as the environment, or they write stories about people, places, or things.

Exercise

Think about an issue that concerns you or a story you'd like to tell.

1. Brainstorm a list of ideas, keying your ideas in the open screen of the word processor. Remember, **no editing!** Just quickly list as many ideas as come to mind.
2. Choose one idea from your list and draft a short rap. Print and save the document. Name it "Rap."
3. Process your work with your writing team.
4. Make final revisions to the rap. Prepare the final for presentation. Print and save a copy. Replace "Rap."

Extended Activity

5. If time permits, each writing team can choose one rap and create a "shape poem." Post your work on the bulletin board. An example of a rap in a shape poem is shown below.

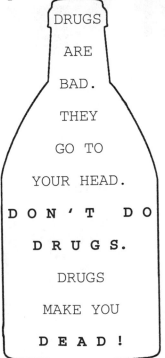

Keep up the good work!

Key each line two times before moving on to key the next line.

1 If it is in the car, Keri may drive it.

2 Roy Rogers is his favorite cowboy star.

3 Jose's dad said, "Do they want to eat?"

4 George quit his part-time job Saturday.

5 Franco said, "I'll need seven tickets."

Destination—The Exclamation Point Key

Strike the keys quickly.

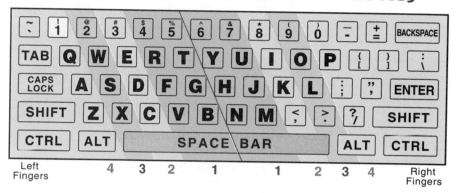

An **exclamation point** (!) is used after an expression of strong feeling or after a command. Space twice after an exclamation point at the end of a sentence. The exclamation point is placed inside the quotation mark when the exclaimed material is part of the quoted material, and outside the quotation mark when it is not part of the quoted material.

Here is the exclamation point (!) key. It is the shift of the 1 and is keyed with your A finger. Place your fingers in a curved, upright position on the home keys. Look at your A finger and practice the reach to the exclamation point. Keep your other fingers curved and resting lightly on the home keys.

a!a a!a a!a a!a a!a a!a a!a a!a a!a a!a

Now look away from the keyboard and practice. Look at your text, not the keyboard.

a!a a!a a!a a!a a!a a!a a!a a!a a!a a!a

Key each line two times before moving on to key the next line.

1 a!a a!a a!a Sari yelled, "Fire!" Stop!

2 We hate to study on Saturdays! We won!

3 No way! The car is still moving! Yes!

4 My team won the championship! Success!

1. When you are finished, proofread your text on the screen and then press Alt-P (⌘-P) to print a copy. Press Alt-S (⌘-S) to save a copy and name it "Lesson77."
2. Proofread your printed copy and then make any needed corrections on the computer.
3. When you are satisfied with your work, press Alt-G (⌘-G) to have UKey2 check your work. Press Enter to save your work and select yes to print a final copy. Press Esc to exit the *Galaxy Gazette*.

Mission Assessment

Take two 2-minute timings on the following paragraphs. Study the material; then following the copy in your book, key the lines on the computer or your typewriter.

1   Before writing a composition, you

2   need to decide on its purpose. The

3   purpose may be to entertain, to inform

4   or tell, to describe, or to explain.

5   Once you have selected a purpose,

6   the next stage in planning is to make

7   a list of ideas related to the topic.

8   Look at your list and group ideas that

9   go together. This grouping can become

10   the basis for the outline of the

11   paper. For each group of words, think

12   of a heading that may be used in an

13   outline.

14   Next decide on the best order to

15   present these ideas. The ideas could

16   be given in the order that they occur,

17   in order of importance, or in order

18   from simple to complex. The length of

19   your final composition may vary based

20   on the subject and how much

21   information you present.

| 1 | 2 | 3 | 4 | 5 | 6 | 7 | 8 |

Destination—The Parentheses Keys

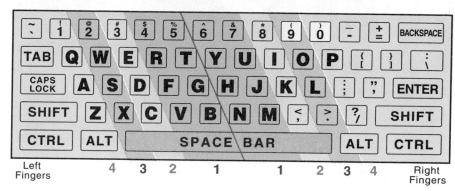

Left Fingers   4   3   2   1   1   2   3   4   Right Fingers

TOP-NOTCH TRAINING TIP

Parentheses are used to set off points in a sentence that expand, explain, or stray from the main concept of the sentence.

Here is the left parenthesis key. It is the shift of the 9 and is keyed with your L finger. Place your fingers in a curved, upright position on the home keys. Look at your L finger and practice the reach to the left parenthesis key. Keep your other fingers curved and resting lightly on the home keys.

```
l(l  l(l  l(l  l(l  l(l  l(l  l(l  l(l. l(l  l(l
```

Now look away from the keyboard and practice. Look at your text, not the keyboard.

```
l(l  l(l  l(l  l(l  l(l  l(l  l(l  l(l  l(l  l(l
```

Key each line two times before moving on to key the next line.

```
1  l(l  l(l  l(l  (a  (dawn  (your  (right  (quit

2  (and  (for  (but  (them  (now  (fury  (flying
```

Now find the right parenthesis key. It is the shift of the 0 and is keyed with your semicolon finger. Place your fingers in a curved, upright position on the home keys. Look at your semicolon finger and practice the reach to the right parenthesis key. Keep your other fingers curved and resting lightly on the home keys.

```
;);  ;);  ;);  ;);  ;);  ;);  ;);  ;);  ;);  ;);
```

Now look away from the keyboard and practice. Look at your text, not the keyboard.

```
;);  ;);  ;);  ;);  ;);  ;);  ;);  ;);  ;);  ;);
```

Key each line two times before moving on to key the next line.

```
1  ;);  ;);  ;);  big)  saw)  zip)  vote)  fazed)

2  gum)  tax)  quota)  zipper)  maybe)  quarts)

3  They must find out (a) how and (b) why.

4  Please (a) call or (b) write Lori soon.
```

LESSON

77 The Writing Process— Brainstorming

MISSION BRIEFING

In this mission, you will:
1. Review word comparisons.
2. Practice writing with a purpose.

Strike the keys quickly.

Keep your eyes on the copy.

TOP-NOTCH TRAINING TIP

Computers—use default margins for all drills unless otherwise indicated.
Typewriters—use these margins unless otherwise indicated: 10 Pitch 2", 12 pitch 2½".
Single-spacing unless otherwise indicated.

Countdown—Get Ready for Blast-off

Review the countdown procedures.

Launch Review

Key each line two times.

1 Johnson & Son stock was $17.45 a share.

2 Perfect pliers pinch pendants properly.

3 Try to stop sneezing loudly. Be quiet.

4 When Cy is ready, we'll go to the game.

Galaxy Gazette—Build Word-Processing Skills

Word Comparisons

Its, It's

Its is the possessive form of it. *It's* is the contraction of it is.

From the main menu, select Mission Report and *Galaxy Gazette*. Study and key each sentence.

1 The boxing team had its banquet at the Adams
   Amusement Park.

2 It's fun to play with my cats, Mason and Frisky.
   Key each sentence with the correct choice of word.

1 (Its, It's) fun to watch baseball games on
   television.

2 Spain would be a wonderful country to visit, and I
   understand that (its, it's) very warm there.

3 Recipes using curry powder make use of (its, it's)
   unusual and delicious flavor.

4 (Its, It's) very important to make good grades.

Skill Exploration

Take two 30-second timings on each of the following lines. Try to reach a new speed goal. Do not worry about errors for now. Work to beat the computer. If you are using a typewriter, you can figure out your speed using the formula in the Introduction.

1 Please remind Quint to go for the mail.

2 Are you able to play tennis with Greta?

3 We require a deposit for each new game.

| 1 | 2 | 3 | 4 | 5 | 6 | 7 | 8 |

Mission Assessment

Take two 1-minute timings on the following paragraph. Following the copy in your book, key the lines on the computer or your typewriter. The computer will figure out the speed. If you are using a typewriter, you can compute your speed using the formula you learned in the Introduction.

1 Early economic systems were based on

2 barter. Barter is a system of trading

3 for goods and services. If you lived

4 in a barter system and wanted to go to

5 the movies, you would not pay cash to

6 get in the theater. Rather you would

7 bring along an item of equal value to

8 the price of the show or offer a

9 service and try to exchange it for a

10 ticket. Can you imagine how long you

11 would have to stand in line while each

12 person bartered with the theater

13 owner? Barter doesn't work very well,

14 which is why money was introduced.

| 1 | 2 | 3 | 4 | 5 | 6 | 7 | 8 |

Minimum goal: 15 wam

Mission Report—Writing in Complete Sentences

Words are the building blocks that we use for communicating. Words build sentences, and sentences are used to build paragraphs. By arranging paragraphs, you then can write full-length letters, reports, and even books.

It is important to learn to write **complete sentences** that contain two elements: a subject (noun or pronoun) and a verb.

Example: Anxiously awaiting the countdown, everyone tense and nervous. (This sentence is incomplete. Can you explain why?)

Correction: Anxiously awaiting the countdown, everyone looked tense and nervous. (This sentence is complete. Explain why.)

Exercise

1. Read the list of words or phrases below and choose any three.

   shopping mall   friend
   dog   brother
   cat   school
   movie   home
   rock group   allowance

2. Using the open screen option in your word processor, key three complete questions relating to each of the three words you chose. Example: "Do you have a brother?" Name your document "Quest."

3. Exchange a printed copy of your three questions with a writing partner.

4. For the three questions you receive from your writing partner, write answers using the word processor. Be certain that you write your answers in complete sentences. Name the document "Ans."

Extended Activities

5. Get together with your writing team. Draw a card to see which role you will play. Discuss the different roles with the team before beginning so that everyone understands his or her role. Work at perfecting your copy and helping your group members with theirs.

6. If time permits, write a complete paragraph to expand on the answer to one question.

REENTRY
BRIEFING

Your mission is complete.

Mission Report

A **synonym** is a word that has nearly the same meaning as another word. For example, a synonym of *fast* is *quick*. From the main menu, select Mission Report and choose the open screen option. Rekey the following sentences, substituting synonyms for the italicized words.

1. A space mission was *organized* to study several planets.
2. In January, the spaceship blasted off and *zoomed* out of our atmosphere.
3. The crew members were *impressed* with the view of Earth from space.
4. The view of Saturn's rings was *fantastic*.
5. The *sleek* spaceship circled Jupiter, the *largest* planet.
6. The astronauts ran *several* tests while they were orbiting the planet.
7. The astronauts exercised *often* while in space so they could keep fit.
8. When they *touched down* three months later, the astronauts were *eager* to be with their families.
9. The *weary* astronauts *stumbled* from the space shuttle.
10. The NASA control center was *excited* about the *success* of the mission.

Press Alt-P (⌘-P) to print your work. Press Alt-N (⌘-N) to save your document. Name it "Lesson19." Press Alt-Q (⌘-Q) to quit.

REENTRY
BRIEFING

You've completed another mission. Congratulations!

20 Learning the Tab Key

Computers—use default margins for all drills unless otherwise indicated.
Typewriters—use these margins unless otherwise indicated: 10 Pitch 2", 12 pitch 2½".
Single-spacing unless otherwise indicated.

Countdown—Get Ready for Blast-off

Review the countdown procedures.

Launch Review

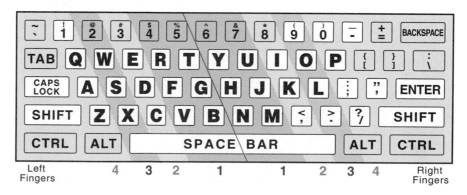

MISSION
BRIEFING

During this mission you will continue to develop keying skill. The purpose of this mission is to:
1. **Review all keys learned.**
2. **Key copy using the tab key.**
3. **Improve keyboarding techniques.**
4. **Improve keyboarding skill.**
5. **Learn to identify keying errors.**

Key each line two times before moving on to key the next line.

1 She told the guys to come to the party.

2 We saw six singing, very fat red birds.

Strike the keys quickly.

3 What did that big, fuzzy bear do today?

4 (May, Can) I have permission to go skating on

Saturday night?

1. When you are finished, proofread your text on the screen and then press Alt-P (⌘-P) to print a copy. Press Alt-S (⌘-S) to save a copy and name it "Lesson76."
2. Proofread your printed copy and then make any needed corrections on the computer.
3. When you are satisfied with your work, press Alt-G (⌘-G) to have UKey2 check your work. Press Enter to save your work and select yes to print a final copy. Press Esc to exit the *Galaxy Gazette*.

Mission Assessment

Take two 2-minute timings on the following paragraphs. Study the material; then following the copy in your book, key the lines on the computer on your typewriter.

| Minimum speed goal: |
| 29 wam |
| Maximum errors allowed: |
| 4 |

1   Desktop publishing software

2 allows users to take documents created

3 in a word processor and combine them

4 with graphics. Documents can be

5 attractively arranged so the pages

6 look as if they were from a magazine

7 or book.

8   With desktop publishing software

9 you can use different kinds of type

10 and place artwork and photographs on

11 the pages. You can have the text wrap

12 around the graphics or the type can be

13 placed in columns.

14   This textbook was written on a

15 word processor. The pages were

16 designed on a desktop publishing

17 system. You can create many different

18 looks with desktop publishing programs.

| | 1 | | 2 | | 3 | | 4 | | 5 | | 6 | | 7 | | 8 | |

Key each line two times.

4 I'll take that part-time position soon.

5 He said, "Where is the antique table?"

6 "Wow, it is so hot today!" said Rafael.

Destination—The Tab Key

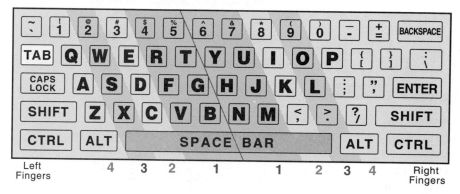

When keying information, sometimes it is necessary to indent paragraphs or arrange text or data in columns. The tab feature of the software allows you to do this. Most microcomputer software packages have preset tabs called default tabs. These default tabs can be changed to allow for variable spacing between columns. In this software, tabs are preset every five spaces. To indent a paragraph, press the tab key once.

Here is the tab key. It is keyed with your A finger. Place your fingers in a curved, upright position on the home keys. Look at your A finger and practice the reach to the tab key. Keep your other fingers curved and resting lightly on the home keys.

a(tab) a(tab) a(tab) a(tab) a(tab)

Now look away from the keyboard and practice. Look at your text, not the keyboard.

a(tab) a(tab) a(tab) a(tab) a(tab)

Strike the tab key to indent each sentence. Key each sentence one time.

1   Software programs save users time.

2   The tab key feature is an example.

3   The tab key can indent paragraphs.

4   Tabs can organize copy in columns.

5   Software normally has preset tabs.

LESSON

76 Writing in Complete Sentences

BRIEFING

In this mission, you will:
1. Review word comparisons.
2. Write complete sentences.

Strike the keys quickly.

Keep your eyes on the copy.

Computers—use default margins for all drills unless otherwise indicated.
Typewriters—use these margins unless otherwise indicated: 10 Pitch 2", 12 pitch 2½".
Single-spacing unless otherwise indicated.

Countdown—Get Ready for Blast-off

Review the countdown procedures.

Launch Review

Key each line two times.

1 A computer talks with others via modem.

2 Modems route data over telephone lines.

3 They can relay and receive information.

4 Communications software runs the modem.

Galaxy Gazette—Build Word-Processing Skills

Word Comparisons

Can, Cannot, May

Can is the ability to do something. *May* indicates that you have permission to do something. *Cannot* is used as one word.

From the main menu, select Mission Report and *Galaxy Gazette.* Study and key each sentence.

1 You cannot help with building the deck until you put

on your safety goggles.

2 Dad said that you may come over after school.

3 You can make a good pie with fresh apples.

Key each sentence with the correct choice of word.

1 Eating the right foods (can, may) help your body be

healthier.

2 Zenia (cannot, can not) go; she is not feeling well.

3 If you go to the top of High Street in Cincinnati,

you (can, may) get a great view of the city.

Skill Exploration

Take two 30-second timings on each of the following lines. Try to reach a new speed goal. Do not worry about errors for now. Work to beat the computer. If you are using a typewriter, you can figure out your speed using the formula in the Introduction.

1 or it la do ha ti by be if at en of ore

2 so on in he is no an so as do up me ask

3 she cut how put ten was its cab too big
| 1 | 2 | 3 | 4 | 5 | 6 | 7 | 8 |

Mission Assessment

Notice that your Mission Assessment now has an accuracy goal as well as the speed goal. You should attempt to key the Mission Assessment at the highest possible speed while meeting the suggested accuracy goal. You will make better progress, if you decide on a specific goal for each timing. That is, decide if you want to try for increased speed or increased accuracy.

Take two 1-minute timings on the following paragraph. Following the copy in your book, key thc lines on the computer or your typewriter. The computer will figure out the speed and indicate keying errors. If you are using a typewriter, you can compute your speed using the formula you learned in the Introduction. Develop your proofreading skills by checking the printout for errors.

1   Computers are very important in

2 our lives today. It is essential that

3 we all become familiar with this great

4 tool. If you want to become an expert

5 on computers, you must learn about

6 their operation. Fast and accurate

7 keying skills will enable you to get

8 the full enjoyment from this machine.
| 1 | 2 | 3 | 4 | 5 | 6 | 7 | 8 |

Galaxy Gazette

It is important to be able to proofread copy in order to work toward producing error-free documents. In some drills, you will need to identify errors by marking them on the printout. In other drills, you will need to identify and correct errors on the screen.

Keying errors usually fall into one of these general groups:

1. Keying a wrong letter.
2. Using the wrong punctuation mark or omitting the punctuation mark.
3. Not spacing between words or using incorrect spacing between sentences.

Minimum speed goal:

15 wam

Maximum errors allowed:

4

The reader collects all responses from the commentators and gives them to the authors. Continue through the writing conference using the following procedure:

1. Revise your copy deciding whether or not to incorporate suggestions from the team. You may edit your existing copy of "Roles" or write new copy. Keep in mind that this is still a rough draft. Print a copy. Replace "Roles" or assign a new name if article is rewritten.
2. Give your draft to your content editor.
3. Take on the role of content editor for the author you have been assigned. Edit the copy for content, organization, and how well it fits the audience. Return the copy to your author.
4. When you get your copy back from your content editor, make any necessary changes to your paper to complete the editing stage. Replace existing copy.
5. Give a draft to your proofreader.
6. Take on the role of proofreader for the author you have been assigned. Proof the draft of your author. As a proofreader you will check for grammar, spelling, and punctuation. Return the draft to your author.
7. When you get back your draft from your proofreader, make any final revisions that are needed. Replace existing copy.
8. Print your copy and proof it yourself. Make any remaining changes to make it the final copy for publication and presentation. Print your final version or prepare it for presentation. See the suggestions on presentations.
9. Give your paper to the Universal Editor. The Universal Editor should hand in the papers to your instructor.

Presenting a Final Paper

As a professional on the *Galaxy Gazette*, you may want to prepare your final papers using one of the following suggestions:

1. Use graphics or artwork on the page.
2. Give an oral reading to your class.
3. Mount your paper on the bulletin board, banner, poster, easel, or fabric.
4. Put your paper in a binding. Add a cover page.
5. Publish your article in the class, school, or community newspaper.
6. Decorate the classroom or school halls.
7. Keep your article in a personal notebook, file, or diary.

REENTRY
BRIEFING

Congratulations on completing your mission!

4. Not capitalizing.
5. Not keying a word or keying a word twice.
6. Not keying a letter or keying a letter more than once.

Use this guideline, when identifying keying errors: Count only one error per word. If errors occur in the punctuation and spacing that follow a word, count the word as an error. Study the following paragraph to see how keying errors are counted.

An efficient computer user (mut) become
(skailld) in the (usr) of the computer's disk
operating system (DOS). The DOS (sysstem) is
loaded into the computer's memory and (allow) the
system (torun) a number of (prorams) and
operations(,) Without the DOS system, ( )the
computer would not operate properly.

From the main menu, select Mission Report and then choose *Galaxy Gazette*. Now key the lines above, correcting the errors as you go. When you are finished, press Alt-G (⌘-G) to have Ukey2 check your work. After reading your score, press Enter to save your document and select yes to print it. Press Esc to exit the *Galaxy Gazette*.

REENTRY
BRIEFING

This mission is complete!

LESSON

21 Review and Skill Building

Computers—use default margins for all drills unless otherwise indicated.
Typewriters—use these margins unless otherwise indicated: 10 Pitch 2", 12 pitch 2½".
Single-spacing unless otherwise indicated.

Countdown—Get Ready for Blast-off

Review the countdown procedures.

Launch Review

MISSION
BRIEFING

During this mission, you do not have any new destinations. You will prepare for the next group of explorations by developing your flight skills. During this lesson, you will:
1. Review all keys learned.
2. Improve keyboarding techniques.
3. Improve keyboarding

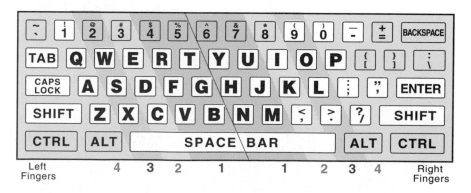

- **Universal Editor:** Each time you meet, in addition to the responsibility of commentator, one of you will be assigned the role of Universal Editor. As the Universal Editor, you will keep the group on task and make sure everyone's assignment is completed and turned in.

Additional Roles

After the reader has presented all of the documents, you will return to your work center and decide how to use the comments given to you by the commentators. You will make corrections to your document and print a copy. At that time, your writing team divides into pairs and you have the following roles:

- **Content Editor:** You will check the copy of another team member and make suggestions about content, organization of thoughts, and how well it fits the audience. You will use the proofreaders's marks you learned in Unit 3 to note suggested changes.

- **Proofreader:** After each team member has had a chance to change the copy according to the editor's suggestions, you will again trade papers and act as a proofreader for one other team member. You will check the copy for grammar, spelling, and punctuation.

Mission Report—"Let's Talk about It": The Writing Conference

The purpose of this activity is to practice the Task Force Writing Team roles. Choose one of the sentence stems below and free write for three minutes using the word processor. Fill up the page as quickly as you can. Even if you think your mind goes blank, key in "My mind is blank...." Keep writing.

Sentence Stems

A. My friends think I am....
B. Secretly I wish....
C. One thing I'm really good at is....

Print and save a copy. Name it "Roles."

Now meet with your writing team and determine role assignments. (You may draw cards, or team members can decide on roles.) As each paper is read aloud, practice your role as commentator and try to write a response, using one or more of the following sentence stems:

A. I liked what you said about....
B. I didn't understand what you said about....
C. Tell me more about....

Strike the keys quickly.

1 The halfback ran quickly off the field.

2 He would like to see the girls all win.

3 Did that queen conquer all the nations?

4 He may take the wet hut for tax credit.

Landing Practice—Review Keys (Part A)

Key each line two times before moving on to key the next line. If time permits, attempt to key each sentence with no more than one incorrect word.

1 Always aspire to be active all of life!

2 Bogus business battles boosted rebates.

3 Careening cars create a crazy accident.

4 Did the death of Dave De deter driving?

5 Eve easily sees an error erases effort.

6 Family was their foundation of fortune.

7 Greg Grant Greson generates good press.

8 How will she heat homes for the hungry?

Landing Practice—Review Keys (Part B)

Key each line two times before moving on to key the next line. If time permits, attempt to key each sentence with no more than one incorrect word.

Take a break. Drop your hands to your sides and shake them gently.

1 I did it! Who will fill it? Eli will.

2 Jan and Jo joyously, jauntily jabbered.

3 Kudos for knowing how to cook kohlrabi.

4 Lighting of liberty lamps lessens loss.

5 Maxi's mean machine mauled the message.

6 New novels never reached the newsstand.

7 Oily oceans are obnoxious for dolphins.

8 Pour a pinch of pepper on top of pasta.

Key each sentence with the correct choice of word.

1 The amount of time you spend riding your bicycle will (affect, effect) how fast you can ride.

2 The government will (affect, effect) growth in the economy by lowering interest rates.

3 If you eat too many fatty foods, there will be an overall (affect, effect) on your health.

4 Sasha has been spending a lot of time talking on the telephone lately, and it has been (affecting, effecting) her grades.

5 The (affect, effect) of not doing my project was that I got a poor grade.

1. When you are finished, proofread your text on the screen and then press Alt-P (⌘-P) to print a copy. Press Alt-S (⌘-S) to save a copy and name it "Lesson75."
2. Proofread your printed copy and then make any needed corrections on the computer.
3. When you are satisfied with your work, press Alt-G (⌘-G) to have UKey2 check your work. Press Enter to save your work and select yes to print a final copy. Press Esc to exit the *Galaxy Gazette*.

Galaxy Gazette Teams

As a worker for the *Galaxy Gazette*, you will be part of a Mission Control Task Force writing team. For activities that involve this writing team, your instructor will divide the class into groups of four. As a member of a team, your efforts will affect the work of the other members. Your roles within your team will be:

• **Author:** Each of you will write an article based on the newspaper assignment you are given.

• **Reader:** Each time you meet, one of you will read all the documents aloud to the group.

• **Commentator:** As the reader reads each document, your role as a commentator is to make suggestions about what you like about the article and what could be improved. There will be three commentators in the group. You will make your comments in writing and give them to the authors of the documents.

Mission Assessment

Take two 1-minute timings on the following paragraphs. Following the copy in your book, key the lines on the computer or your typewriter. Decide on a goal of increased speed or increased accuracy.

1   Batteries are used to run many

2 things such as calculators and radios,

3 but batteries wear out. Solar cells

4 act like batteries, but they do not

5 run down and have to be replaced.

6   Solar cells turn light into

7 electricity. The light can come from

8 the sun or from electric lights. Many

9 calculators run on solar cells. Even

10 some cars do. What other uses can you

11 think of for solar cells?

| 1 | 2 | 3 | 4 | 5 | 6 | 7 | 8 |

Galaxy Gazette

From the main menu, select Mission Report and choose *Galaxy Gazette*. An important part of writing for the *Galaxy Gazette* is to be able to recognize and correct keying errors. Rekey the following paragraph correcting any errors.

Dont you think that it woul be

very exciting to be an astronat.

imagine the excitement of training for

an imporant mission and of the thrill

of your first flight space. i cant

think of a more fasinating carer.

When you are finished, press Alt-G (⌘-G) to have Ukey2 check your work. After reading your score, press Enter to save your document and select yes to print it. Press Esc to exit the *Galaxy Gazette*.

LESSON

75 The Writing Process—Writing Teams

MISSION BRIEFING

Computers—use default margins for all drills unless otherwise indicated.
Typewriters—use these margins unless otherwise indicated: 10 Pitch 2", 12 pitch 2½".
Single-spacing unless otherwise indicated.

Countdown—Get Ready for Blast-off

Review the countdown procedures.

Launch Review

Key each line two times.

1 Discount for cash items was 10 percent.

2 Outdoor outposts are open to outsiders.

Strike the keys quickly.
Keep your eyes on the copy.

3 My two puppies wreak havoc on my place.

4 All students are pleased by the awards.

Galaxy Gazette—Build Word-Processing Skills

Word Comparisons

Affect, Effect

Affect is a verb that means to influence. *Effect* as a verb means to cause something to happen. *Effect* as a noun means a result or consequence.

TOP-NOTCH TRAINING TIP

From the main menu, select Mission Report and *Galaxy Gazette*. Study and key each sentence.

1 Painting my room bright blue has had a positive effect on my mood.

2 Rising costs of plastic will effect a large price increase for water guns.

3 The amount of money you earn will affect your standard of living.

LESSON

22 Review and Skill Building

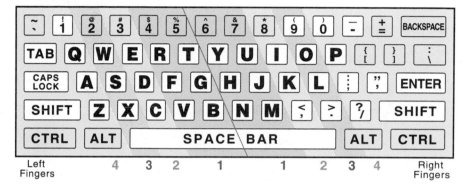

MISSION BRIEFING

During this mission, you do not have any new destinations. You will prepare for the next group of explorations by developing your preflight skills. During this lesson, you will:

1. Review all keys learned.
2. Improve keyboarding techniques.
3. Improve keyboarding skill.

Strike the keys quickly.

Computers—use default margins for all drills unless otherwise indicated.
Typewriters—use these margins unless otherwise indicated: 10 Pitch 2", 12 pitch 2½".
Single-spacing unless otherwise indicated.

Countdown—Get Ready for Blast-off

Review the countdown procedures.

Launch Review

Key each line two times before moving on to key the next line.

1 Jan and Jean sent Kent and Deana a fan.

2 Jacob watched the team leave the field.

3 Kylum drank all the milk before dinner.

4 Tim aimed at meeting the company quota.

5 Every night she dreams of running cats.

Landing Practice—Review Keys (Part A)

Key each line two times before moving on to key the next line. If time permits, attempt to key each sentence with no more than one incorrect word.

1 Queen's quiet question is quite quaint.

2 Really I refused Rathe because of Raye.

3 Salty sailors seek sea sailing sources.

4 The tried technical technique was true.

5 Unions unite to unload usual umbrellas.

6 Vacuum vapors vanished over the valves.

Skill Exploration

Take two 30-second timings on each of the following lines. Try to reach a new speed goal. Do not worry about errors for now. Work to beat the computer. If you are using a typewriter, you can figure out your speed using the formula in the Introduction.

1 Imagine a computer responding to voice.

2 Voice-activated computers are workable.

3 Say an order and the computer responds.

| 1 | 2 | 3 | 4 | 5 | 6 | 7 | 8 |

Mission Assessment

Take two 2-minute timings on the following paragraphs. Study the material; then following the copy in your book, key the lines on the computer or your typewriter.

1   The writing process includes a

2 series of logical activities. Some of

3 these activities take place before the

4 actual writing begins. During the

5 beginning stages, information is

6 gathered. The writer also thinks

7 creatively about the way to present

8 facts. Ideas and details supporting

9 the main topics are planned.

10   How the topics will be presented

11 is decided. For example, topics may

12 be introduced in the order in which

13 they occurred. They also may be given

14 in order of importance. The most

15 important ideas may come first. In

16 some cases, you may want to give the

17 least important ideas first and build

18 to the important ones.

| 1 | 2 | 3 | 4 | 5 | 6 | 7 | 8 |

REENTRY
BRIEFING

Very good work.

Landing Practice—Review Keys (Part B)

Key each line two times before moving on to key the next line. If time permits, attempt to key each sentence with no more than one incorrect word.

1 When the war was won, where was Warsaw?

2 X-ray exams excel as exacting examples.

3 You always yearn for yummy yellow yams.

4 ZIP codes zip zany letters to zoo zone.

5 I remember Ed's advice, "Be a success!"

6 Can she use the word-processing system?

Skill Exploration

Take two 30-second timings on each of the following lines. Try to reach a new speed goal. Do not worry about errors for now. Work to beat the computer. If you are using a typewriter, you can figure out your speed using the formula in the Introduction.

1 The dog begs for the bone and cats cry.

2 Fry the eggs in oil but do not eat ham.

3 Tag the bat and don the hat for a gnat.

| 1 | 2 | 3 | 4 | 5 | 6 | 7 | 8 |

Mission Assessment

Take two 1-minute timings on the following paragraph. Following the copy in your book, key the lines on the computer or your typewriter. Decide on a goal of increased speed or increased accuracy.

1   Now that you have learned to use

2 the letter keys, you will begin to

3 learn the number keys. As you

4 continue, your speed will increase

5 slowly until you have reached your

6 desired goal. You should be pleased

7 with your progress and able to use

8 your keyboarding skill with other

9 school subjects.

| 1 | 2 | 3 | 4 | 5 | 6 | 7 | 8 |

Minimum speed goal:

16 wam

Maximum errors allowed:

4

---

3 Her mother said the dress was (to, too, two) expensive, and she would have to find a less expensive one for the dance.

4 For doing my evaluation sheet, my teacher gave me (to, too, two) passes to the library.

5 Carol will go with us, (to, too, two).

1. When you are finished, proofread your text on the screen and then press Alt-P (⌘-P) to print a copy. Press Alt-S (⌘-S) to save a copy and name it "Lesson74."
2. Proofread your printed copy and then make any needed corrections on the computer.
3. When you are satisfied with your work, press Alt-G (⌘-G) to have UKey2 check your work. Press Enter to save your work and select yes to print a final copy. Press Esc to exit the *Galaxy Gazette*.

Landing Practice—Review All Keys (Part A)

Key each drill line two times. Try to increase your speed on the second try.

1 A man mailed the main mandate to malls.

2 Neither neighbor nor friend noticed it.

3 Our organization owns the outer outlet.

4 Peg, pick up the pod partners promptly.

5 Quickly and quietly question the queen.

6 Recreation and relaxation revive Roger.

7 Saul and Sue sing sad songs for school.

Landing Practice—Review All Keys (Part B)

Key each line two times before moving on to key the next line.

1 The tense tennis team tends to triumph.

2 Uniformed umpire utters untimely yells.

3 As vile vapors vanish, the values vary.

4 Winter walk was waived because of wind.

5 Exhibit xylophones next to extra exits.

6 Yani cooks yellow yams on yonder yacht.

7 Zapped ozone indicates zero protection.

After completing all of the drill lines for speed and if time permits, key each line again until it can be keyed with no more than one error.

Mission Report

An **antonym** is a word that means the opposite of another word. From the main menu, select Mission Report and choose the open screen option. Key the following sentences substituting antonyms for each italicized word.

1. The astronauts found the climate on the moon to be *sultry*.
2. The *good* air filled their lungs.
3. The terrain they saw was *mountainous*.
4. *Warm* breezes swept through the land.
5. Chan was an *excellent* skier on the moon's mountains.
6. Yumi discovered a *prehistoric* organism.
7. Sometimes the crew felt *glad* to be so far from home.
8. There was an *excess* of water on the moon from an *abundance* of lakes.
9. When they finished their research, the crew *slowly* piloted their spaceship back to Earth.
10. The captain said she thought the trip was a *failure*.

When you are finished, press Alt-P (⌘-P) to print your work. Press Alt-N (⌘-N) to save your document. Name it "Lesson22." Press Alt-Q (⌘-Q) to quit.

You have completed this mission. You are now ready to learn the number keys. Keep up the good work.

LESSON

74 Review and Skill Building

BRIEFING

In this mission, you will:
1. **Review word comparisons.**
2. **Improve straight-copy skill building.**

Strike the keys quickly.

Keep your eyes on the copy.

Computers—use default margins for all drills unless otherwise indicated.
Typewriters—use these margins unless otherwise indicated: 10 Pitch 2", 12 pitch 2½".
Single-spacing unless otherwise indicated.

Countdown—Get Ready for Blast-off

Review the countdown procedures.

Launch Review

Key each line two times before moving on to key the next line.

1 She sent me 10 1" x 2" x 8' oak boards.

2 Nan's new novels are nicely nonviolent.

3 My zippy lizard is a hazard to Arizona.

4 Thousands of fans cheered the new hero.

Galaxy Gazette—Build Word-Processing Skills

Word Comparisons

Many words are often confused. For the next few lessons, we will look at some of the most commonly confused words and practice sentences in which you will decide which word is correct.

To, Too, Two

To is a preposition. *Too* is an adverb meaning also or to an excessive extent. *Two* is a number.

From the main menu, select Mission Report and *Galaxy Gazette*. Study and key each sentence.

TOP-NOTCH TRAINING TIP

1 I went to Virginia Beach with my dad.

2 Wong will go with us to the skating rink, too.

3 Two of her friends stayed at her house on Friday

night.

Key each sentence with the correct choice of word.

1 She put (to, too, two) pairs of socks in the dryer.

2 He rode his bicycle (to, too, two) Innsbrook

Stadium.

UNIT 2

LEARNING TOP-ROW NUMBERS

The purpose of Unit 2 is to teach you to key the top-row numbers and symbols by touch. When you complete this unit, you should have complete command of the keyboard. You will be able to key paragraph copy containing any alphabetic character, punctuation mark, number, and symbol by touch. You should be able to key straight-copy material at a minimum of 20 words a minute with no more than four errors.

In this unit, you will continue to develop your composition and writing skills. You should begin to use the keyboard for as many assignments from other classes as possible. The extra practice will make you an excellent keyboarder (and probably earn you better grades).

Continue to follow UKey2's advice. Thumbs up!

Skill Exploration

Take two 30-second timings on the following lines. Try to reach a new speed goal.

1 Data and records can be saved on disks.

2 The paperless office will be a reality.

3 Many trees will be saved in the future.

| 1 | 2 | 3 | 4 | 5 | 6 | 7 | 8 |

Mission Assessment

Take two 2-minute timings on the following paragraphs. Study the material; then following the copy in your book, key the lines on the computer or your typewriter.

1   Composing your papers and reports

2 directly on the keyboard will save you

3 time. You will use your keying skill

4 and the ability to write at the

5 keyboard all of your school career.

6   When you write a paper for a

7 class, first do your research. Draft

8 your document directly on the keyboard

9 when you are ready to write. While

10 writing this draft, do not become

11 bogged down in the details of writing.

12 Just attempt to get your thoughts down.

13   Print your draft and read it for

14 content and errors. Mark any changes

15 on the draft. Using your word-

16 processing skills, add and delete

17 words as necessary. If desired, you

18 also can move text using the word

19 processor. You will like this new,

20 efficient way of writing.

| 1 | 2 | 3 | 4 | 5 | 6 | 7 | 8 |

REENTRY
BRIEFING

Great job!

LESSON

23 Learning Numbers 5 and 0

Computers—use default margins for all drills unless otherwise indicated.
Typewriters—use these margins unless otherwise indicated: 10 Pitch 2", 12 pitch 2½".
Single-spacing unless otherwise indicated.

Countdown—Get Ready for Blast-off

Launch Review

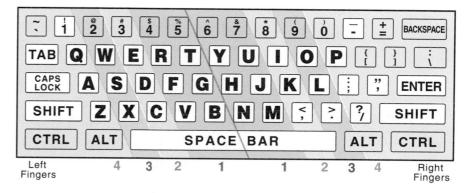

Key each line two times before moving on to key the next line.

1 She saw the men walking down that lane.

2 ISU's new pass/fail systems are unique.

3 We realized that ozone is not too warm.

4 Their excited pony bit the quiet woman.

5 We'll discover unique prizes or extras.

Destination—The 5 Key

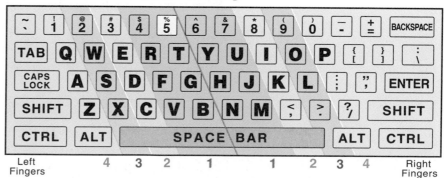

Here is the 5 key. It is keyed with your F finger. Place your fingers in a curved, upright position on the home keys. Look at your F finger and

2 In New England, we saw (4, four) windmills and (12, twelve) lighthouses.

3 At the pool, they sell (4, four) types of soft drinks and (15, fifteen) types of candy.

4 The track team had (14, fourteen) students who participated in high jump, (3, three) people who participated in the 50-yard dash, and (16, sixteen) who participated in the mile run.

1. When you are finished, proofread your text on the screen and then press Alt-P (⌘-P) to print a copy. Press Alt-S (⌘-S) to save a copy and name it "Lesson73."
2. Proofread your printed copy and then make any needed corrections on the computer.
3. When you are satisfied with your work, press Alt-G (⌘-G) to have UKey2 check your work. Press Enter to save your work and select yes to print a final copy. Press Esc to exit the *Galaxy Gazette*.

Landing Practice—Review All Keys

Key each drill line two times. Try to increase your speed on the second try. After completing all of the drill lines for speed and if time permits, key each line again until it can be keyed with no more than one error.

1 Average annual income data were absent.

2 Bigger bonus buys brought back baggage.

3 Catch a crazy calf and carry it calmly.

4 Daffy ducklings enjoy dim, deep diving.

5 Educate everyone about the environment.

6 Find funds for saving our fine forests.

7 The governor fosters great land grants.

8 Who heats the homes for all the hungry?

9 Initiate the immediate investment bill.

10 Jili joyfully jumped on Jupiter's moon.

11 Katy knows how to knit the knotty kite.

12 Lofty lab was laden with loose lichens.

practice the reach to 5. Keep your other fingers curved and resting lightly on the home keys.

```
f5f f5f f5f f5f f5f f5f f5f f5f f5f f5f
```

Now look away from the keyboard and practice. Look at your text, not the keyboard.

```
f5f f5f f5f f5f f5f f5f f5f f5f f5f f5f
```

Key each line two times before moving on to key the next line.

1 f5f f5f f5f 5 55 555 5555 fan 55 of 555

2 fur 55 fir 55 fat 55 for 55 fun 555 555

3 fire 555 form 555 fast 555 feat 555 555

4 Send 55 receipts for the first 55 fans.

5 Wow, number 5 scored 5,555 game points!

Destination—The 0 Key

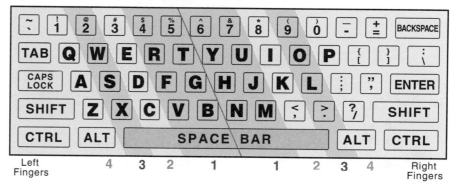

Here is the 0 key. It is keyed with your semicolon finger. Place your fingers in a curved, upright position on the home keys. Look at your semicolon finger and practice the reach to 0. Keep your other fingers curved and resting lightly on the home keys.

```
;0; ;0; ;0; ;0; ;0; ;0; ;0; ;0; ;0; ;0;
```

Now look away from the keyboard and practice. Look at your text, not the keyboard.

```
;0; ;0; ;0; ;0; ;0; ;0; ;0; ;0; ;0; ;0;
```

Key each line two times before moving on to key the next line.

1 ;0; ;0; ;0; 00 00 000 ;00; 0000 or 0000

2 and; 00 the; 000 for; 000 old; 000 0000

3 but; 000 aim; 000 put; 000 can; 000 000

4 5 0 0 5 05 005 50 500 505 050 5005 0550

LESSON

73 Review and Skill Building

Computers—use default margins for all drills unless otherwise indicated.
Typewriters—use these margins unless otherwise indicated: 10 Pitch 2", 12 pitch 2½".
Single-spacing unless otherwise indicated.

Countdown—Get Ready for Blast-off

Review the countdown procedures.

Launch Review

In this mission, you will:
1. Review number usage.
2. Improve straight-copy skill building.

Strike the keys quickly.

Keep your eyes on the copy.

Key each line two times.

1 Items #18, #19, and #320 were $1.19 ea.

2 Making machines mimic me is mysterious.

3 Tow autos from yellow no-parking zones.

4 He thinks he'll be able to go with her.

Galaxy Gazette

Number Review—Related Numbers

Study the following rule.

When numbers in a series are used in a document, they should be expressed in the same form. That is, when numbers that normally are spelled out (one-ten) are used with those normally given in figures (11 and up), use figures for all of them.

From the main menu, select Mission Report and *Galaxy Gazette*. Study and key each of these examples.

TOP-NOTCH TRAINING TIP

1 Kelly practiced playing the saxophone 8 minutes

   on Monday, 45 minutes on Tuesday, and 15 minutes

   on Wednesday.

2 Of the 25 plants she bought, 3 were not blooming.

Now key each of the following sentences, choosing the correct way to express the numbers.

1 Rashad planted (15, fifteen) broccoli plants,

   (10, ten) tomato plants, and (3, three)

   eggplants.

Key each line two times.

1 Taylor was born on 5/05/55 at 5:05 p.m.

2 She ordered 500 of Items 5505 and 0050.

3 The 55 horses ran a race in 50 minutes.

Landing Practice

Improve your skill in reading and keying numbers.

To key numbers more efficiently, practice the following number reading techniques.

1. For one-digit numbers, say the number to yourself as you key it.
   Example: 5   Say five.
2. For two-digit numbers, say the numbers as a unit.
   Example: 55   Say fifty-five.
3. For three-digit numbers, say the first digit as a separate unit and the other two as a unit.
   Example: 550   Say five/fifty.
   Example: 555   Say five/fifty-five.
4. For four-digit numbers, say the first two digits. as a unit and then the last two as a unit.
   Example: 5511   Say fifty-five/eleven.
   Example: 5555   Say fifty-five/fifty-five.
5. For five-digit numbers, say the first two as a unit followed by a group of three.
   Example: 51155   Say fifty-one/one fifty-five.
   Example: 11511   Say eleven/five eleven.
6. If the numbers have other characters included in them, read the character as a separate unit and then continue with the pattern.
   Example: 1,511   Say one/comma/five eleven.
   Example: 243-58-9743   Say two forty-three/hyphen/fifty-eight/hyphen/ninety-seven/forty-three.

Practice reading the following numbers following the number reading techniques.

1 5 0 05 55 550 555 5050 5555 50505 55550

2 5,500 5:55 50.55 555.50 55 5-550-55-550

Now key the numbers while reading them according to the described steps. Key each line two times before moving on to key the next line.

1 5 0 05 55 550 555 5050 5555 50505 55550

2 5,500 5:55 50.55 555.50 55 5-550-55-550

Skill Exploration

Take two 30-second minute timings on each of the following lines. Try to reach a new speed goal. Do not worry about errors for now. Work to beat the computer. If you are using a typewriter, you can figure out your speed using the formula in the Introduction.

1 Computer spreadsheets are very helpful.

2 They perform math and accounting tasks.

3 You can budget and track costs quickly.

| | 1 | 2 | 3 | 4 | 5 | 6 | 7 | 8 | |

Mission Assessment

Take two 2-minute timings on the following paragraphs. Study the material; then following the copy in your book, key the lines on the computer or your typewriter.

1   There are three major types of

2 paragraphs. One type tells a story.

3 The second type describes an event or

4 person. The third type explains how

5 to do something.

6   You will get practice in keying

7 articles using these three types of

8 paragraphs. Before you begin to

9 write, you need to decide the purpose

10 of your writing and then choose the

11 suitable kind of paragraph. In some

12 instances, you may need to combine

13 the types of paragraphs.

14   Another important point to think

15 about is who your readers will be.

16 Articles should be written on a level

17 to suit them. Check to be sure that

18 the vocabulary fits your reader.

| | 1 | 2 | 3 | 4 | 5 | 6 | 7 | 8 | |

Minimum speed goal:
29 wam
Maximum errors allowed:
4

Happy landing!

Minimum speed goal:
16 wam
Maximum errors allowed:
4

Mission Assessment

Take two 1-minute timings on the following paragraphs. Following the copy in your book, key the lines on the computer or your typewriter. Decide on a goal of increased speed or increased accuracy.

1   Data can be entered into a computer

2 system in a variety of ways. You can

3 input data from a soft or hard disk.

4 You can type in alpha and numeric data

5 on the keyboard. Light pens can be

6 used to touch or draw on the screen.

7   Graphics can be entered using a

8 graphics tablet or special software.

9 In the future, computers will have

10 voice input that will allow the user

11 to enter data more efficiently.

| 1 | 2 | 3 | 4 | 5 | 6 | 7 | 8 |

REENTRY
BRIEFING

Great job! You have completed this mission!

Jupiter is the largest and heaviest of the planets. Eleven Earths could fit across the face of Jupiter.

2 In order to purchase the house, they needed to pay a

20 (percent, %) down payment.

3 Statistical Table

Movie(tab)Checked Out

Bambi   30(percent, %)

1. When you are finished, proofread your text on the screen and then press Alt-P (⌘-P) to print a copy. Press Alt-S (⌘-S) to save a copy and name it "Lesson72."
2. Proofread your printed copy and then make any needed corrections on the computer.
3. When you are satisfied with your work, press Alt-G (⌘-G) to have UKey2 check your work. Press Enter to save your work and select yes to print a final copy. Press Esc to exit the *Galaxy Gazette*.

Landing Practice—Skill Review

Review—Space Bar

Key each drill line two times. Try to increase your speed on the second try.

1 a b c d e f g h i j k l m n o p q r s t

2 me to or of it as if an we by so go the

3 but can yet set jet let wax bug nut van

4 Kim will go to her new job in one hour.

Review—Tabulation

Use the tab key to put the words in columns.

1 five   land   rest   exit   even   quit   have   time

2 also   gate   mane   sale   type   lazy   taxi   fair

3 keep   quad   coca   idea   jade   kale   kiln   milk

4 user   band   mane   nine   zero   zany   post   firm

5 pale   very   when   deed   open   rain   wind   snow

Review—Top-Row Numbers

Use the tab key to put the numbers in columns.

1 319   934   8935   8953   90873

2 109   965   6739   9873   09483

Remember to read the numbers in units.

3 190   946   9012   8956   03861

4 389   678   9834   6734   95620

LESSON

24 Learning Numbers 1 and 7

BRIEFING

This mission will enable you to:
1. Key copy using top-row numbers 1 and 7.
2. Improve keyboarding skill.

Computers—use default margins for all drills unless otherwise indicated.
Typewriters—use these margins unless otherwise indicated: 10 Pitch 2", 12 pitch 2½".
Single-spacing unless otherwise indicated.

Countdown—Get Ready for Blast Off

Review the countdown procedures.

Launch Review

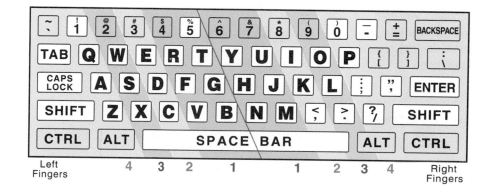

Left Fingers   4   3   2   1   1   2   3   4   Right Fingers

Key each line two times before moving on to key the next line.

Strike the keys quickly. Keep your eyes on the copy.

1 There are two red tables for Zackory G.

2 Roxey bought oil wells and topaz rings.

3 Volume 05, page 55 says that she is 50.

4 Please order: 50 desks and 505 chairs.

5 My number is 550,505. Hers is 550,500.

Destination—The 1 Key

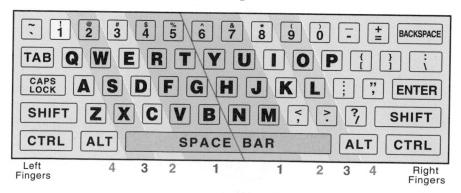

Left Fingers   4   3   2   1   1   2   3   4   Right Fingers

LESSON

72 Review and Skill Building

Computers—use default margins for all drills unless otherwise indicated.
Typewriters—use these margins unless otherwise indicated: 10 Pitch 2", 12 pitch 2½".
Single-spacing unless otherwise indicated.

Countdown—Get Ready for Blast-off

Review the countdown procedures.

Launch Review

Key each line two times.

1 The costs were 7 @ $6.42 and 9 @ $3.51.

2 Lillian lights lava lamps for a living.

3 Max Qui is quite vexed by her laziness.

4 Cooking can be a success with a recipe.

Galaxy Gazette

Number Review—Percentages

Study the following rules.

Percentages should be written in figures followed by the word percent. The percentage symbol (%) should only be used in statistical or technical tables or forms.

From the main menu, select Mission Report and *Galaxy Gazette*. Study and key each of these examples. Use the tab key in the table.

1 He earned 95 percent on the Spanish final exam.

2 Statistical Table

Honor

Roll	Students
Grade 6	25%
Grade 7	30%
Grade 8	18%

Now key each of the following sentences, choosing the correct form.

1 In industry, about 55 (percent, %) of employees use

computers every day.

TOP-NOTCH TRAINING TIP

MISSION BRIEFING

In this mission, you will:
1. **Review number usage.**
2. **Improve straight-copy skill building.**

Strike the keys quickly.

Keep your eyes on the copy.

The 1 key is keyed with your A finger. Place your fingers in a curved, upright position on the home keys. Look at your A finger and practice the reach to 1. Keep your other fingers curved and resting lightly on the home keys.

Keep your fingers in home key position so you don't lose your place.

```
a1a a1a a1a a1a a1a a1a a1a a1a a1a a1a
```

Now look away from the keyboard and practice. Look at your text, not the keyboard.

```
a1a a1a a1a a1a a1a a1a a1a a1a a1a a1a
```

Review the procedure for reading numbers in Lesson 23 before keying this drill.

Key each line two times before moving on to key the next line.

```
1  a1a a1a a1a 1 1 ask 111 and 11 air 1111

2  11 at 11 and 11 a 111 11,111 and 11.111

3  The appointments were for 1/11 and 11/1.

4  Send me Nos. 1, 10, 11, 15, 51, and 550.

5  The list included:  515, 1015, and 5105.

6  The address was 115 N. 50 Street, Yumaz.
```

Destination—The 7 Key

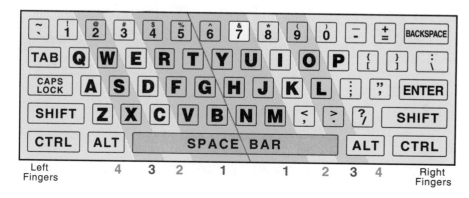

Here is the 7 key. It is keyed with your J finger. Place your fingers in a curved, upright position on the home keys. Look at your J finger and practice the reach to 7. Keep your other fingers curved and resting lightly on the home keys.

```
j7j j7j j7j j7j j7j j7j j7j j7j j7j j7j
```

Now look away from the keyboard and practice. Look at your text, not the keyboard.

```
j7j j7j j7j j7j j7j j7j j7j j7j j7j j7j
```

Skill Exploration

Take two 30-second timings on each of the following lines. Try to reach a new speed goal. Do not worry about errors for now. Work to beat the computer. If you are using a typewriter, you can figure out your speed using the formula in the Introduction.

1 Good exercise keeps you physically fit.

2 Proper muscle tone can improve posture.

3 Regular exercise helps maintain health.

| 1 | 2 | 3 | 4 | 5 | 6 | 7 | 8 |

Mission Assessment

Take two 2-minute timings on the following paragraphs. Study the material; then following the copy in your book, key the lines on the computer or your typewriter.

1   In any writing, planning is very

2 important. Paragraph writing is no

3 exception. The well-written paragraph

4 is carefully planned. The subject of

5 the paragraph is introduced in the

6 topic sentence, and the ideas that

7 relate to the topic then follow.

8   Details, examples, logical

9 reasons, and feelings may all be used

10 to support the topic sentence. Every

11 sentence in a paragraph should support

12 the main idea.

13   When a paragraph is long and

14 complex, a concluding or summary

15 sentence may be written. This

16 sentence restates or sums up the main

17 idea or topic of the paragraph.

| 1 | 2 | 3 | 4 | 5 | 6 | 7 | 8 |

REENTRY

BRIEFING

Great job!

Key each line two times before moving on to key the next line.

1 j7j j7j j7j 7 77 777 jar 77 jam 777 777

2 77 jaw 77 jeer 77 jack 77 joke 777 jury

3 7 1 71 7 55 75 7 0 70 771 775 770 17/77

4 1 7 17 1 5 15 1 0 10 7 55 75 57 70 07 7

5 The letter of 7/17/70 included 7 of 17.

6 Order 750 for 70, 71, 57, 07, 17, or 7.

Skill Exploration

Take two 30-second timings on each of the following lines. Try to reach a new speed goal. Do not worry about errors for now. Work to beat the computer. If you are using a typewriter, you can figure out your speed using the formula in the Introduction.

1 The bug in the jar was happy to escape.

2 The fox ran the rabbits under the bush.

3 Place the tray on the blue wire holder.

| 1 | 2 | 3 | 4 | 5 | 6 | 7 | 8 |

Mission Assessment

Take two 1-minute timings on the following paragraphs. Following the copy in your book, key the lines on the computer or your typewriter. Decide on a goal of increased speed or increased accuracy.

1   Volcanos cause many problems on

2 Earth. They release ash and gases

3 into the air. When it rains, the ash

4 covering the ground turns into mud.

5 The mud slide flows rapidly and

6 destroys many buildings.

7   After a volcano explodes, the

8 people must attempt to resume their

9 normal lives. Many times this is not

10 possible because they may have lost all

11 their personal property.

| 1 | 2 | 3 | 4 | 5 | 6 | 7 | 8 |

REENTRY
BRIEFING

This orbit is complete. Proceed to the next destination.

1. When you are finished, proofread your text on the screen and then press Alt-P (⌘-P) to print a copy. Press Alt-S (⌘-S) to save a copy and name it "Lesson71."
2. Proofread your printed copy and then make any needed corrections on the computer.
3. When you are satisfied with your work, press Alt-G (⌘-G) to have UKey2 check your work. Press Enter to save your work and select yes to print a final copy. Press Esc to exit the *Galaxy Gazette*.

Landing Practice—Skill Review

Key each drill line two times. Try to increase your speed on the second try. After completing all of the drill lines for speed and if time permits, key each line again until it can be keyed with no more than one error.

Review—Double-Letter Words (Part A)

1 all call tall fall ally equally falling

2 cuff offer effect affect suffer muffler

3 paddle buddy toddle caddie daddy saddle

Review—Up Reaches (Part B)

Strike the keys quickly as though they were hot.

1 led fed nod act edge edit edict educate

2 jut jug jag juice judo jump jumbo judge

3 kid kit kiln king kite skill kind kicks

Review—Down Reaches (Part C)

1 avid save have pave stave avenue avoids

2 bat back bank badly bacon ballot bakery

3 cake care carp cargo cable carts carton

Review—Out Reaches (Part D)

1 tear easy bean fears feast nears learns

2 hill high hide shirt shine hiked shifts

3 rate rail race rides rally straw trains

LESSON

25 Learning Numbers 3 and 9

BRIEFING

The top-row number destinations continue. In this mission, you will:
1. Key copy using top-row numbers 3 and 9.
2. Improve keyboarding skill.

Computers—use default margins for all drills unless otherwise indicated.
Typewriters—use these margins unless otherwise indicated: 10 Pitch 2", 12 pitch 2½".
Single-spacing unless otherwise indicated.

Countdown—Get Ready for Blast-off

Review the countdown procedures.

Launch Review

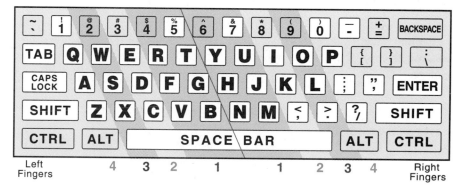

Key each line two times before moving on to key the next line.

1 Jackie is excited about having a truck.

2 Rachael was taking Elaine to the movie.

3 Will a solid background ensure success?

4 Send that letter by 7:50 a.m. on 10/15.

5 Send us tickets 571, 701, 105, and 755.

Strike the keys quickly.

Keep your eyes on the copy.

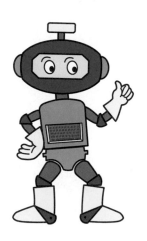

Destination—The 3 Key

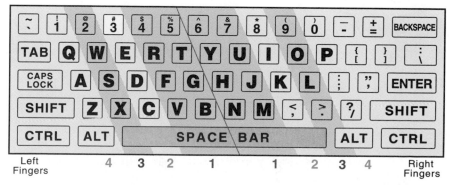

LESSON

##
71 Review and Skill Bulding

Computers—use default margins for all drills unless otherwise indicated.
Typewriters—use these margins unless otherwise indicated: 10 Pitch 2", 12 pitch 2½".
Single-spacing unless otherwise indicated.

Countdown—Get Ready for Blast-off

Review the countdown procedures.

Launch Review

Key each line two times.

1 Order new pens #4786, #1523, and #7562.

2 Kindness keeps that king knowledgeable.

3 The quiz was quite fair; Rexi got an A.

4 I do all the work with my own computer.

Galaxy Gazette

Number Review—Clock Time

Study the following rules.

Numbers are used with *a.m.* and *p.m.* to express clock time. A colon is used between the hour and minutes. For even time, do not use the colon or any zeros.

From the main menu, select Mission Report and *Galaxy Gazette*. Study and key each of the following examples.

1 She will meet me at the Trellis for lunch at 1 p.m.

2 Make sure you take your medicine at 8:30 a.m., 1

p.m., and 5:30 p.m.

Now key each of the following sentences, choosing the correct way of expressing the time.

1 The florist will deliver the flowers no later than

(1 p.m., 1:00 p.m.) today.

2 My radio is set on a timer to go off at (11:00

p.m., 11 p.m.) every night.

MISSION
BRIEFING

In this mission you will:
1. Review number usage.
2. Improve straight-copy skill building.

Strike the keys quickly.

Keep your eyes on the copy.

TOP-NOTCH TRAINING TIP

The 3 key is keyed with your D finger. Place your fingers in a curved, upright position on the home keys. Look at your D finger and practice the reach to 3. Keep your other fingers curved and resting lightly on the home keys.

d3d d3d d3d d3d d3d d3d d3d d3d d3d d3d

Now look away from the keyboard and practice. Look at your text, not the keyboard.

d3d d3d d3d d3d d3d d3d d3d d3d d3d d3d

Key each line two times before moving on to key the next line.

Remember to practice reading in units.

1 33 did 33 dam 33 dog 33 data 33 day 333

2 333 dark 333 dorm 333 door 333 decks 33

3 373 735 035 350 351 137 300 370 735 153

4 Process receipts 33, 137, 350, and 351.

5 The 531 team scored 135 points earlier.

6 What is the total of 703, 135, and 371?

Destination—The 9 Key

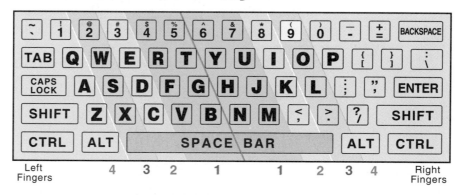

Here is the 9 key. It is keyed with your L finger. Place your fingers in a curved, upright position on the home keys. Look at your L finger and practice the reach to 9. Keep your other fingers curved and resting lightly on the home keys.

191 191 191 191 191 191 191 191 191 191

Now look away from the keyboard and practice. Look at your text, not the keyboard.

191 191 191 191 191 191 191 191 191 191

Review—Alternate-Hand Words (Part C)

1 an or if so is of it on to for the furl

2 paid idle clay kept mane paid corn oaks

3 fix pans their handy world rights ivory

Skill Exploration

Take two 30-second timings on each of the following lines. Try to reach a new speed goal. Do not worry about errors for now. Work to beat the computer.

1 Word processing is vital for students.

2 It also has uses in your private life.

3 School could be easier with computers.

| 1 | 2 | 3 | 4 | 5 | 6 | 7 | 8 |

Mission Assessment

Take two 2-minute timings on the following paragraphs. Study the material; then following the copy in your book, key the lines on the computer or your typewriter.

1 The paragraph is a basic building

2 block of all reports and stories. All

3 of your writing will include paragraph

4 copy. Both short and lengthy articles

5 require the same writing skills.

6 Practice your paragraph writing skills,

7 and you will see improvement.

8 A paragraph is a series of

9 sentences developing a single topic.

10 The main topic of the paragraph is

11 usually stated in the first sentence.

12 This first sentence is called the

13 topic sentence. The sentences that

14 follow the topic sentence give details

15 to support the main idea.

| 1 | 2 | 3 | 4 | 5 | 6 | 7 | 8 |

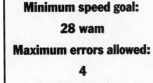

Minimum speed goal:
28 wam
Maximum errors allowed:
4

BRIEFING

You have completed this mission!

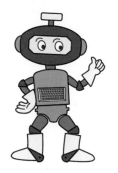

Key each line two times before moving on to key the next line.

1 191 191 9 99 999 law 99 low 999 lit 999

2 lift 999 love 999 level 999 last 999 99

3 1 9 19 3 9 39 7 9 79 5 9 59 590 095 509

4 9795 95 75 9051 1095 3790 7990 7931 709

5 Jim sent 95; Sally, 93; and Judith, 91.

Landing Practice—Improve Keying Speed

Key each line two times before moving on to key the next line. Try to increase your speed as you repeat the line.

1 got say day aim big way hat sit bet did

2 ever walk upon them when they only gone

3 She is to do all the work for the town.

4 To do the right job is your goal today.

Key each line two times before moving on to key the next line. Say the phrases to yourself.

1 if it is, it is to, as is, as it, if he

2 of all, at us, of his, so he, and if it

Mission Assessment

Take two 1-minute timings on the following paragraphs. Following the copy in your book, key the lines on the computer or your typewriter. Decide on a goal of increased speed or increased accuracy.

1   There are many word-processing

2 programs on the market. Each brand

3 has different features. Some are

4 easier to learn than others.

5   The ability to store basic

6 paragraphs and form letters is a great

7 business convenience. The added

8 features of format changes, typeface

9 changes, and spelling checks are very

10 attractive to users.

| 1 | 2 | 3 | 4 | 5 | 6 | 7 | 8 |

Minimum speed goal:
17 wam
Maximum errors allowed:
4

Now key each of the following sentences, choosing the correct way of expressing the numbers.

1 When I checked the prices for a permit, knee pads, helmet, and in-line skates,

2 I was given the following prices: ($.99, $20, $25, and $100) (99 cents, $20.00, $25.00 and $100.00).

3 My uniform costs ($54, $54.00), and I need to pay for it tomorrow.

4 Antonio had (70 cents, $.70) with him but needed more for the peanuts.

5 A very popular music teacher charges ($20, $20.00) per half hour for drum lessons.

1. When you are finished, proofread your text on the screen and then press Alt-P (⌘-P) to print a copy. Press Alt-S (⌘-S) to save a copy and name it "Lesson70."
2. Proofread your printed copy and then make any needed corrections on the computer.
3. When you are satisfied with your work, press Alt-G (⌘-G) to have UKey2 check your work. Press Enter to save your work and select yes to print a final copy. Press Esc to exit the *Galaxy Gazette*.

Landing Practice—Skill Review

Key each drill line two times. Try to increase your speed on the second try. After completing all of the drill lines for speed and if time permits, key each line again until it can be keyed with no more than one error.

Review—One-Hand Words (Part A)

1 jump fear fare upon pull tear card hill

2 join east hump pony loop face vest date

3 dear lump weed vest mill noon card rare

Review—Adjacent-Key Words (Part B)

1 are new try pan buy yule lion dirt here

2 news quiz trip suit over part true view

3 art opt car oil gas open base milk vase

26 Review and Skill Building

This mission is a flight review. In this review, you will:

1. **Review the number keys learned.**
2. **Improve keyboarding techniques.**
3. **Improve keyboarding skill.**

Computers—use default margins for all drills unless otherwise indicated.
Typewriters—use these margins unless otherwise indicated: 10 Pitch 2", 12 pitch 2½".
Single-spacing unless otherwise indicated.

Countdown—Get Ready for Blast-off

Review the countdown procedures.

Launch Review

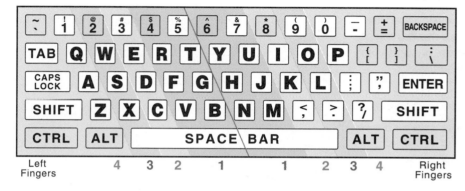

Left Fingers   4   3   2   1   1   2   3   4   Right Fingers

Key each line two times before moving on to key the next line.

1 One form states parts 55, 139, and 507.

2 Did you buy a size 3, 5, 7, or 9 shirt?

3 Henry wanted to reward the arctic crew.

4 Christine keys 70 wam and Lori keys 55.

5 Comets come here every 100 years or so.

Landing Practice—Review Numbers

Key each line two times before moving on to key the next line.

1 15 53 50 55 75 17 37 57 70 79 19 39 591

2 Li accepted a job from 7 a.m. to 5 p.m.

3 The profit is 3,975 points of the deal.

4 Handle the 15 marble statues with care.

5 Did you run the race as entry 50 or 05?

6 We asked for 39 bananas and 171 lemons.

LESSON

70 Review and Skill Building

Countdown—Get Ready for Blast-off

Review the countdown procedures.

Launch Review

Key each line two times before moving on to key the next line.

1 The new orders were #81, #32, and #386.

2 Jonathan jumps joyously and jubilantly.

3 The quarry yielded an excess of quartz.

4 You know how long it takes to complete.

Galaxy Gazette

Number Review—Money

Study the following rules.

Express even dollars with a dollar sign and no decimal point or zeros. (Example: $10.) Express amounts less than a dollar in numbers followed by the word *cents*. (Example: 55 cents.) If several amounts of money are used together in a sentence, they are all keyed in the same style. (Example: $.45, $1.25, and $6.75.)

From the main menu, select Mission Report and *Galaxy Gazette*. Study and key each of the following example sentences. Press Enter at the end of each line to divide the sentences as shown.

1 The video game is on sale for $42.45.

2 At the game, a soft drink is 55 cents.

3 The candy, gum, and lemonade cost $.65, $.85, and

$1.25 at the snack bar.

4 The computer I want costs $1,595.

MISSION BRIEFING

In this mission you will:
1. Review number usage.
2. Improve straight-copy skill building.

Strike the keys quickly.

Keep your eyes on the copy.

TOP-NOTCH TRAINING TIP

Skill Exploration

Take two 30-second timings on each of the following lines. Try to reach a new speed goal. Do not worry about errors for now. Work to beat the computer. If you are using a typewriter, you can figure out your speed using the formula in the Introduction.

1 Tyronne was runner 13 in the last race.

2 McStrat opened a new CD stop yesterday.

3 Chicago, IL, is famous for tasty pizza.
   | 1 | 2 | 3 | 4 | 5 | 6 | 7 | 8 |

Minimum speed goal:

17 wam

Maximum errors allowed:

4

Mission Assessment

Take two 1-minute timings on the following paragraphs. Following the copy in your book, key the lines on the computer or your typewriter. Decide on a goal of increased speed or increased accuracy.

1   Saturn is the second largest planet

2 in our solar system. Its volume is

3 more than 700 times greater than

4 Earth's. Saturn is made mostly

5 of gases. It is very cold on Saturn.

6 The planet rotates once every 17

7 hours. Saturn is well known for its

8 rings. The rings are made of chunks

9 of rock and ice.
   | 1 | 2 | 3 | 4 | 5 | 6 | 7 | 8 |

Mission Report

A **simile** is a figure of speech comparing two unlike things. For example:

The horse's mane shone like gold.

The idea went over like a ton of bricks.

From the main menu, select Mission Report and the open screen option. Key the following sentences completing each one with a word or phrase that is a simile. Key each sentence on a new line. Do not key the numbers.

1. The storm blew in like _____.

2. His laughter was like _____.

3. The team played the game like _____.

4. Carrie hit the ball like _____.

5. Lonnie knew the road like _____.

Minimum speed goal:
28 wam
Maximum errors allowed:
4

Mission Assessment

Take two 2-minute timings on the following paragraphs. Study the material; then following the copy in your book, key the lines on the computer or your typewriter.

1   With practice, everyone can

2 become a better writer. If you follow

3 the writing steps given in this text,

4 your writing skills should improve

5 greatly.

6   The use of word processing has

7 changed the writing process from one

8 of boredom to one of excitement.

9 Changes can be made to the text in

10 minutes. Before word processing, it

11 was often necessary to completely

12 retype the whole paper.

13   Your keyboarding and writing

14 skills will provide you with a

15 valuable tool that can help you

16 improve your grades in your classes.

17 Use your computer in as many writing

18 activities as possible. The more you

19 use your skills, the more skillful you

20 will become.

| 1 | 2 | 3 | 4 | 5 | 6 | 7 | 8 |

REENTRY
BRIEFING

You have completed this mission!

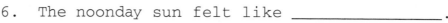

BRIEFING

Mission complete! You can proceed to more numbers.

6. The noonday sun felt like _____ .
7. The children grew like _____ .
8. The racehorse ran like _____ .
9. The rumor spread like _____ .
10. Getting an answer from her is like _____ .

When you are finished, press Alt-P (⌘-P) to print your work. Press Alt-N (⌘-N) to save your document. Name it "Lesson26." Press Alt-Q (⌘-Q) to quit.

LESSON

27 Learning Numbers 2 and 8

BRIEFING

After completing this mission, you will be able to:
1. **Key copy using top-row numbers 2 and 8.**
2. **Improve keyboarding skill.**

Computers—use default margins for all drills unless otherwise indicated.
Typewriters—use these margins unless otherwise indicated: 10 Pitch 2", 12 pitch 2½".
Single-spacing unless otherwise indicated.

Countdown—Get Ready for Blast-off

Review the countdown procedures.

Launch Review

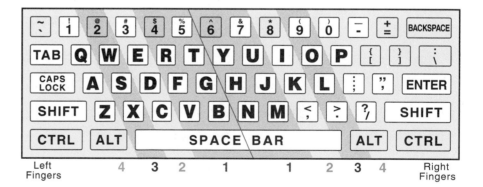

Left Fingers   4 3 2 1   1 2 3 4   Right Fingers

Key each line two times before moving on to key the next line.

Strike the keys quickly.

Keep your eyes on the copy.

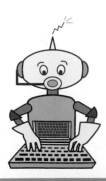

1 Store my materials on the floppy disks.

2 Raze the Yorktown building for hazards.

3 Were the 1790 items delivered on 10/19?

4 Can you add 1597, 7903, 3159, and 1379?

5 My race time was 19 minutes, 5 seconds.

6 Ask Roberta if her time was 39 seconds.

3 Kiri and (4, four) other musicians get together to

practice playing the guitar.

4 LeAnn chose a beautiful turquoise sequined dress

after looking at dresses in (11, eleven) stores.

1. When you are finished, proofread your text on the screen and then press Alt-P (⌘-P) to print a copy. Press Alt-S (⌘-S) to save a copy and name it "Lesson69."
2. Proofread your printed copy and then make any needed corrections on the computer.
3. When you are satisfied with your work, press Alt-G (⌘-G) to have UKey2 check your work. Press Enter to save your work and select yes to print a final copy. Press Esc to exit the *Galaxy Gazette*.

Landing Practice—Skill Review

Key each drill line two times. Try to increase your speed on the second try. After completing all of the drill lines for speed and if time permits, key each line again until it can be keyed with no more than one error.

Review Phrases (Part A)

1 as/as it/as it is/as it can/as it will/

2 if/if we/if we do/if we can/if we were/

3 so/so to/so to go/so to go on/so it is/

4 and to/the man/the man has/the man was/

5 at a/at that/at that time/at that hour/

Review Word Families (Part B)

Key each line two times.

1 ate late gate mate rate date fate crate

2 bear tear fear near hear year sear dear

3 sill hill mill pill dill fill kill gill

4 vail mail sail rail tail jail bail nail

5 our sour tour four hour pour dour flour

Destination—The 2 Key

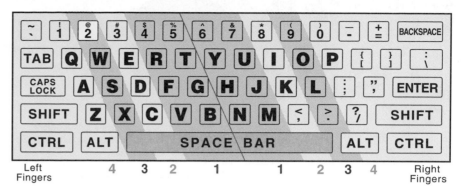

Here is the 2 key. It is keyed with your S finger. Place your fingers in a curved, upright position on the home keys. Look at your S finger and practice the reach to 2. Keep your other fingers curved and resting lightly on the home keys.

s2s s2s s2s s2s s2s s2s s2s s2s s2s s2s

Now look away from the keyboard and practice. Look at your text, not the keyboard.

s2s s2s s2s s2s s2s s2s s2s s2s s2s s2s

Key each line two times before moving on to key the next line.

1 s2s s2s 2 22 22 saw 222 see 222 set 222

2 shoe 222 sure 222 slit 222 same 222 222

3 2 5 25 2 0 20 2 9 29 2 1 21 2 7 27 2 23

4 2/25 2/90 2/79 2/12 2/35 2/70 2/29 2 50

5 Flight 233 left Rome at 2:27 on 2/2/72.

Destination—The 8 Key

Here is the 8 key. It is keyed with your K finger. Place your fingers in a curved, upright position on the home keys. Look at your K finger and practice the reach to 8. Keep your other fingers curved and resting lightly on the home keys.

k8k k8k k8k k8k k8k k8k k8k k8k k8k k8k

LESSON

69 Review and Skill Building

MISSION BRIEFING

In this mission, you will:
1. **Review number usage.**
2. **Improve straight-copy skill building.**

Strike the keys quickly.

Keep your eyes on the copy.

Computers—use default margins for all drills unless otherwise indicated.
Typewriters—use these margins unless otherwise indicated: 10 Pitch 2", 12 pitch 2½".
Single-spacing unless otherwise indicated.

Countdown—Get Ready for Blast-off

Review the countdown procedures.

Launch Review

Key each line two times.

1 Get 13 lbs. of #1 nails @ $1.45 per lb.

2 Are the initial items inclined to exit?

3 A quiet, anxious engineer voted for it.

4 It's easy for us to leave a purse here.

Galaxy Gazette

Number Review

Study the following rule.

Write out numbers from one through ten when used in general text. Use figures to express numbers above ten.

From the main menu, select Mission Report and *Galaxy Gazette*. Study and key each of the example sentences.

1 There are 24 people on the track team this spring.

2 Jane invited eight people to her party on Saturday night.

3 The art contest for the county included work from 13 of our students.

Now key each of the following sentences and choose the correct way of expressing the numbers.

1 Karl and Ross went on a camping trip with (14, fourteen) other Boy Scouts.

2 The swim team will participate in (8, eight) swim meets this summer.

Now look away and practice.

k8k k8k k8k k8k k8k k8k k8k k8k k8k k8k

Key each line two times before moving on to key the next line.

1 k8k k8k 8 88 888 kit 88 key 88 keg 8 88

2 88 kite 88 kick 88 kazoo 88 kettle 8 88

3 It was 8:15 p.m. in Phoenix and Denver.

4 Item 859 on page 80 placed at 2,389.95.

5 At 12:15, Flight 1848 was an hour late.

Skill Exploration

Take two 30-second timings on each of the following lines. Try to reach a new speed goal. Do not worry about errors for now. Work to beat the computer. If you are using a typewriter, you can figure out your speed using the formula in the Introduction.

1 Please come to the birthday party, Lil.

2 Sailing in a hot air balloon is superb!

3 Do they enjoy playing soccer in summer?

| 1 | 2 | 3 | 4 | 5 | 6 | 7 | 8 |

Mission Assessment

Take two 1-minute timings on the following paragraphs. Following the copy in your book, key the lines on the computer or your typewriter. Decide on a goal of increased speed or increased accuracy.

1   Have you ever been up in a hot air

2 balloon? Hot air balloons are fun.

3 When lifted in one, all your worries

4 disappear. As you gently float across

5 the sky, the only thing you hear is

6 the sound of the burner.

7   Everything looks like small

8 dollhouses perfectly placed below. As

9 you pass over, all the people on the

10 ground yell to you hoping that you

11 will land in their yard.

| 1 | 2 | 3 | 4 | 5 | 6 | 7 | 8 |

Minimum speed goal: 17 wam

Maximum errors allowed: 4

BRIEFING

Mission control reports that your mission is accomplished.

UNIT 5

THE COMPUTER AND THE WRITING PROCESS

In this unit, you will have the opportunity to improve your composing and writing skills and apply the knowledge and skills that you already have developed.

The unit begins with several lessons that concentrate on developing straight-copy skill building. While completing these lessons, you should attempt to improve your speed rate and the accuracy of your keying. By the end of this unit, you should be keying at a minimum of 30 wam for 2 minutes with no more than four errors.

This unit will cover steps in the writing process. You will complete exercises including prewriting activities in which you let your imagination and creativity assist you in developing topics. You will learn to group these ideas in a logical sequence depending on the type of writing you are doing. Finally, you will discover ways to make your document ready for presentation.

With permission of your instructor, you are encouraged to substitute assignments from other classes for any exercises in this unit. You will find writing using this process fun and exciting. Your writing skills will improve, and you may find that grades in your other classes will improve, too.

LESSON

28 Learning Numbers 4 and 6

This mission will complete the destinations to the top-row numbers. In this mission, you will:
1. Key copy using top-row numbers 4 and 6.
3. Improve keyboarding skill.

Strike the keys quickly.

Keep your eyes on the copy.

Computers—use default margins for all drills unless otherwise indicated.
Typewriters—use these margins unless otherwise indicated: 10 Pitch 2", 12 pitch 2½".
Single-spacing unless otherwise indicated.

Countdown—Get Ready for Blast-off

Review the countdown procedures.

Launch Review

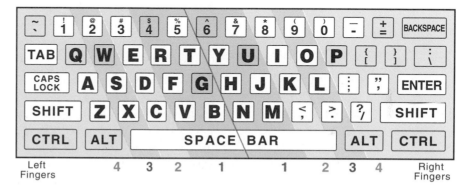

Left Fingers   4   3   2   1   1   2   3   4   Right Fingers

Key each line two times before moving on to key the next line.

1 Chris asked Sarah to meet by 12:38 p.m.

2 The tax yields qualified budget extras.

3 That series contained 1, 2, 33, and 57.

4 Did over 10,000 people attend at 12:13?

5 Did you draw the number 98, 99, or 100?

6 Meet me at the baseball field by 12:15.

Destination—The 4 Key

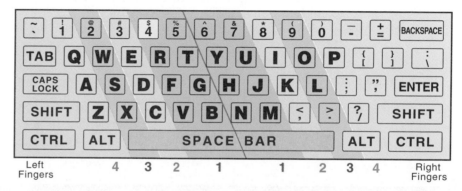

Left Fingers   4   3   2   1   1   2   3   4   Right Fingers

JUANITA R. MOZINGO
4298 ANDERSON ROAD
CHICAGO, IL 60607
(312) 555-9843

Career Objective

To gain experience in microcomputer technology and ultimately become a microcomputer specialist.

Education

Prairie Community College, Associate Degree, expected June 1995; majoring in Computer Information Systems. Maintain a 3.4 grade point average. President of Microcomputer Club.

Lincoln High School, diploma, May 1993; graduated with honors. Vice President of Beta Club; President of Future Business Leaders of America.

Qualifications

Knowledge of COBOL, C language, WordPerfect, Lotus, Microsoft, and accounting software.

Experience

Computer Information Systems Lab Assistant-- worked 20 hours per week in the computer laboratory at Prairie Community College from September 1, 1994, to present. Assist students with computer programs and software packages.

Central Community Bank--worked summers of 1991, 1992, and 1993 in CIS department.

Special Skills

Fluent in Spanish.

References

References, including work supervisors and instructors, will be provided on request.

The 4 key is keyed with your F finger. Place your fingers in a curved, upright position on the home keys. Look at your F finger and practice the reach to 4. Keep your other fingers curved and resting lightly on the home keys.

```
f4f  f4f  f4f  f4f  f4f  f4f  f4f  f4f  f4f  f4f
```

Now look away from the keyboard and practice. Look at your text, not the keyboard.

```
f4f  f4f  f4f  f4f  f4f  f4f  f4f  f4f  f4f  f4f
```

Key each line two times before moving on to key the next line.

Remember the number reading procedures!

```
1  f4f  f4f  4  44  444  far  44  fig  44  for  4  44

2  44  fire  44  file  44  fold  44  four  444  fig

3  4 1 41 4 2 42 4 5 45 4 0 40 4 9 49 4 54

4  4 7 47 4 8 48 8 4 84 440 445 489 432 42

5  4/47 4/41 4/94 4/04 4:14 4:84 4:74 4:48

6  Bring me items 4, 42, 48, 149, and 294.
```

Destination—The 6 Key

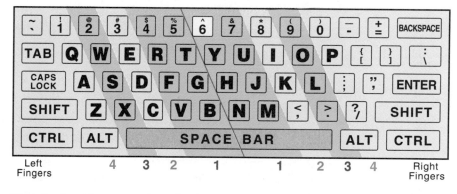

Left Fingers   4   3   2   1   1   2   3   4   Right Fingers

Here is the 6 key. It is keyed with your J finger. Place your fingers in a curved, upright position on the home keys. Look at your J finger and practice the reach to 6. Keep your other fingers curved and resting lightly on the home keys.

```
j6j  j6j  j6j  j6j  j6j  j6j  j6j  j6j  j6j  j6j
```

Now look away from the keyboard and practice. Look at your text, not the keyboard.

```
j6j  j6j  j6j  j6j  j6j  j6j  j6j  j6j  j6j  j6j
```

2. **Career Objective.** This area of the resume lists what type of job you would like. The heading *Career Objective* starts at the left margin. It is printed in bold. Double-space before listing your objective. The line frequently starts with the word *To*. Lines of the objective are indented five spaces.

3. **Education.** In this part, you list all of your education, starting with the most recent. Follow the same formatting guidelines as for Career Objective. Double-space between each entry.

4. **Qualifications.** For qualifications, list specific skills you have that would be helpful for the type of job you want. For example, if you want a job as a singer you could mention voice lessons and experience in a choir or singing group.

5. **Experience.** Jobs that you held are listed in order from the most recent to the first. Remember, if you have not held any jobs yet, you can list work in your neighborhood or volunteer work.

6. **Special Skills.** In this section, you would list any other skills you have that do not pertain directly to the job you are applying for but that are helpful.

7. **References.** References are people who will tell employers about your character and quality of work. In most cases, you do not list the references on the resume but state that they will be provided. Before using any person as a reference, be sure to get his or her permission. People for whom you have worked are good references. Teachers, coaches, religious leaders, and club leaders are also good.

Exercise

1. In the *Galaxy Gazette*, key the model resume on page 258. Follow the steps outlined above. Use the default side margins. Begin the name line setting a two-inch top margin. Press tab to indent the lines as shown.

2. After you finish keying the letter, proofread your document on the screen. Correct any keying errors.

3. Select Alt-P (⌘-P) to print a copy. Press Alt-S (⌘-S) to save the document. Name it "Resume." Proofread the printed copy; mark all undetected errors on the printout. Correct any errors you found in your proofreading.

4. Select Alt-G (⌘-G) and UKey2 will check your document to see how well you completed your task. After you read your score and status, press Enter to save the document. Next, select yes to print a copy.

Good landing. Congratulations, you have completed this unit. Prepare to take off on a new tour.

Read the numbers in units.

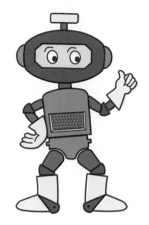

Key each line two times before moving on to key the next line.

1 j6j j6j 6 66 666 jar 66 jig 666 jaw 666

2 66 jury 66 juice 66 judge 66 jostle 666

3 6 7 67 6 8 68 6 9 69 6 0 60 06 86 56 67

4 466 567 896 362 126 945 960 060 635 623

5 476 368 296 687 906 306 246 193 356 685

6 Ticket sales are for rows 6, 7, and 86.

Landing Practice—Increase Keying Speed

Key each line two times before moving on to key the next line. Try to increase your speed as you repeat the line.

1 bunt take here want make sale true area

2 fort quit move room ware exit vote bare

3 Can Meri key all of the drills in time?

4 Anne Lyn was born at 2:02 p.m. on 4/22.

Key each line two times before moving on to key the next line. Silently say the phrases as you key them.

1 to it, as it, do it, on it, and for, an

2 by my, on it, is not, in so, so she is,

Mission Assessment

Take two 1-minute timings on the following paragraphs. Following the copy in your book, key the lines on the computer on your typewriter. Decide on a goal of increased speed or increased accuracy.

1   How are we doing with all the new

2 orders? We must fill them quickly.

3 The only way we can keep ahead is to

4 fill our orders faster than other

5 companies. If there is a problem, we

6 must all pitch in and work overtime.

7   When we ship the items, please

8 ensure that everything is correct.

9 Correct addresses are very important.

| 1 | 2 | 3 | 4 | 5 | 6 | 7 | 8 |

Minimum speed goal:
18 wam
Maximum errors allowed:
4

Mission accomplished!

Minimum speed goal:
27 wam
Maximum errors allowed:
6

Mission Assessment

Take two 2-minute timings on the following paragraphs. Following the copy in your book, key the lines on the computer or your typewriter.

1   When you want to apply for a job,

2 you will need a resume. A resume is a

3 written account of your previous jobs

4 and skills. The resume gives only the

5 most important facts about your work

6 experience and education. If you are

7 trying to get your first job and do

8 not have any previous jobs to list,

9 you can include work you have done in

10 your neighborhood or volunteer work.

11   It is important that your resume

12 not have any errors in grammar,

13 misspelled words, or words that are

14 used incorrectly. Resumes should be

15 formatted properly, too. Your resume

16 will be the first impression you make

17 on any employer and you want that

18 impression to be a good one.

| 1 | 2 | 3 | 4 | 5 | 6 | 7 | 8 |

Destination—Learn to Format a Resume

A resume is single-spaced with double-spaces used between main parts. A resume should be attractively arranged on the page, centered vertically. That means if it is short, leave a bigger top margin. In general, leave a two-inch top margin.

The parts of the resume are:
1. **Name and Address.** In capital letters and centered at the top of the page, you key your name; street address; city, state, and zip code; and telephone number. Print these lines in bold. Double-space after the phone number line.

LESSON

29 Learning the Ampersand, Number Sign, Percent Sign, and Asterisk

BRIEFING

After completing this mission, you will be able to:

1. **Key copy using the symbols for the ampersand, number sign, percent sign, and asterisk.**

2. **Improve keyboarding skill.**

Computers—use default margins for all drills unless otherwise indicated.
Typewriters—use these margins unless otherwise indicated: 10 Pitch 2", 12 pitch 2½".
Single-spacing unless otherwise indicated.

Countdown—Get Ready for Blast-off

Review the countdown procedures.

Launch Review

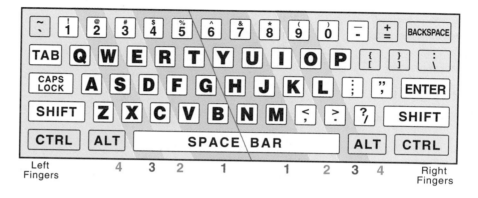

Key each line two times before moving on to key the next line.

Strike the keys quickly.

Keep your eyes on the copy.

1 Kirby and Taxi are Jac's two sheepdogs.

2 Amazon parrots like to eat fresh fruit.

3 Cathie lives in a suburb of Boston, MA.

4 Oregon's coastal highway is attractive.

5 Texas is nicknamed the Lone Star State.

Destination—The Ampersand Key

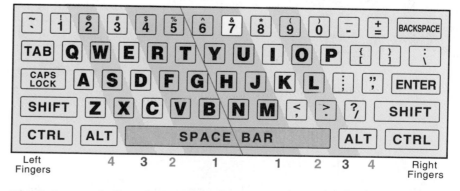

The & is a symbol used to mean "and." It is called an **ampersand**. Here is the ampersand key. It is the shift of the 7 key. It is keyed with your J finger.

LESSON

68 Format a Resume

MISSION
BRIEFING

In this mission you will:
1. **Improve free-writing skills.**
2. **Format a resume.**

Strike the keys quickly.

Don't forget proper posture.

Computers—use default margins for all drills unless otherwise indicated.
Typewriters—use these margins unless otherwise indicated: 10 Pitch 2", 12 pitch 2½".
Single-spacing unless otherwise indicated.

Countdown—Get Ready for Blast-off

Review the countdown procedures.

Launch Review

Key each line two times.

1 Chi Lee wrote her new novel in 15 days.

2 Minnesota's named Land of 10,000 Lakes.

3 The Sphinx in Egypt is 9,000 years old.

4 My huge dog wants to swim in the river.

Mission Report—Free Writing

Using the word processor, write your journal entry. Write about a hobby you like or a sport you like to play. Describe the hobby or sport to the readers and help them understand why you like it. Double-space your copy. Print and save a copy. Name it "Jour68."

Place your fingers in a
curved, upright position
on the home keys.

Look at your J finger and practice the reach to the ampersand. Keep your other fingers curved and resting lightly on the home keys.

j&j j&j j&j j&j j&j j&j j&j j&j j&j j&j

Now look away from the keyboard and practice.

j&j j&j j&j j&j j&j j&j j&j j&j j&j j&j

Key each line two times before moving on to key the next line.

1 j&j j&j j&l k&f r&r d&k u&n e&k w&m q&s

2 Can you add 104 & 290 & 310 & 705 & 15?

3 Zarro & Hodge, Inc. did the tax return.

4 Leah & Lowell offer special trip fares.

Destination—The Number Sign Key

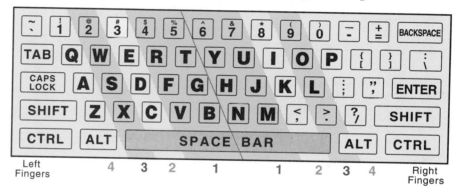

The # is a symbol for "number" if it is used with a numeral, such as #2. You do not leave a space between the number sign and the numeral that follows it. Here is the number sign key. The # is the shift of 3. It is keyed with your D finger. Place your fingers in a curved, upright position on the home keys. Look at your D finger and practice the reach to the number sign. Keep your other fingers curved and resting lightly on the home keys.

d#d d#d d#d d#d d#d d#d d#d d#d d#d d#d

Now look away from the keyboard and practice.

d#d d#d d#d d#d d#d d#d d#d d#d d#d d#d

Key each line two times before moving on to key the next line.

1 #3 #33 #2 #23 #4 #45 #55 #11 #22 #23 #3

2 Compare #63 with #861 for price quotes.

3 Biker #64 will win the race before #36.

4 Racehorse #23 is ridden by Eileen Cord.

were asked to answer on a scale of 1 to 10 with 10 being the best. The survey included:

1. comfort of the suit.

2. attractiveness of the suit.

3. ease of care.

4. durability of the suit (how well made it is).

     After all 20 people answered, We Ask You averaged the numbers. The results were:

COMPARISON OF SPACE SUITS

Criteria	Glow Gear	Zippy Gear	Difference
Comfort	6	8	(compute)
Attractiveness	9	8	(compute)
Ease of care	5	8	(compute)
Durability	6	9	(compute)

Tab Settings:
10 pitch: 33, 46, and 60
12 pitch: 43, 56, and 70.

Results

     From the survey, Space Gear, Inc. found out that customers like the look of the Glow Gear, but it is not as comfortable, easy to take care of, or durable as Zippy Gear. Based on these results, Space Gear, Inc. decided to remake the Glow Gear suits using some of the features of the Zippy Gear.

↑ 2
1"

Destination—The Percent Sign Key

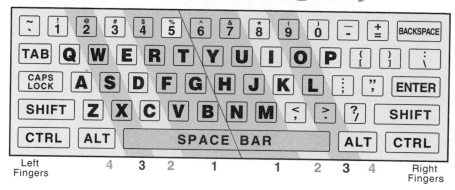

Left Fingers   4   3   2   1   1   2   3   4   Right Fingers

Place your fingers in a curved, upright position on the home keys.

The % is a symbol for "percent." It is called a **percent sign** and is used with numerals. Here is the percent key. It is the shift of 5. It is keyed with your F finger. Look at your F finger and practice the reach to percent. Keep your other fingers curved and resting lightly on the home keys.

f%f f%f f%f f%f f%f f%f f%f f%f f%f f%f

Now look away from the keyboard and practice.

f%f f%f f%f f%f f%f f%f f%f f%f f%f f%f

Key each line two times before moving on to key the next line.

1 Can you figure out what 5% of 1,345 is?

2 The man added the city sales tax of 6%.

3 Only 10% of that class has voted today.

4 She donated 20% of profit to a charity.

Destination—The Asterisk Key

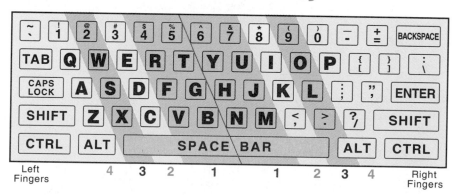

Left Fingers   4   3   2   1   1   2   3   4   Right Fingers

TOP-NOTCH TRAINING TIP

Place your fingers in a curved, upright position on the home keys.

The * is a symbol used as a reference mark to alert the reader to a footnote. This symbol is called an **asterisk**. It is placed after the period. Here is the asterisk key. It is the shift of 8. It is keyed with your K finger. Look at your K finger and practice the reach to the asterisk. Keep your other fingers curved and resting lightly on the home keys.

k*k k*k k*k k*k k*k k*k k*k k*k k*k k*k

CONSUMER SATISFACTION REPORT

Introduction

Space Gear, Inc. asked that their two main lines
of space suits be compared to find out which one
customers liked better. We Ask You Opinion Service
was given the job of finding out. We Ask You
arranged to give to 20 different customers space
suits and have them try out the suits for one month.
At the end of that time the wearers would allow in-
depth interviews and fill out a form about the
product.

Population

Twenty of the people living on the space station
were chosen by the computer at random. Half of the
20 were given Glow Gear space suits. The others were
given Zippy Gear.

Survey Forms

We Ask You made an interview guide and survey
form. To make the forms easy to use, the wearers

Now look away from the keyboard and practice.

```
k*k k*k k*k k*k k*k k*k k*k k*k k*k k*k
```

Key each line two times before moving on to key the next line.

1 k*k ill* sic* des* num* red* ask* lack*

2 it* fizz* deal* feel* well* quit* gone*

3 Dave was famous for his speech of 3/2.*

4 Tanya won the vote by a narrow margin.*

Mission Assessment

Take two 1-minute timings on the following paragraphs. Following the copy in your book, key the lines on the computer. Decide on a goal of increased speed or increased accuracy.

1   Do you like animals? Do you ever

2 wonder why they do funny things?

3 Animal behaviorists are people who

4 study the way animals behave. They

5 can help other people understand why

6 animals act as they do.

7   By understanding animal behavior,

8 people can help protect wildlife.

9 They will know how animals live and

10 learn how to preserve the environment

11 to save animal habitat.

| 1 | 2 | 3 | 4 | 5 | 6 | 7 | 8 |

BRIEFING

Mission Control reports that your mission is accomplished.

Saturn is well-known for its rings made of ice and rock. On the planet itself, winds blow at an amazing 870 MPH.

LESSON

67 Format a Rough Draft Report with a Table

In this mission, you will:
1. Improve free-writing skills.
2. Format a rough draft with a table.

Strike the keys quickly.

Keep your eyes on the copy.

Computers—use default margins for all drills unless otherwise indicated.
Typewriters—use these margins unless otherwise indicated: 10 Pitch 2", 12 pitch 2½".
Single-spacing unless otherwise indicated.

Countdown—Get Ready for Blast-off

Review the countdown procedures.

Launch Review

Key each line two times.

1 The plants will close at 11 a.m. today.

2 When summer arrives, we like to travel.

3 Kathy and Mark live outside of Chicago.

4 Solar energy does not pollute the city.

5 They decorated floats for the carnival.

Mission Report—Free Writing

Using the word processor, write your journal entry. You may choose any topic you want. You may want to take a topic from an earlier lesson and expand upon it. Double-space your copy. Print and save a copy. Name it "Jour67."

Destination—Keying a Rough Draft Report with a Table

1. Key the following draft report in correct format in the *Galaxy Gazette*. Make corrections as you key and compute the figures for the differences in the table. Leave four spaces between the columns. Do not set a top margin; press Enter.
2. Proofread the screen copy. Use the editing keys to make corrections.
3. Select Alt-P (⌘-P) to print a copy. Press Alt-S (⌘-S) to save the document. Name it "Reptsur." Proofread the printed copy; mark all undetected errors on the printout. Compare your printout with the model table. If it is not spaced properly, try it again. Correct any errors you found in your proofreading.
4. Select Alt-G (⌘-G) and UKey2 will check your document to see how well you completed your task. After you read your score and status, press Enter to save the document. Next, select yes to print a copy.

You've really made great progress!

LESSON

30 Learning the Dollar Sign, At Symbol, Caret, and Equals and Plus Signs

BRIEFING

After completing this mission, you will be able to:

1. Key copy using the dollar sign, at symbol, caret, and equals and plus signs.
2. Improve keyboarding skill.

Strike the keys quickly.

Keep your eyes on the copy.

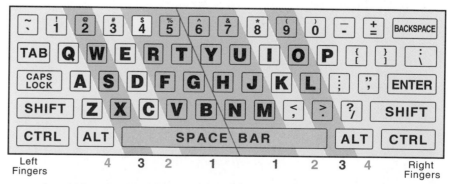

Computers—use default margins for all drills unless otherwise indicated.
Typewriters—use these margins unless otherwise indicated: 10 Pitch 2", 12 pitch 2½".
Single-spacing unless otherwise indicated.

Countdown—Get Ready for Blast-off

Review the countdown procedures.

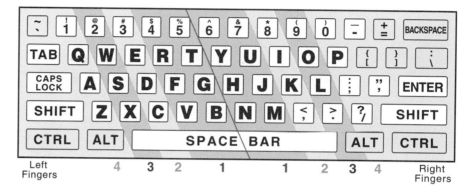

Launch Review

Key each line two times before moving on to key the next line.

1 Katie's brother got married in Phoenix.

2 Ron's 13-year-old daughter is a singer.

3 Sarah went on a two-week trip to Paris.

4 Bruce and Joni are local baseball fans.

5 Flights #356 & #902 were only 60% full.

6 Figures 33 & 89* denote the loss of it.

Destination—The Dollar Sign Key

AVERAGE DISTANCE FROM THE SUN

Body	Miles*	Kilometers*
Mercury	36	(Compute)
Venus	67	(Compute)
Earth	93	(Compute)
Mars	141	(Compute)
Jupiter	483	(Compute)
Saturn	886	(Compute)
Uranus	1,783	(Compute)
Neptune	2,793	(Compute)
Pluto	3,666	(Compute)

Tab Settings
In 10 Pitch: 22, 35, and 52
In 12 pitch: 32, 45, and 62

* computed in millions of miles/kilometers

The $ is a symbol used to mean "dollar." It is called a **dollar sign.** The dollar sign key is the shift of the 4 key. It is keyed with your F finger. Place your fingers in a curved, upright position on the home keys. Look at your F finger and practice the reach to the dollar sign. Keep your other fingers curved and resting lightly on the home keys.

f$f f$f f$f f$f f$f f$f f$f f$f f$f f$f

Now look away from the keyboard and practice. Look at your text, not the keyboard.

f$f f$f f$f f$f f$f f$f f$f f$f f$f f$f

Key each line two times before moving on to key the next line.

1 $1 $4 $43 $56 $75 $15 $90 $89 $123 $555

2 Jim bought his new tape player for $99.

3 Freida made $25 in overtime at her job.

4 Season tickets for the theater are $40.

Destination—The At Symbol Key

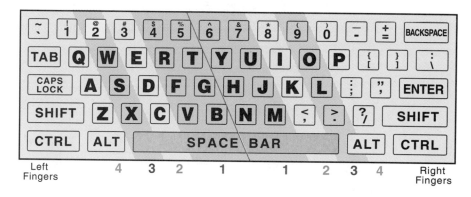

The @ is a symbol for "at" and "each." It is called the **at symbol.** Here is the at symbol key. It is the shift of 2. It is keyed with your S finger. Place your fingers in a curved, upright position on the home keys. Look at your S finger and practice the reach to the at symbol. Keep your other fingers curved and resting lightly on the home keys.

s@s s@s s@s s@s s@s s@s s@s s@s s@s s@s

Now look away from the keyboard and practice. Look at your text, not the keyboard.

s@s s@s s@s s@s s@s s@s s@s s@s s@s s@s

TOP-NOTCH TRAINING TIP

Line 27 ⟶ PLANNED EXPLORATIONS

Geological survey of Mars	December
Rendezvous with <u>Voyager</u>	February
Sample collection from Kepler	August
Measurement of Olympus Mons	September
Photograph Jupiter and Io	November
Visit new space station	December

Key each line two times before moving on to key the next line.

1 @ 2 @ 5 @ 9 @ 0 @ 1 @ 3 @ 4 @ 7 @ 8 @ 2

2 Char bought five apples & pears @ $.25.

3 Tickets for the circus ride are @ $.99.

4 He wants a milk chocolate malt @ $1.99.

Destination—The Caret Key

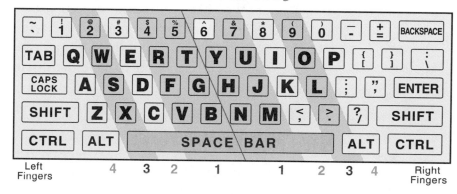

Left Fingers   4   3   2   1   1   2   3   4   Right Fingers

TOP-NOTCH TRAINING TIP

The ^ is a symbol that can represent the place where something is to be inserted and is called a **caret**. The ^ symbol also can represent an **exponent** in mathematical terms, which means a number is multiplied by itself. For example, 2^3 means multiply 2 by 2 three times, which equals 8.

Here is the ^ key. It is the shift of 6. It is keyed with your J finger. Place your fingers in a curved, upright position on the home keys. Look at your J finger and practice the reach to ^. Keep your other fingers curved and resting lightly on the home keys.

j^j j^j j^j j^j j^j j^j j^j j^j j^j j^j

Now look away from the keyboard and practice. Look at your text, not the keyboard.

j^j j^j j^j j^j j^j j^j j^j j^j j^j j^j

Key each line two times before moving on to key the next line.

1 What does 5^2 equal? What about 15^15?

2 Is the earth 10^30 miles from a quasar?

3 A ^ can help a programmer locate files.

4 The rate of inflation is 5^2 in Brazil.

Destination—Key Additional Tables

1. In the *Galaxy Gazette,* key the table "Planned Explorations" in correct format centered vertically and horizontally. Double-space. Leave eight spaces between columns.
2. Proofread the copy and use the editing keys to make corrections.
3. Select Alt-P (⌘-P) to print a copy. Press Alt-S (⌘-S) to save the document. Name it "Table2." Proofread the printed copy; mark all undetected errors on the printout. Compare your printout with the model table. If it is not spaced properly, try it again. Correct any errors you found in your proofreading.
4. Select Alt-G (⌘-G) and UKey2 will check your document to see how well you completed your task. After you read your score and status, press Enter to save the document. Next, select yes to print a final copy.

Extended Activity

1. In the open screen of the Mission Report, key the table "Average Distance from the Sun" in correct format centered vertically and horizontally. Double-space. Leave six spaces between columns. You must compute the distance in kilometers. A kilometer is 0.62 of a mile; a mile is 1.61 kilometers.
2. Select Alt-P (⌘-P) to print a copy. Press Alt-S (⌘-S) to save the document. Name it "Table3." Proofread the printed copy; mark all undetected errors on the printout. Compare your printout with the model table. If it is not spaced properly, try it again. Correct any errors you found in your proofreading.
3. Select Alt-P (⌘-P) to print your table. Proof the copy, make any corrections to your document, save it again, and print a final copy.

REENTRY
BRIEFING

Mission accomplished.

Destination—The Equals and Plus Sign Key

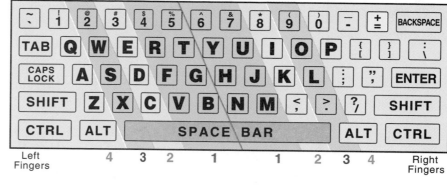

Left Fingers   4   3   2   1   1   2   3   4   Right Fingers

TOP-NOTCH TRAINING TIP

The = is a symbol used to represent "equals." The + is a symbol that means plus. Here is the **equals sign** key. The **plus sign** key is the shift of the equals sign. Both are keyed with your semicolon finger. Place your fingers in a curved, upright position on the home keys. Look at your semicolon finger and practice the reach to the equals and plus sign keys. Keep your other fingers curved and resting lightly on the home keys.

;=; ;=; ;=; ;=; ;=; ;+; ;+; ;+; ;+; ;+;

Now look away from the keyboard and practice. Look at your text, not the keyboard.

;=; ;=; ;=; ;=; ;=; ;+; ;+; ;+; ;+; ;+;

Key each line two times before moving on to key the next line.

1 2 + 2 = 4 1 + 6 = 7 13 + 13 = 26 1 + 1

2 Jan writes that 3 + 11 = 14. Does it?

3 Doral calculates that 123 + 126 = 249.

4 His bill was 3 + 146 + 190 + 23 = 362.

Skill Exploration

Take two 30-second timings on each of the following lines. Try to reach a new speed goal. Do not worry about errors for now. Work to beat the computer. If you are using a typewriter, you can figure out your speed using the formula in the Introduction.

1 The ozone is thin above the South Pole.

2 World's oldest song was dated 1800 B.C.

3 Amundsen was first to reach South Pole.

| 1 | 2 | 3 | 4 | 5 | 6 | 7 | 8 |

Minimum speed goal:
27 wam
Maximum errors allowed:
6

Mission Assessment

Take two 2-minute timings on the following paragraphs. Study the material; then following the copy in your book, key the lines on the computer.

1   Some plants and animals have

2 protective colors that disguise them

3 from enemies. For example, snakes

4 that live in the grass are green, and

5 those that live in the desert are gray

6 or sand colored. Some rabbits and

7 weasels have seasonal changes in the

8 coloring of their fur coats. For

9 instance, they are brown in the summer

10 and white during the winter.

11   Other defenseless animals are

12 mimics. They have coloring that makes

13 them look like an animal their enemies

14 avoid. For instance, some moths and

15 flies look like bees and wasps. The

16 viceroy butterfly has a wing pattern

17 similar to the monarch butterfly, which

18 birds do not like to eat.

19   Coloring serves other purposes,

20 too. For example, brightly colored

21 flowers attract birds and bees. The

22 birds and bees that feed on nectar and

23 pollen transfer pollen from one flower

24 to another. The process, known as

25 cross pollination, is necessary for the

26 reproduction of some plants.

| 1 | 2 | 3 | 4 | 5 | 6 | 7 | 8 |

Minimum speed goal:
18 wam
Maximum errors allowed:
4

Mission Assessment

Take two 1-minute timings on the following paragraph. Following the copy in your book, key the lines on the computer or on your typewriter. Decide on a goal of increased speed or increased accuracy.

1   Solar power plants make electricity

2 by using energy from the sun. Large

3 panels of mirrors serve as collectors

4 to capture the sun's energy. The

5 collectors reflect the sunlight onto

6 pipes with oil in them. The sunlight

7 heats the oil. The heat in the oil is

8 used to change water into steam. The

9 steam runs machines called generators,

10 and the generators make electricity.

11 The electricity can then reach

12 thousands of homes. Is there a solar

13 power plant near your home?

| 1 | 2 | 3 | 4 | 5 | 6 | 7 | 8 |

BRIEFING

Mission Control reports that your mission is accomplished.

The Sun is about eight million miles in diameter or about 2,000 Earths. Energy from the core of the Sun takes nearly one million years to reach the Sun's surface. That energy, which we know as "light," then reaches the Earth in just eight minutes.

LESSON

66 Review Simple Tables

MISSION
BRIEFING

In this mission, you will:
1. **Improve free-writing skills.**
2. **Review simple tables.**

Strike the keys quickly.

Keep your eyes on the copy.

Computers—use default margins for all drills unless otherwise indicated.
Typewriters—use these margins unless otherwise indicated: 10 Pitch 2", 12 pitch 2½".
Single-spacing unless otherwise indicated.

Countdown—Get Ready for Blast-off

Review the countdown procedures.

Launch Review

Key each line two times.

1 We placed an order for 14 quick copies.

2 What is the value of that antique ring?

3 Our profits were 120% higher this year.

4 You should be able to key without care.

Landing Practice—Free Writing

Using the word processor, write your journal entry. Think about something that you are really glad happened to you. Was it a special event or a special way you were treated? Was it an award or something unexpected? Describe to your readers the event and how it made you feel at the time and how it makes you feel now. Double-space your copy. Print and save a copy. Name it "Jour66."

LESSON

31 Review and Skill Building

Computers—use default margins for all drills unless otherwise indicated.
Typewriters—use these margins unless otherwise indicated. 10 Pitch 2", 12 pitch 2-½".
Single spacing unless otherwise indicated.

Countdown—Get Ready for Blast-off

Review the countdown procedures.

Launch Review

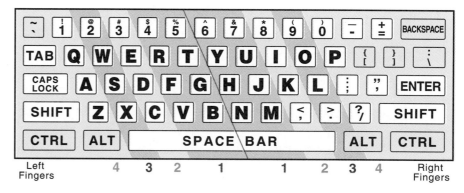

Key each line two times before moving on to key the next line.

1 The combination is 421, 2790, and 3601.

2 The numbers were 749-3841 and 371-3301.

3 Take a 10% discount on items #78 & 802.

4 The price was $90.95 for the blue bike.

5 Item 290 @ $40.36 was the worst choice.

6 Check these prices: $379.63 & $628.13.

Landing Practice—Keying Numeric Tabulation

Use the tab key between the groups of numbers. Key each line two times before moving on to key the next line. Remember to read the numbers in groups of two. For example: 2652 is read twenty-six/fifty two. Press Enter at the end of each line.

1 2652	4893	3903	7832	0821
2 0984	1610	1794	1510	4264
3 4290	6247	7304	2956	9040
4 3629	3429	1985	1793	6383

MISSION BRIEFING

Congratulations! You have completed all the top-row number and symbol destinations. You will now prepare for the next missions by reviewing your flight information. During this mission you will:

1. Review all top-row numbers and symbols.
2. Improve keyboarding skill.

Strike the keys quickly.

Keep your eyes on the copy.

TYPEWRITER TIP

Review the Introduction material on setting tabs.

STUDENT GOVERNMENT OFFICERS   ← Line 25
                          double-space

President   Sarah Jenkins

Vice President   Jay Lincoln

Secretary   Mateo Vargas

Treasurer   Janet Farrell

Class Representative   Li Chin

Class Representative   June Strickland

Class Representative   Louisa Romano
↑   ↑   ↑
tab   8 spaces   tab
(10 pitch: 21)   (10 pitch: 49)
(12 pitch: 30)   (12 pitch: 58)

Keep your eyes on the copy!

5	3983	3905	3893	2106	4593
6	4902	3902	3894	6854	6031
7	4021	6734	8932	9032	8920

Skill Exploration

Take two 30-second timings on each of the following lines. Try to reach a new speed goal. Do not worry about errors for now. Work to beat the computer. If you are using a typewriter, you can figure out your speed using the formula in the Introduction.

1 Ezrim went to the movie with his class.

2 I practiced to refine my keying skills.

3 Yuril jogged downtown to the local gym.

| 1 | 2 | 3 | 4 | 5 | 6 | 7 | 8 |

Mission Assessment

Take two 1-minute timings on the following paragraphs. Following the copy in your book, key the lines on the computer or your typewriter. Decide on a goal of increased speed or increased accuracy.

1   Since 1945, Japan has grown into an

2 economic leader. Foreign trade played

3 a major role in Japan's economic

4 recovery. Foreign trade is important

5 to Japan because of its small size and

6 large population.

7   Japan is equal to California in

8 size and imports most of its needed

9 raw materials. Look for Japan to be a

10 major economic power for many years.

| 1 | 2 | 3 | 4 | 5 | 6 | 7 | 8 |

Minimum speed goal:
19 wam
Maximum errors allowed:
4

BRIEFING

You have completed this mission!

c. Change tab settings as follows: Set a tab for column 1 at position 21 and a tab for column 2 at position 49.

d. Delete the key line.

5. To key the table, press tab and then key *President*. Press tab and then key *Sarah Jenkins*. Key across the columns; press Enter at the end of each line.

6. Proofread and make corrections.

7. Select Alt-P (⌘-P) to print a copy. Press Alt-S (⌘-S) to save the document. Name it "Table1." Proofread the printed copy; mark all undetected errors on the printout. Correct any errors you found in your proofreading. Compare your printout with the model table. If it is not spaced properly, try it again.

8. Select Alt-G (⌘-G) and UKey2 will check your document to see how well you completed your task. After you read your score and status, press Enter to save the document. Next, select yes to print a copy.

Great work.

LESSON

MISSION BRIEFING

You will continue your flight preparation in this mission. When you complete this mission, you will:

1. Improve keyboarding skill.
2. Improve keyboarding technique.
3. Improve composition skill.

Strike the keys quickly.

Keep your eyes on the copy.

Computers—use default margins for all drills unless otherwise indicated.
Typewriters—use these margins unless otherwise indicated: 10 Pitch 2", 12 pitch 2½".
Single-spacing unless otherwise indicated.

Countdown—Get Ready for Blast-off

Review the countdown procedures.

Launch Review

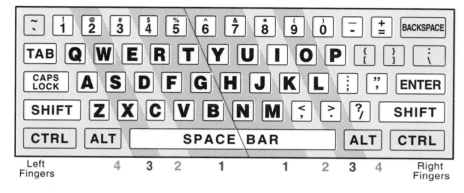

Key each line two times before moving on to key the next line.

1 it no as if he at us do an me am up bye

2 Being able to key is a workplace skill.

3 Take the town's star apart for repairs.

4 Can you add 1, 2, 3, 4, 5, 6, 22, & 89?

5 Bring 46 cards, 28 folders, and 7 pens.

6 Does $38,942 and $42,689 equal $81,631?

Launch Review—The Tab Key

Use the tab key between the words. Key each line twice, trying to increase your speed. Press Enter at the end of each line.

1 abbe	bank	cane	deed	even
2 four	gate	have	ices	jack
3 keep	lane	made	navy	open
4 pane	quad	rush	said	type
5 ugly	vote	when	exit	zero

4. Center the columns horizontally, leaving the same amount of space between each column. This space usually ranges from 4 to 12 spaces. It is easier to work with even spacing between the columns.
5. Align word columns on the left and numerical columns on the right or at the decimal point.

Example:

Watches	$134.90
Rings	98.07
Bracelets	15.95
Chains	9.89

Exercise

Follow these step-by-step directions to key the model table. The table is two columns with eight spaces between the columns. It is double-spaced. Use the *Galaxy Gazette*.

1. Compute the vertical center. To do so:
   a. Determine the number of vertical lines available on the paper on which you will be printing. There are 6 lines per inch, so standard 8½ by 11-inch paper has 66 vertical lines (11 x 6 lines per inch). Refer to the Introduction.
   b. Determine the number of printed and blank lines in the copy to be keyed. The table you will key has 15 lines (including blank lines).
   c. Subtract the lines to be keyed from the total lines available on the page.

Available	66
Used	-15
Unused	51

   d. Divide the unused lines by two to determine the number of blank lines to leave for the top and bottom margins. If your number includes a fraction, round it up.

   $$51 \div 2 = 25\frac{1}{2} \text{ (round up to 26)}$$

   e. To leave the corrrect amount of space in the top margin, begin keying on line 25. (Remember, your software automatically leaves 6 blank lines in the top margin.)
2. Set the line spacing to double-space.
3. Press Enter until your cursor is on line 25. Center and key the title in all caps. Press Enter one time.
4. Compute the settings for tabs. To do so:
   a. Identify the **key line.** The key line is the one with the longest item in each column plus the number of spaces to be left between columns. This table has eight spaces between columns. The key line for this table is Class Representative (eight spaces)June Strickland
   b. Key and center this key line. Note the position on the status line where the *C* in *Class* and the *J* in *June* begins. *Class* should begin at position 21, and *June* should begin at position 49.

TYPEWRITER TIP

Typewriters see the Introduction.

Do not worry about errors for now. Work to beat the computer.

If you are using a typewriter, you can figure out your speed using the formula in the Introduction.

Landing Practice—Improve Keying Speed

Key each line two times before moving on to key the next line. If time permits, key each line again until it can be keyed with no more than one error.

1 Violet checks the new oil heater meter.

2 Avoid avenues with new cargo cable car.

3 Trains hit the rail for one easy shift.

4 "Don't be surprised," she said briskly.

5 The stock price @ $75.38 seemed unfair.

Skill Exploration

Take two 30-second timings on each of the following lines. Try to reach a new speed goal.

1 If they make a visit, it may end there.

2 It was up to us to set the right price.

3 Hills allow you to fall with odd calls.

| 1 | 2 | 3 | 4 | 5 | 6 | 7 | 8 |

Mission Assessment

Take two 1-minute timings on the following paragraphs. Following the copy in your book, key the lines on the computer or your typewriter. Decide on a goal of increased speed or increased accuracy.

1   There are many word-processing

2 software packages on the market. All

3 users should field test them before

4 buying. Find out how long it will

5 take to learn to use the package.

6 Good keying skills will help.

7   A portable computer can be a big

8 help when people must travel. Some

9 laptops can now fit into a briefcase.

10 Although they are small, they are

11 quite powerful. You can now prepare

12 reports while traveling.

| 1 | 2 | 3 | 4 | 5 | 6 | 7 | 8 |

**Minimum speed goal:
19 wam
Maximum errors allowed:
4**

LESSON 65 Format Simple Tables

MISSION BRIEFING

In this mission, you will:
1. **Improve free-writing skills.**
2. **Format simple tables.**

Strike the keys quickly.

Keep your eyes on the copy.

Computers—use default margins for all drills unless otherwise indicated.
Typewriters—use these margins unless otherwise indicated: 10 Pitch 2", 12 pitch 2½".
Single-spacing unless otherwise indicated.

Countdown—Get Ready for Blast-off

Review the countdown procedures.

Launch Review

Key each line two times.

1 Buy 18 cups, 204 plates, & 615 napkins.

2 His version of the battle amazed Zarah.

3 She said, "Hello Ms. Guy," to the lady.

4 Shay told me to come home after dinner.

Landing Practice—Free Writing

Using the word processor, write your journal entry. Think about a movie you have seen recently or a book you have read that you enjoyed. Describe the movie or book in such a way that your reader will want to see or read it. Double-space your copy. Print and save a copy. Name it "Jour65."

Destination—Learn to Format Simple Tables

Tables are a concise way of presenting data, which is often difficult to read in text format. Tables may be presented alone on a page or included in letters and reports. Tables may range from simple two-column tables with a main heading to those with several levels of headings and many columns.

  Study the two-column table on page 246, and review these general guidelines for formatting it.
1. Center tables horizontally and vertically on the page. (If the table is included in another document such as a letter or report, you do not need to center it vertically.)
2. Center the main heading, and key it in all capital letters. Double-space after it.
3. Format the body of the table in columns. The body may be single-spaced or double-spaced.

Galaxy Gazette

Because of your excellent keyboarding progress, you have been promoted to Star Reporter! You are now ready to begin more advanced composition activities. As a part of that preparation, you need to practice some prewriting activities. Free thinking or brainstorming is an essential prewriting activity. During this stage of the writing process, you will rely on your own imagination, thoughts, and feelings.

1. To practice this process, select one of the following topics:
   School Is Fun
   River Pollution
   Violence on Television
   Students' Rights
   Teamwork Is Great

   From the main menu, select Mission Report and then choose the open screen option. Key any ideas that come to mind as you think about the topic you selected. List at least 20 words that relate to the topic. Key them directly on your keyboard. Do not write them on paper first. Do not worry about errors at this time.

2. Compose five draft sentences about the topic you selected using one or more of the words from your list in each sentence. Key the sentences directly on the keyboard. Do not worry about errors, just try to get your thoughts down.

3. When you are finished, press Alt-P (⌘-P) to print your work. Press Alt-N (⌘-N) to save it and name it "Lesson32." Press Alt-Q (⌘-Q) to exit the word processor.

Great job!

Uranus orbits the Sun on its side. That means it points one or the other of its poles toward the Sun during its 84-year orbit.

MEMORANDUM

DATE: September 4, 2010

TO: All Class Members

FROM: Joan Temple, Class President

SUBJECT: Mars Theater Trip

Reservations for 45 have been made for the evening performance of "Black Hole Odyssey" on November 12. The tickets will be $22.50 each and round-trip transportation by charter shuttle will be $17.85 each.

Please reserve your tickets by 5 p.m. September 25 by depositing $15 with Jack Poole, the class treasurer. The deposits are nonrefundable.

This promises to be a great trip, so make your reservations early as space is limited. First come, first serve.

LESSON

33 Review and Skill Building

BRIEFING

You will continue your flight skill building during this mission. When you complete this mission, you will:

1. Improve keyboarding skill.
2. Improve keyboarding technique.
3. Improve composition skill.

Strike the keys quickly.
Keep your eyes on the copy.

Computers—use default margins for all drills unless otherwise indicated.
Typewriters—use these margins unless otherwise indicated: 10 Pitch 2", 12 pitch 2½".
Single-spacing unless otherwise indicated.

Countdown—Get Ready for Blast-off

Review the countdown procedures.

Launch Review

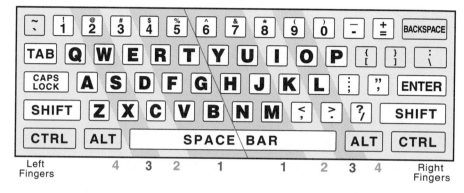

Key each line two times before moving on to key the next line.

1 The mail system speeds fall deliveries.

2 A new computer disk made our work easy.

3 Bring the crazy zoo zebra home quickly.

4 Was that purchase for $36.95 & $102.89?

5 Wild mustangs roam Wyoming and Montana.

Landing Practice—Numeric Copy

Use the tab key between the groups of numbers. Key each line twice, trying to increase your speed. Press Enter at the end of each line.

1	2903	9031	7882	9032	9034
2	2093	1043	9046	9831	1294
3	1095	9832	6734	8965	8673
4	8912	8923	8943	8475	8734
5	3903	9499	3681	7320	8943
6	8223	4156	8561	8934	8933

1½"
↓

MEMORANDUM   ← Center

3 blank lines

↓ tab (10 spaces)

DATE: January 30, 2032
double-space

TO: All Members of Mission Control Task Force
double-space

FROM: Nadlia L. Balear
double-space

SUBJECT: Task Force Meeting

2 blank lines

1" → There will be a Mission Control Task Force meeting on   ← 1"
February 15. The purpose of this meeting will be to
plan our next exploration. Please come to the
meeting prepared to discuss the following topics:
          1. Purpose of the next exploration.
          2. Destination of the next exploration.
tabs   3. Timing to include date and length.
          4. Estimated cost.
          5. Special equipment needed.

double-space

jsb

Landing Practice—Improve Keying Speed

Key each line two times before moving on to key the next line. Try to reach a new speed goal. If time permits, key each line again until it can be keyed with no more than one error.

1 race fear fare pull wade hump weed earn

2 hall call off odd fall adds tall alloys

3 teen allows effect suffer offer toddler

4 pony tear upon raft noon dear vest jilt

5 That tear in the shirt was only feared.

6 A raft trip at noon loomed upon Wendal.

Minimum speed goal:
20 wam
Maximum errors allowed:
4

Mission Assessment

Take two 1-minute timings on the following paragraphs. Following the copy in your book, key the lines on the computer or your typewriter. Decide on a goal of increased speed or increased accuracy.

1   You are making excellent progress

2 in your keyboarding program. Now you

3 can key by touch any word or number

4 that you desire. Did you ever think

5 that you would have this much skill?

6   When you go to the next unit, you

7 will learn to use the word processor.

8 You will be able to key your own

9 papers and make corrections to them

10 using this software. This will save

11 you a lot of time in writing for your

12 other classes.

| 1 | 2 | 3 | 4 | 5 | 6 | 7 | 8 |

1. Center and key the word *memorandum* in capital letters 1½ inches from the top of the page. (You may wish to bold *memorandum* in the title.)
2. Leave three blank lines between the word *memorandum* and the heading.
3. Key the headings *Date, To, From,* and *Subject* in all caps. Double-space the headings. Press the tab key to reach ten spaces to align the heading fill-in information.
4. Leave two blank lines between the subject heading and the body. Single-space the body. Default margins are generally used.
5. The initials of the operator are keyed at the bottom, double-space from the last line of the body.

Exercise

1. Use the *Galaxy Gazette* to key the memorandum on page 241 following the formatting directions. Use the default side margins. Set the top margin. Press the tab key for each listing in the body.
2. After you finish keying the memo, proofread your document on the screen. Correct any keying errors.
3. Select Alt-P (⌘-P) to print a copy. Press Alt-S (⌘-S) to save the document. Name it "Memo1." Proofread the printed copy; mark all undetected errors on the printout. Correct any errors you found in your proofreading.
4. Select Alt-G (⌘-G) and UKey2 will check your document to see how well you completed your task. After you read your score and status, press Enter to save the document. Next, select yes to print a copy.

Destination—Keying an Unarranged Memorandum

1. Use the open screen word processor to key the unarranged memorandum on page 242, following the formatting directions. Use the default side margins and set the top margin.
2. After you finish keying the memorandum, proofread your document on the screen. Correct any keying errors.
3. Select Alt-P (⌘-P) to print a copy. Press Alt-S (⌘-S) to save the document. Name it "Memo2." Proofread the printed copy; mark all undetected errors on the printout. Correct any errors you found in your proofreading.
4. Select Alt-P (⌘-P) to print a final copy and exit the word processor.

REENTRY
BRIEFING

Good work.

Galaxy Gazette

When writing for the *Galaxy Gazette*, you can make your writing more interesting by using **descriptive words.** Descriptive words include action verbs, adverbs, and adjectives. These words may discuss color, size, and shape. Words are most vivid when they appeal to the senses of sight, smell, sound, taste, and touch. Look at the following list of descriptive words:

soft	cool	throw	sour
harsh	blue	walk	sweet
silent	scarlet	drive	rough
green	hot	carry	scratchy
red	pink	hold	smooth
plush	loud	touch	cool
torn	black	get	

From the main menu, select Mission Report and choose the open screen option. Using the list of words, compose five sentences that vividly describe a person, place, object, or event that you have experienced or imagined. All five of the sentences can be about the same thing or you could write about different things. Kcy the draft sentences directly on the keyboard without worrying about errors for now.

When you are finished, press Alt-P (⌖-P) to print your work. Press Alt-N (⌖-N) to save your document and name it "Lesson33." Press Alt-Q (⌖-Q) to exit the word processor.

REENTRY
BRIEFING

Mission is a A-OK.

Mission Assessment

Take two 2-minute timings on the following paragraphs. Study the material; then following the copy in your book, key the lines on the computer.

1   When employees of the same company

2 need to communicate in writing, they use

3 a memorandum. Memorandums are usually

4 simply called memos.

5   Memos have many uses in an office.

6 Employees can pass on information, make

7 an announcement, and provide a record of

8 a decision. Many times employees

9 communicate with each other by phone.

10 In some cases, though, people need

11 written notice. Sending memos helps

12 prevent misunderstandings among

13 employees.

14   This is very important in large

15 companies where a number of employees

16 need the information. In offices where

17 employees use computers that are

18 networked, they can communicate by

19 electronic mail.

1	2	3	4	5	6	7	8

Destination—Learn to Format Memorandums

Communications going outside a company or school are usually keyed in letter format. Internal communications are keyed in memorandum format. The style of a memo may change from company to company, but the basic information included in the heading is standard. The standard heading for a memorandum includes the date, the name of the addressee, the name of the sender, and the subject. When keying memorandums, follow these guidelines:

UNIT 3

LEARNING WORD-PROCESSING SKILLS

You are a member of a team being sent to a space station. Your team will be responsible for communicating with Mission Control. Your primary method of communication will be by computer. To use the computer effectively, you need to learn to use the word processor. This is the primary purpose of Unit 3. When you complete this unit, you will be able to key documents in the word processor, make format changes, make corrections to the text, and print final copy. You will learn proofreader's marks and be able to key documents containing them.

In this unit, you will continue to develop your composition skills. You will review punctuation including the comma, semicolon, and colon rules.

At the end of the unit, your straight-copy keying rate should be a minimum of 25 words a minute with no more than six errors on a two-minute timed writing.

You also can begin to use the word processor to key assignments for other classes. The more you practice your skill, the more proficient you will become.

LESSON

64 Format Memorandums

MISSION
BRIEFING

In this mission, you will:
1. Improve free-writing skills.
2. Format memorandums.

Strike the keys quickly.

Keep your eyes on the copy.

Computers—use default margins for all drills unless otherwise indicated.
Typewriters—use these margins unless otherwise indicated: 10 Pitch 2", 12 pitch 2½".
Single-spacing unless otherwise indicated.

Countdown—Get Ready for Blast-off

Review the countdown procedures.

Launch Review

Key each line two times.

1 What do 51,820 pencils @ $.50 ea. cost?

2 BLT sandwiches taste delicious in July.

3 Are San Jose & San Diego located in CA?

4 A dog or cat or bird makes a great pet.

Landing Practice—Free Writing

Using the word processor, write your journal entry. Describe an embarrassing moment of your life that you now think is funny. Try to use descriptive words that will make your reader laugh with you. Double-space your copy. Print and save a copy. Name it "Jour64."

LESSON

34 Learning the Cursor Movement Keys

BRIEFING

In this mission, you will:
1. Review comma usage.
2. Use the cursor movement keys.

Strike the keys quickly.

Keep your eyes on the copy.

Computers—use default margins for all drills unless otherwise indicated.
Typewriters—use these margins unless otherwise indicated: 10 Pitch 2", 12 pitch 2½".
Single-spacing unless otherwise indicated.

Countdown—Get Ready for Blast-off

Review the countdown procedures.

Launch Review

Key each line two times before moving on to key the next line.

1 If it is easy for you, you should play.

2 Jill said, "I'll need $5 for the trip."

3 What good movies did you see last year?

4 Carry the brown credenza to the house.

5 Add 1, 2, 30, 40, 50, 60, 70, 80, & 90.

Galaxy Gazette—Build Word-Processing Skills

Punctuation Review—Comma

Study the following rule.

Use a comma before *and, but, or, nor, for,* and *yet* when they join independent clauses. (An independent clause is a complete thought, therefore it could be a separate sentence.)

From the main menu, select Mission Report and *Galaxy Gazette.* Key each of the following sentences.

1 The train is fast, yet it's late today.

2 Ed likes pie, but he doesn't like cake.

Key this example.

3 Bob likes tennis but doesn't like golf.

Key each sentence punctuating as necessary. Key each sentence once.

Do not use a comma before a compound verb joined by a conjunction. In this case the thought could not be a separate sentence because it is missing the second subject.

1 The Milky Way is made up of billions of stars and
the Sun is just one of these stars.

2 Some stars are called quasars and pulsars and send
out radio waves.

TOP-NOTCH TRAINING TIP

Space Center Command

Intergalactic Central Zone, Milky Way

2½"
↓

→ **4 to 4½"**
(10 pitch: 40 to 45 spaces)
(12 pitch: 48 to 54 spaces)

MS JUDITH MCINTYRE DIRECTOR
MISSION CONTROL SPACE CENTER
1505 SPACE DRIVE
HOUSTON TX 77062

Good mission.

Exercise

1. Using the word processor, key an envelope for each business letter that you keyed. Use the guidelines for #10 envelopes. Save each one after keying and proofreading it by pressing Alt-N (⌘-N). Name them "Busenv1," "Busenc2," "Busenv3."

2. Ask your instructor how to load an envelope into the printer. Envelopes may also be keyed on a typewriter.

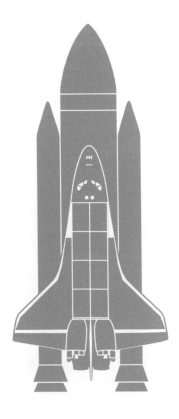

3 Quasars and pulsars are a puzzle to astronomers but there are also many other mysteries in space.

1. When you are finished, proofread your text on the screen and then press Alt-P (⌘-P) to print a copy. Press Alt-S (⌘-S) to save a copy and name it "Lesson34."
2. Proofread your printed copy and then make any needed corrections on the computer.
3. When you are satisfied with your work, press Alt-G (⌘-G) to have UKey2 check your work. Press Enter to save your work and select yes to print a final copy. Exit the *Galaxy Gazette*.

Mission Assessment

Take two 2-minute timings on the following paragraphs. Following the copy in your book, key the lines on the computer or on your typewriter. Decide on a goal of increased speed or increased accuracy.

1   After the Civil War, there was a
2 period of great economic growth in the
3 United States. Railroads provided
4 cheap transportation and allowed a
5 steady flow of goods from the eastern
6 factories to western consumers.
7   Western beef and grain flowed to the
8 East for use by the large cities. The
9 rise of the railroads created a bond
10 between East and West. Even though
11 railways are still an important method
12 of transportation, they have now been
13 surpassed by the trucking industry.

| 1 | 2 | 3 | 4 | 5 | 6 | 7 | 8 |

Destination—The Cursor Movement Keys

This activity should be completed using the word processor. Select Mission Report from the main menu and then select the open screen option. Complete the following activity using the word-processing screen.

Top-Notch Training Tip
The names Earth, Sun, and Moon are capitalized when tied in with the other bodies of the Solar System. Other times, they are not capitalized.

Minimum speed goal:
20 wam
Maximum errors allowed:
6

TYPEWRITER TIP

If you are using a typewriter, you will not be able to complete the following sections. Consult your instructor for the proper method to be used in correcting errors.

3. Key the address single-spaced, in all capitals, and with all punctuation marks omitted. Include the two-letter state abbreviation and the zip code. (Use the nine-digit zip code if known.)

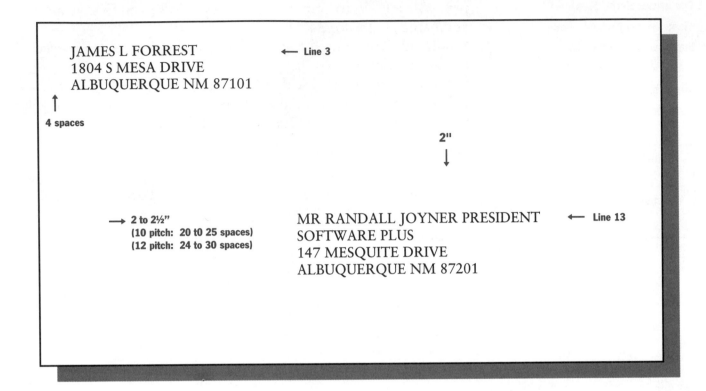

Exercise

1. Use the word processor to key an envelope for each personal business letter that you keyed in the last lessons. Use the guidelines for #6¾ envelopes. Save each envelope by pressing Alt-N (⌘-N). Name them "Perenv1," "Perenv2," and "Perenv3."
2. Ask your instructor how to place the envelope in the printer. Envelopes may also be keyed on a typewriter.

Destination—Learn to Format Large Business Envelopes (#10)

1. Many businesses have envelopes printed with their name and address. If a printed envelope is not available, key the return address using the same instructions as for a small envelope.
2. Begin the address 4 to 4½ inches from the left edge (40 to 45 spaces for 10 pitch, 48 to 54 spaces for 12 pitch). Leave 2½ inches (15 lines) of blank space above the address. Begin the mailing address on line 16.

The cursor movement or arrow keys allow you to move around in text documents you have keyed on the computer. These cursor movement keys are sometimes located on the numeric keypad and are activated by turning off the Num Lock key. On some computers, they may be located on the alphabetic keys or on a separate set of keys.

Find the cursor movement or arrow keys on your computer.

Exercise

Read the following paragraph and then key it.

```
It is easy to make corrections when you use

computer software.  If you make a keying error or

decide to change a word, you simply move the cursor

to that place and make the change.  The cursor

movement or arrow keys are used to move the cursor.
```

After keying in that paragraph, return to the top of your document by pressing the home key or clicking with the mouse. Then practice moving around in the paragraph using the cursor movement keys by doing the following:

Anytime you want to return to the top of your document, you easily can do so by pressing the home key or ⌘-up arrow.

1. Move the cursor using the right arrow key to the *t* in *corrections*.
2. Move the cursor to the *e* in *keying*.
3. Move the cursor up using the up arrow and over using the arrow to the *w* in *when*.
4. Move the cursor down using the down arrow and over to the *s* in *cursor* in line 3.
5. Move the cursor over using the left arrow to the *s* in *simply*.
6. Move the cursor up using the up arrow and over to the *e* in *error*.
7. Move to the bottom of the document by pressing the end key or clicking the mouse.

Practice moving the cursor to other locations until you are comfortable with the operation of the cursor movement keys.

When keying documents in the word processor, you will be able to move the cursor to different locations in the document. You then will be able by using other keys to add or delete text if you desire. You will not be able to use the cursor movement keys when keying drills.

Exit

When finished with this exercise, exit the word processor by pressing the Alt-F keys for file or use the mouse to access the pulldown file menu. Select Alt-Q (⌘-Q) for quit. Indicate no when asked if you want to save this document.

LESSON 63 Format Envelopes

BRIEFING

In this mission, you will:
1. Improve free-writing skills.
2. Format envelopes.

Strike the keys quickly.

Keep your eyes on the copy.

Computers—use default margins for all drills unless otherwise indicated.
Typewriters—use these margins unless otherwise indicated: 10 Pitch 2", 12 pitch 2½".
Single-spacing unless otherwise indicated.

Countdown—Get Ready for Blast-off

Review the countdown procedures.

Launch Review

Key each line two times.

1 We can take 14 @ $6.50 and 29 @ $18.47.

2 Laura Eun wants to move to Mississippi.

3 We'll be happy to receive your request.

4 When birds sing, spring has come again.

Mission Report—Free Writing

Using the word processor, write your journal entry. Think of times that you have been angry. Pick one of those times and describe it. Write about the event that made you angry and how you reacted. Double-space the copy. Print and save a copy. Name it "Jour63."

Destination—Learn to Format Small Envelopes (#6¾)

To speed the processing of mail, the U. S. Postal Service recommends that all envelopes be keyed and formatted in OCR style. (**OCR** stands for optical character recognition and means a machine that is programmed to sense printed letters.) Envelopes addressed in OCR style can be sorted by machine more quickly.

   Use the following procedure to format a small envelope for personal business letters:
1. Key the return address single-spaced in the upper left corner of the envelope in block style. Begin the return address on line 3. Start 4 spaces from the left edge.
2. Start the address 2 to 2½ inches from the left edge (20 to 25 spaces for 10 pitch, 24 to 30 spaces for 12 pitch). Leave 2 inches (12 lines) of blank space above the address; key the address beginning on line 13.

Shortcut Method

A note about **shortcut keys.** When you are using the word processor and the *Galaxy Gazette,* many times you can use shortcut keys for functions. For example, to exit the word processor, you simply can press Alt-Q (⌘-Q). You will learn other shortcut keys as you use the word processor. You also can use the tutorial in the software to help you learn more about your word processor.

LESSON

35 Learning Backspace, Delete, Insert, Save, and Print

Computers—use default margins for all drills unless otherwise indicated.
Typewriters—use these margins unless otherwise indicated: 10 Pitch 2", 12 pitch 2½".
Single-spacing unless otherwise indicated.

mission
BRIEFING

You will continue your flight preparation. In this mission you will:
1. **Review comma usage.**
2. **Correct copy using the backspace/delete and delete keys.**
3. **Print and save from the word processor**

Strike the keys quickly.

Keep your eyes on the copy.

Countdown—Get Ready for Blast-off

Review the countdown.

Launch Review

Key each line two times before moving on to key the next line.

1 of to no in or so up fa go am em be dot

2 day may can did end let two sad but jar

3 line mark dude list buzz zero exam quad

4 Orders #149, #236, #621, & #871 are in.

Galaxy Gazette—Build Word-Processing Skills

Punctuation Review—Comma

Study the following rule.

Use a comma to separate items in a series. A comma also should be used before the conjunction (and, nor, or).

From the main menu, select Mission Report and *Galaxy Gazette.* Key each sentence once.

1 We read poems by Dickinson, Browning, and Whitman.

2 We had fun all summer at the beach, at the pool, and at the water slide.

3 The sea looked cold, grey, and angry during the storm.

Universal Ceramics Engineering
10 Pluto Drive
Trinton, Neptune 00320

2"
↓

August 29, 2011

Fantastic Tours, Inc.
1597 Dock Street
Newark, NJ 07102

Ladies and Gentlemen:

We have received your brochure about the voyage of
Enterprise, your new cruise ship. The planet
stopovers sound great. I am really interested in
1" → the one with the adventureland theme park. I've   ← 1"
heard that the Black Hole roller coaster is the trip.
                                          ^ worth

I would like to book a cabin on deck nine on the
  port
starboard side. The advanced deposit is enclosed, and
I would like confirmation as soon as possible for the
voyage dates advertised. If the dates requested are
unavailable, please send the second space cruise
dates.
      ^ and destinations
Sincerely yours,

R. D. Smythe
Space Chemist

↑
1"

Key each sentence once, punctuating as necessary.

1 The Sun is 100 times bigger than Earth has an
   internal temperature of about 30 million degrees and
   a day about 27 Earth-days long.

2 The planets that are farthest from the Sun are
   Uranus Neptune and Pluto.

3 The rings around Saturn are composed of rocks ice
   and dust.

1. When you are finished, proofread your text on the screen and then
   press Alt-P (⌥-P) to print a copy. Press Alt-S (⌥-S) to save a copy
   and name it "Lesson35."
2. Proofread your printed copy and then make any needed corrections
   on the computer.
3. When you are satisfied with your work, press Alt-G (⌥-G) to have
   UKey2 check your work. Press Enter to save your work and select
   yes to print a final copy. Exit the *Galaxy Gazette*.

Mission Assessment

Take two 2-minute timings on the following paragraphs. Following the copy in your
book, key the lines on the computer or your typewriter.

Minimum speed goal:
20 wam
Maximum errors allowed:
6

1   Thomas Edison is considered to be

2 the father of motion pictures. He made

3 the first workable camera and viewer for

4 motion pictures. In 1891, Edison and a

5 friend obtained film stock that would

6 work with their machine.

7   The first movies were brief and

8 silent. As the pictures were used to

9 tell stories, the process became more

10 complex. We owe our modern world of

11 movies and videos to Edison. Can you

12 imagine a world without movies or

13 television?

| | 1 | 2 | 3 | 4 | 5 | 6 | 7 | 8 | |

under the computer warranty. It was my
understanding that the whole system was warrantied:
keyboard, monitor, computer, and printer.

I purchased a system designed and packaged by your
company. I feel that if any part of the system
doesn't work, then the whole system is useless.

I would appreciate your attention to this problem
and a clarification in regard to your system's
warranty.

Sincerely yours,/Malcolm D. Ross/President

ecs

Good progress.

Destination—Correcting Errors

Use the open screen section of Mission Report to complete the next sections.

1. Select Mission Report from the main menu.
2. Select the open screen option.
3. Do not exit the word processor until you have completed all of the destinations in this lesson. You will be instructed when to exit the word processor.

When using the word processor, at times you will need to correct text that has been keyed. The most frequently used correction technique is to delete copy that already has been keyed and insert the new text. Text is deleted with the backspace/delete or delete key. Text is inserted by moving the cursor to the position where you wish to insert text and then keying in the text.

Destination—The Backspace/Delete Key

Your keyboard has a backspace/delete key. It is keyed with your right little finger. The backspace/delete key is used to correct keying errors. When you press the backspace/delete key, the character to the left of the cursor is deleted. Text to the left of the cursor will continue to be deleted as long as you depress this key.

Exercise

1. Find the backspace/delete key on your keyboard. (It's backspace on IBM and compatible computers and delete on Apple computers.)
2. Practice using the backspace/delete key by following these steps.
   a. Key the words `this program` and do not press Enter.
   b. Using the semicolon finger, backspace four times. Notice that the characters *gram* were deleted.
   c. Key the characters `blem` to create the word *problem*.
3. Notice that you have changed *this program* to *this problem*.
4. You will be able to use the backspace key in the word processor and *Galaxy Gazette*. Consult your instructor to determine if you may use the backspace key in drill copy.

Destination—The Delete Key

On some computers (IBM and compatibles), keying errors also can be corrected using a separate delete key. Locate this delete key on your keyboard. When the delete key is pressed, the character over the cursor is deleted. Complete the following exercise using the delete key. (If you do not have a separate delete key, complete this drill using the backspace/delete key following the instructions presented above.) Find the delete key on your keyboard (if available).

Destination—Format Business Letters from Edited Copy

1. Use the *Galaxy Gazette* to key the letter on page 234 following the formatting directions. Do not forget to turn off the page numbering. Use the default margins. Set the top margin.
2. After you finish keying the letter, proofread your document on the screen. Correct any keying errors.
3. Select Alt-P (⌘-P) to print a copy. Press Alt-S (⌘-S) to save the document. Name it "Buslet2." Proofread the printed copy; mark all undetected errors on the printout. Correct any errors you found in your proofreading.
4. Select Alt-G (⌘-G) and UKey2 will check your document to see how well you completed your task. After you read your score and status, press Enter to save the document. Next, select yes to print a copy.

Destination—Format Unarranged Business Letters

1. Use the open screen word processor to key the letter below, following the formatting directions.
2. After you finish keying the letter, proofread your document on the screen. Correct any keying errors.
3. Select Alt-P (⌘-P) to print a copy. Press Alt-S (⌘-S) to save the document. Name it "Buslet3." Proofread the printed copy; mark all undetected errors on the printout. Correct any errors you found in your proofreading.
4. Save your document if changes were made and print a final copy. Exit the word processor.

3012 Market Street/Elgin, IL/61082

November 19, 1996/Computer Service, Inc./1500 Star

Street/Suite 7000/Chicago, IL/60607

Ladies and Gentlemen:

On January 17, 1995, I purchased a 386 SX Speedo

computer from your southside store #178. The

warranty registration card was mailed as instructed.

Last week, November 12, 1996, I began to experience

difficulties with the keyboard. A number of the

letters stick and do not work. I contacted the

store and was told that the keyboard is not covered

Exercise

1. Key the words `Microcampiter Keiboardang` with the errors shown.
2. Identify the keying errors in the words (*Microcomputer Keyboarding*).
3. Correct the keying errors using the delete key. You must delete the incorrect character first, then key the correct character. Follow these steps:
    a. Move the cursor to the *a* in *Microcampiter*. Before you can key the correct character, you must delete the *a*. With the cursor under the *a*, press the delete key. Now key the *o*.
    b. Move the cursor to the *i*, delete the *i*, and key the correct character *u*.
    c. Move the cursor to the *i* in *Keiboardang*. Delete the *i* and key the correct character *y*. Now correct the *a* using the same steps.
4. When keying in the word processor and *Galaxy Gazette,* you will be able to use the cursor movement keys and the backspace/delete and delete (if available) keys to make corrections.

Destination—Inserting Text

To insert text, move the cursor to the position where you wish to add the text. As you key the new text, the software will automatically make space for the text being inserted.

Exercise

Key the following sentence.

`The Earth is old.`

Correct the sentence to read:

`The Earth is very old.`

Follow these instructions.
1. Place the cursor under the *o* in the word *old*.
2. Key the word *very* and the space following it.
3. Notice the software automatically adjusts the space needed for the word.

Key the following sentences.

`Each turn of the Earth takes one day.`

`Each orbit takes one year.`

Correct these sentences by inserting the additional text.

1 `Each full turn of the Earth on its axis takes one`

`day.`

2 `Each full orbit around the Sun takes one year.`

Take two 2-minute timings on the following paragraphs. Study the material; then following the copy in your book, key the lines on the computer or your typewriter.

1 One of the most populous nations

2 in the world, after China, India, and

3 the United States, is the Republic of

4 Indonesia. About 180 million people

5 live there. The Indonesians make up

6 at least 300 ethnic groups, speaking

7 250 different languages.

8 The country consists of five main

9 islands and 30 smaller islands

10 stretching across 3,200 miles of

11 water. The islands separate the

12 Indian Ocean from the Pacific Ocean.

13 Indonesians gained independence

14 in 1949. At the time the islands were

15 not under a central government. There

16 was little sense of national identity

17 and few leaders. Today, the national

18 slogan is "Unity in Diversity." The

19 official language is called Bahasa

20 Indonesia. Most Indonesians are

21 Muslims. Other religions practiced

22 include Christianity, Hinduism, and

23 Buddhism.

| 1 | 2 | 3 | 4 | 5 | 6 | 7 | 8 |

Destination—Printing and Saving from the Word Processor

1. Key Alt-F (use the mouse to access the file menu). Select Alt-P (⌘-P) to print the exercises. Be sure the printer is on. Press Enter to start printing.
2. To save your file, press Alt-F (mouse) to access the pulldown file menu. Select Alt-S (⌘-S) to save the file. Press Enter to accept the current path. Name the document "Edit."
3. After the computer has saved your document, you will return to your text screen. To quit the word processor, select Alt-F (mouse) and then Alt-Q (⌘-Q) or use the shortcut of Alt-Q (⌘-Q).

Shortcut Method

1. Press Alt-P (⌘-P) to print the exercises. You will get a message reminding you to be sure the printer in on.
2. Press Alt-S (⌘-S) to save your document without accessing the pulldown file menu. Key in the name of your document.
3. Press Alt-Q (⌘-Q) to exit the word processor.

REENTRY
BRIEFING

Mission completed!

LESSON

36 Learning to Retrieve, Edit, Replace, and Print Documents

Computers—use default margins for all drills unless otherwise indicated.
Typewriters—use these margins unless otherwise indicated: 10 Pitch 2", 12 pitch 2½".
Single-spacing unless otherwise indicated.

Countdown—Get Ready for Blast-off

Review the countdown procedures.

Launch Review

Key each line two times before moving on to key the next line.

MISSION
BRIEFING

During this mission you will:
1. Review comma usage.
2. Retrieve and edit files.
3. Replace and print files.

Strike the keys quickly.

Keep your eyes on the copy.

1 The cheerful dog licked the calico cat.

2 Billy awarded six prizes at the bazaar.

3 Over 64% of our class voted for reform.

4 Your usual 62% discount is still valid.

5 We want to go to our fall class picnic.

LESSON

62 Review Business Letters

MISSION BRIEFING

In this mission, you will:
1. **Improve free-writing skills.**
2. **Review business letters.**

Strike the keys quickly.

Keep your eyes on the copy.

Computers—use default margins for all drills unless otherwise indicated.
Typewriters—use these margins unless otherwise indicated: 10 Pitch 2", 12 pitch 2½".
Single-spacing unless otherwise indicated.

Countdown—Get Ready for Blast-off

Review the countdown procedures.

Launch Review

Key each line two times.

1 Does 25 (3 + 2) = 125 and 25 x 5 = 125?

2 Dozens of vultures flew around the bow.

3 Tomas, Grace, and Sammy went to Greece.

4 A big ball is in the Avila's back yard.

Mission Report—Free Writing

Using the word processor, write your daily journal entry. Describe how you felt about a new experience. Some suggestions could be when you hit your first home run, when you learned how to ride a bicycle, when you were first called upon in class, when your parents brought home your new baby brother or sister, or the first dance you attended. Try to help the reader feel what you felt by using descriptive writing. Double-space the copy. Print and save a copy. Name it "Jour62."

Galaxy Gazette—Build Word-Processing Skills

Punctuation Review—Comma

Study the following rule.

Use a comma to separate two or more adjectives preceding a noun when the word *and* is omitted.

From the main menu, select Mission Report and *Galaxy Gazette.* Key each sentence once, punctuating as shown.

1 Midnight is a gentle, beautiful horse.

2 We love to run over the cool, wet sand.

3 John was elected SGA president because of his logical, organized thinking.

Key each sentence once, punctuating as necessary.

1 The planet Saturn has a set of huge flat rings around it.

2 The Moon has high sharp peaks.

3 The Viking spacecraft revealed that Mars is a rough rocky planet.

1. When you are finished, proofread your text on the screen and then press Alt-P (⌘-P) to print a copy. Press Alt-S (⌘-S) to save a copy and name it "Lesson36."
2. Proofread your printed copy and then make any needed corrections on the computer.
3. When you are satisfied with your work, press Alt-G (⌘-G) to have UKey2 check your work. Press Enter to save your work and select yes to print a final copy. Press Esc to exit the *Galaxy Gazette.* On Macintosh computers, select Mission Control from the file menu.

NEPTUNE

Neptune is 17 times more massive than Earth. Images of the surface show the Great Dark Spot, which is a storm about the size of Earth.

Space Station Command ← Letterhead
Intergalactic Central Zone, Milky Way

2"
↓

February 21, 2021   ← Date

4 blank lines

Ms. Judith McIntyre, Director   **Inside**
Mission Control Space Center ← **Address**
1505 Space Drive
Houston, TX 77062
double-space
Dear Ms. McIntyre: ← Salutation
double-space
1" → The Mission Control Task Force performed admirably   ← 1"
last week in the satellite rescue effort. You should
be very proud of the team you have assembled.
double-space
Even though the project was an extremely difficult
one, it was accomplished according to the plan   Body
presented by Mission Control. The task required
extreme precision and caution. Needless to say, it
is very difficult to "harness" a giant satellite.
double-space
I have presented the crew with medals. These medals
are given only in special cases of outstanding
performance.
double-space
Sincerely yours,   ← Closing

4 blank lines

Joseph R. Richards   ← Signature Block
Space Station Commander
double-space
kbo   ← Operator's Reference Initials
double-space
Enclosure   ← Enclosure Notation

↑
1"

Mission Assessment

Take two 2-minute timings on the following paragraphs. Following the copy in your book, key the lines on the computer or your typewriter.

1   Today all people need a basic

2 understanding of how to use a computer

3 system. It is also necessary for people

4 to have a knowledge of computer terms.

5 In the near future, persons who do not

6 have computer skills will be limited in

7 their school, home, and work lives.

8   People will use computers in their

9 homes to keep budgets, checking

10 accounts, menus, and time schedules.

11 These functions will help people become

12 better organized.

| 1 | 2 | 3 | 4 | 5 | 6 | 7 | 8 |

Destination—Learn to Retrieve, Edit, Replace, and Print Documents

Select Mission Report and the open screen option to complete this activity.

Exercise 1

1. Key the paragraph below. You may use the editing keys to make corrections to keying errors as you key the paragraph.
    NOTE: When you print a document from the word processor, page numbers will be automatically printed on the document. You also can set the computer to indent paragraphs. To do so, press Alt-R (use the mouse to access the format menu). Use the arrow key to move the highlight bar to indent paragraphs and change it to yes.

The time before records were recorded is called

prehistory. Many symbols are evidence of life.

People search for objects made by humans during this

time.

2. Proofread the paragraph on the screen and use the editing keys to make any corrections needed.
3. Select Alt-P (⌂-P) to print the document.

Exercise

1. Use the *Galaxy Gazette* to key the letter on the next page, following the formatting directions. Use the default side margins. Set the top margin.

2. After you finish keying the letter, proofread your document on the screen. Correct any keying errors.

3. Select Alt-P (⌘-P) to print a copy. Press Alt-S (⌘-S) to save the document. Name it "Buslet1." Proofread the printed copy; mark all undetected errors on the printout. Correct any errors you found in your proofreading.

4. Select Alt-G (⌘-G) and UKey2 will check your document to see how well you completed your task. After you read your score and status, press Enter to save the document. Next, select yes to print a copy.

Message transmitted.

4. Save a copy of the file by pressing the Alt-F keys (mouse) and then the Alt-N (⌘-N) keys. Press Enter to accept the current path and name the document "History." The Alt-N (⌘-N) keys allow you to save your current document and clear the screen for a new file. You would use this method to save and file a document before starting a new document in your word processor.

Shortcut Method

To save your current document in the word processor and open a new one without using the pulldown menu, press Alt-N (⌘-N) from the text screen.

Exercise 2

1. Key the paragraph below. You may use the editing keys to make corrections to keying errors as you key the paragraph.

```
    We enjoy one of the highest standards in

the world, and our country is a leader.  Even

though this is the case, we have a number of

problems that we need to solve.  Problems such

as crime, poverty, and drugs need attention to

help solve them.
```

2. Proofread the paragraph on the screen and make any additional corrections needed.
3. Select Alt-P (⌘-P) to print the document. Be sure the printer is on. Press Enter to start printing.
4. Save a copy of the file by pressing the Alt-N (⌘-N) keys. Press Enter to accept the current path and name the document "Country."

Exercise 3

1. Retrieve the "History" file you created in Exercise 1. To do so, press Alt-F (mouse) and select Alt-O (⌘-O). Press Enter to accept the path. Move the highlight bar with the down arrow until the file "History" is highlighted. Press Enter.
2. Use the editing keys to make the following corrections to the paragraph.

LESSON

61 Format Business Letters

MISSION BRIEFING

In this mission, you will:
1. Improve free-writing skills.
2. Format business letters.

Countdown—Get Ready for Blast-off

Review the countdown procedures.

Launch Review

Key each line two times.

1 We ordered #39, #693, & #852 @ $.06 ea.

2 Crazy Zelda zoomed high above treetops.

3 Mary reads classic novels for pleasure.

4 You know how to ride a dirt wheel bike.

Mission Report—Free Writing

Using the word processor, write your daily journal report. Describe in your writing the way you used to look, think, or act two years ago as compared to the way you look, think, or act now. Use colorful adjectives to describe yourself so that someone who does not know you would be able to form a picture of you from your writing. Double-space the copy. Print and save a copy. Name it "Jour61."

Destination—Learn to Format Business Letters

The format for a business letter is very similar to a personal business letter. The primary differences are:
1. The business letter is keyed on printed letterhead stationery that includes the company's address. Therefore, no return address is keyed on the letter.
2. The business letter often includes the writer's title in the signature block.
3. If the letter is keyed by someone other than the writer, the operator's reference initials are keyed at the left margin a double-space below the signature block.
4. If additional items are to be mailed with the letter, an enclosure notation is keyed at the left margin a double-space below the reference initials.

The time before written records were recorded is called prehistory. Many nonwritten symbols were used as evidence of life before written records. Many people today search for articles made by humans during that time.

3. Select Alt-P (⌘-P) to print a copy of the revised file.
4. Save the revised file by pressing Alt-N (⌘-N). Press Enter to accept the current path. Press Enter to accept the current name "History." When asked if you want to save over the document already named "History," press Enter to accept yes.

Shortcut Method

To open a file you already have created, press Alt-O (⌘-O). You will then see the list of files from which you can choose. Select the document you want by moving the highlight bar and pressing Enter.

Exercise 4

1. Retrieve the "Country" file you created in exercise 2. Press Alt-O (⌘-O). Press Enter to accept the path. Move the highlight bar with the down arrow until the file "Country" is highlighted. Press Enter.
2. Use the editing keys to make the following corrections to the paragraph.

We enjoy one of the highest standards of living in the world, and our country is a world leader in many ways. Even though this is the case, we still have a number of problems that we need to resolve. Our social problems such as crime, poverty, and drugs need additional resources to help solve them.

3. Select Alt-P (⌘-P) to print the file.
4. Save the revised file by pressing Alt-S (⌘-S). Press Enter to accept the current path. Press Enter to accept the current name "Country." When asked if you want to save over the document already named "Country," press Enter to accept yes.
5. Exit the word processor by pressing Alt-Q (⌘-Q).

REENTRY
BRIEFING

You have completed this mission!

5207 Shore Drive
Nantucket, MA 02554
April 2, 1999

Mr. Gerald Fitzsimmons
Bay Yacht Service
1218 Dock Street
Boston, MA 02101

Dear Mr. Fitzsimmons:

1" →   I understand that your company has a summer Hire the   ← 1"
Youth Program. Our school will be out May 30, and I
would like very much to have a summer ~~job~~ with your
company.
                                            position

                                Hire the Youth
Please send me information about the ∧program and the
required application forms. I have just completed a
computer keyboarding program and can operate a
personal computer. *My keyboarding skill is approximately*
50 wam.
I look forward to receiving the required information
and possibly working with you this summer. *I will be pleased*
to come in for an interview at your convenience.
Sincerely yours,

James R. Johnson

James R. Johnson

LESSON

37 Learning to Change Margins

MISSION BRIEFING

In this lesson you will:
1. Review comma usage.
2. Change left and right margins.
3. Change top and bottom margins.

Strike the keys quickly.

Keep your eyes on the copy.

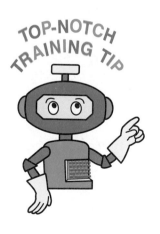

TOP-NOTCH TRAINING TIP

Computers—use default margins for all drills unless otherwise indicated.
Typewriters—use these margins unless otherwise indicated: 10 Pitch 2", 12 pitch 2½".
Single-spacing unless otherwise indicated.

Countdown—Get Ready for Blast-off

Review the countdown procedures.

Launch Review

Key each line two times before moving on to key the next line.

1 "Warm up quickly! Relax your muscles!"

2 Nathan said, "Stop the loud music, Jo!"

3 He says that the zoo zebras are unique.

4 We produced 10% more at a cost of $501.

5 Today (Monday) we will practice rowing.

Galaxy Gazette—Build Word-Processing Skills

Punctuation Review—Comma

Study the following rules.

   Use commas to set off phrases and clauses that are not necessary to the meaning of the sentence. Do not use commas with phrases or clauses that are necessary to the meaning.

Study and key each sentence. From the main menu, select Mission Report and *Galaxy Gazette.*

1 Mrs. Nina Ray, who is the assistant principal, met
  with all the parents.

2 Summer, which is the hottest season, is still
  enjoyed by all students.

3 Students who finish their work early may leave class
  five minutes before the bell rings.

Destination—Format Block Style Personal Business Letters from Unarranged Copy

1. In the open screen word processor, key the personal business letter below. Follow the procedures outlined in the last lesson.
2. After you finish keying the letter, proofread your document on the screen. Correct any keying errors.
3. Select Alt-P (⌘-P) to print a copy. Press Alt-S (⌘-S) to save the document. Name it "Perbus3." Proofread the printed copy; mark all undetected errors on the printout. Correct any errors you found in your proofreading.
4. Save your document again if changes were made and print a final copy. Exit the word processor.

1905 W. Park Place/Outpost 3, Saturn 18105/June 10, 2010

Majestic Theater/4200 New Broadway/Outpost 2, Mars 10001

Ladies and Gentlemen:

Our class of 45 students will be coming to Mars to see the "Black Hole Odyssey" evening performance on November 12. We wish to participate in the special student program that you are currently offering. Please reserve a block of tickets in the "Starlight Tier" area with as many adjoining seats as possible. We understand that the cost of each ticket will be $22.50. Please confirm the reservations as soon as possible so that we may proceed with our travel reservations. If there are any problems with this request, please contact me at 215-555-4236.

Sincerely yours,/Joan Temple/Class President

REENTRY
BRIEFING
Good progress.

Key each sentence once, punctuating as necessary.

1 The tilt of the Earth's axis which is slanted a little to one side causes the different seasons.

2 Light that is reflected by the Sun is the source of the Moon's light.

3 The Moon which seems small when viewed from Earth is actually about 2,000 miles in diameter.

1. When you are finished, proofread your text on the screen and then press Alt-P (⌘-P) to print a copy. Press Alt-S (⌘-S) to save a copy and name it "Lesson37."
2. Proofread your printed copy and then make any needed corrections on the computer.
3. When you are satisfied with your work, press Alt-G (⌘-G) to have UKey2 check your work. Press Enter to save your work and select yes to print a final copy. Exit the *Galaxy Gazette*.

Mission Assessment

Take two 2-minute timings on the following paragraphs. Following the copy in your book, key the lines on the computer or your typewriter.

1   Software quality is often not as

2 good as we would like. Many programs

3 have flaws or "bugs" in them. You

4 should try out software before buying

5 it. Software to be used in schools

5 needs to be very dependable.

7   The term "bug" comes from the past

8 when computers had magnetic switches.

9 The heat from the switches attracted

10 bugs and lint, so "debugging" actually

11 meant removing the bugs. This term is

12 still used to refer to software that

13 does not work properly.

| 1 | 2 | 3 | 4 | 5 | 6 | 7 | 8 |

Minimum speed goal:
21 wam
Maximum errors allowed:
6

Mission Assessment

Take two 2-minute timings on the following paragraphs. Study the material; then following the copy in your book, key the lines on the computer or your typewriter.

1   Personal business letters can be

2 written in several styles. The style

3 is often chosen based on the image one

4 wants. As you learned, the block

5 letter style has a more modern image.

6 It is easy to key because all lines

7 begin at the left margin.

8   Other styles are not as easy to

9 key as the block letter style. Lines

10 must be indented, and it is more

11 difficult to align them. Letters with

12 indented lines require tab sets at the

13 proper points. These styles are not

14 as efficient as the block letter

15 style. Most people today prefer the

16 block letter style.

| 1 | 2 | 3 | 4 | 5 | 6 | 7 | 8 |

Destination—Format Personal Business Letters from Edited Copy

1. In the *Galaxy Gazette,* key the personal business letter on page 226. Follow the steps in the previous lesson. Use the default side margins. Set the top margin. Turn off the page numbering. Begin the return address leaving a two-inch top margin.
2. After you finish keying the letter, proofread your document on the screen. Correct any keying errors.
3. Select Alt-P (♔-P) to print a copy. Press Alt-S (♔-S) to save the document. Name it "Perbus2." Proofread the printed copy; mark all undetected errors on the printout. Correct the errors.
4. Select Alt-G (♔-G) and UKey2 will check your document to see how well you completed your task. After you read your score and status, press Enter to save the document. Next, select yes to print a copy.

TYPEWRITER TIP

See the Introduction for directions on changing margins.

Shortcut Method:
You can access the document formatting menu by pressing Alt-D (⌂-D).

COMPUTER TIP

It is wise to save longer documents as you are working on them. When you save a document it is protected. For example, say that you just saved your document and then the power goes out. Your document is safe. If you have not saved, you would lose all of your work. Be smart—save often.

Destination—Learn to Change Left and Right Margins

When you key documents in the word processor, you will sometimes need to change the margin settings. Review the margin chart in the Introduction. Follow the steps below to change margins in the word processor.

1. Select Mission Report from the main menu, then the open screen option.
2. Margin changes are made from the format pulldown menu. Access this menu with Alt-R or the mouse. When document, Alt-D (⌂-D), is highlighted, press Enter.
3. Use the up and down arrows to move the highlight bar to the margin settings. Use the left and right arrows to change the margin settings. The left arrow decreases the margin setting; the right increases it.
4. For this exercise change the left and right margin settings to 20 left and 20 right. That will make each margin 2 inches. Press Enter when finished.
5. Key the following paragraph, correcting keying errors as you enter the information.

```
When keying documents, the appearance can often
be improved by adjusting the amount of space left on
either side.  This space can be adjusted by setting
the margins to leave the desired amount of space on
each side.
```

6. Proofread the document on the screen and correct any keying errors.
7. Select Alt-P (⌂-P) to print a copy.
8. Press Alt-S (⌂-S) to save the document. Name it "Margins." Alt-S (⌂-S) is used to save a document when you wish it to remain on the screen for future use. Alt-S (⌂-S) does not clear the document from the screen.

You can change margins before you key a document as in the last exercise or at any time after a document has been keyed. Try changing the margins in document "Margins." Follow these steps:

1. Position the cursor at the top of the document and press Alt-D (⌂-D). Change both side margins to 1½ inches (left, 15; right, 15).
2. Select Alt-P (⌂-P) to print the document.
3. Save the revised file by pressing Alt-S (⌂-S). You do not need to clear the screen because you are going to use the document again.

LESSON

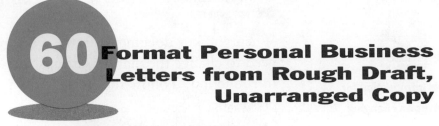

60 Format Personal Business Letters from Rough Draft, Unarranged Copy

MISSION BRIEFING

In this mission, you will:
1. Improve free-writing skills.
2. Format personal business letters from rough draft, unarranged copy.

Computers—use default margins for all drills unless otherwise indicated.
Typewriters—use these margins unless otherwise indicated: 10 Pitch 2", 12 pitch 2½".
Single-spacing unless otherwise indicated.

Countdown—Get Ready for Blast-off

Review the countdown procedures.

Launch Review

Key each line two times.

1 Please meet Vic on July 15 at 8:30 a.m.

2 Li's van provided extra transportation.

3 What a day! The bright sun is radiant.

4 Bab Broten is going to have a baby boy.

Mission Report—Free Writing

Using the word processor, write your journal entry. Write about one of the saddest times in your life. Describe what happened and how you felt. How did other people and family members help you? Double-space the copy. Print and save a copy. Name it "Jour60."

Press Enter to accept the current path. Press Enter to accept the current name "Margins." When asked if you want to save over the document already named "Margins," press Enter to accept yes.

4. Compare the two documents. Does the first one have 2-inch margins and the second one 1½-inch margins? If not, try the exercise again.

Destination—Learn to Change Top and Bottom Margins

You will notice when you print documents from the word processor that the software automatically leaves a blank 1-inch top and bottom margin. That is because the top and bottom margins have been preset to leave 6 lines (1-inch) blank. Review vertical spacing in the Introduction. Follow the steps below to change top and bottom margins in the word processor.

1. Position the cursor at the top of the "Margins" document and press Alt-D (⌘-D). Use the down arrow key to move to the top margin setting. Use the right arrow to increase the top margin setting to 12 lines (2 inches). (If needed, the same procedure would be used to change the bottom margin.)
2. Select Alt-P (⌘-P) to print the document.
3. Save the revised file by pressing Alt-S (⌘-S). Press Enter to accept the current path. Press Enter to accept the current name "Margins." When asked if you want to save over the document already named "Margins," press Enter to accept yes.
4. Check your printed document. Does it have a 2-inch top margin? If not, consult your instructor to determine whether the paper was properly placed in the printer, and try the exercise again.
5. Press Alt Q (⌘-Q) to quit the word processor.

REENTRY BRIEFING

You have completed this mission!

Pluto is 64 times smaller than Earth. Very little is known about Pluto because it is so small and so far away.

Return Address → 1804 S. Mesa Drive
Albuquerque, NM 87101
Date → August 20, 1999

4 blank lines

Inside Address → Mr. Randall Joyner, President
Software Plus
147 Mesquite Drive
Albuquerque, NM 87201

double-space

Salutation → Dear Mr. Joyner:

double-space

On June 14, 1999, I purchased a video game from your store on East Bowling Street. After repeated attempts, I have not been able to get the game to load and run. I believe the disk is defective.

double-space   ←1"

1" →

Several times I have returned to your store for assistance and advice concerning loading the game. The last time I went in, August 17, I asked that I be given a new game or a refund. My request was refused by Ms. Justin Seron, the store manager.

Body

double-space

I feel that since the disk cannot be loaded that you should replace it and send the defective disk back to your supplier. I would appreciate anything you can do to assist me with this problem that I feel has already caused me considerable trouble.

double-space

Closing → Sincerely yours,

4 blank lines

Signature Block →

LESSON

38 Review Editing Skills and Double-Space Copy

In this mission you will:
1. Review comma usage.
2. Review editing skills.
3. Key double-spaced copy.

Strike the keys quickly.

Keep your eyes on the copy.

Computers—use default margins for all drills unless otherwise indicated.
Typewriters—use these margins unless otherwise indicated: 10 Pitch 2", 12 pitch 2½".
Single-spacing unless otherwise indicated.

Countdown—Get Ready for Blast-off

Review the countdown procedures.

Launch Review

Key each line two times before moving on to key the next line.

1 hex her vie gas has set new way run day

2 brat open buzz exit vote mark card good

3 If the reply is returned, pay your dues.

4 By voting, all citizens become involved.

Think and key each of these phrases:

as it is/at my/by my/go to do/to no one

Mission Report—Build Word-Processing Skills

Punctuation Review—Comma

Study the following rule.

   Use a comma after an introductory dependent clause. Even though introductory dependent clauses include both a subject and verb, they cannot stand alone. Introductory dependent clauses usually begin with one of the following words:

as	if	when	after	although	because
before	since	unless	until	while	so

From the main menu, select Mission Report and the open screen option. Study and key each sentence.

1 When fall comes, football games begin.

2 As we decided, Nekosha will babysit for the Wongs on

   Thursday.

3 Although I would like to go to the movie with you,

   my homework isn't done.

1. In the *Galaxy Gazette,* key the model personal business letter on page 222. Follow the steps outlined above. Use the default side margins. Turn off the page numbering. Begin the return address setting a two-inch top margin. Leave four lines between the date and the inside address. Press Enter after the short lines, but use wordwrap on the paragraph copy.

2. After you finish keying the letter, proofread your document on the screen. Correct any keying errors.

3. Select Alt-P (⌘-P) to print a copy. Press Alt-S (⌘-S) to save the document. Name it "Perbus1." Proofread the printed copy; mark all undetected errors on the printout. Correct any errors you found in your proofreading.

4. Select Alt-G (⌘-G) and UKey2 will check your document to see how well you completed your task. After you read your score and status, press Enter to save the document. Next, select yes to print a copy.

Good landing.

A dependent clause that comes at the end of a sentence does not usually need a comma. For example:

```
Football season will begin when fall comes.
```

Key each sentence once, punctuating as necessary.

1 When astronauts visited the Moon they discovered no
  air or water.

2 The Moon is difficult to inhabit because it is very
  hot on the sunny side and cold on the shady side.

3 If you traveled in a very fast spacecraft you could
  reach the Moon in about two days.

When you are finished, press Alt-P (⌘-P) to print your work. Press Alt-S (⌘-S) to save your document. Name it "Lesson38." Exit the word processor.

Mission Assessment

Take two 2-minute timings on the following paragraphs. Following the copy in your book, key the lines on the computer or your typewriter.

```
 1       Your keying skill is gradually
 2  improving.  Very soon you probably will
 3  be keying faster than 25 words a minute.
 4  As you progress, your speed and accuracy
 5  will improve.  You will be very pleased
 6  with your progress.  You will be able to
 7  key papers for other classes.
 8       You should find it much easier to
 9  use the computer now that you have a
10  touch keying skill.  Continue to use
11  proper techniques, and you will find
12  using the computer fun and exciting.
13  Use the computer as often as you can to
14  build your skill.
     | 1 | 2 | 3 | 4 | 5 | 6 | 7 | 8 |
```

Top-Notch Training Tip
Remember, the names
Earth, Sun, and Moon are
capitalized when tied in
with the other bodies of the
Solar System. Other times,
they are not capitalized.

Minimum speed goal:
21 wam
Maximum errors allowed:
6

Block Style

The example letter is keyed in block style. In block style, all lines begin at the left margin. This is a very popular and modern letter style. It is easy to key because no indentions are necessary. In word-processing software, the default margins are usually used. You vary the space between some of the parts of the letter to get the proper vertical placement. For example, you may add extra lines before the return address and between the dateline and the inside address.

Punctuation

The example letter is shown with standard punctuation. In standard punctuation, a colon follows the salutation; a comma follows the closing.

Parts of a Block Style Personal Business Letter

1. **Return Address.** The return address is keyed at the left margin, leaving about two inches blank at the top of the page. This space may be adjusted depending on the length of the letter. When using letterhead, do not key the return address. **Letterhead** is stationery that has the name and address of a company printed on it. Use the two-letter state abbreviation. Leave one space between the state and the zip code.

2. **Date.** Key the date a single-space below the return address. This line includes the month (spelled out), the day, and the year.

3. **Inside Address.** Key the inside address approximately four to eight lines below the date. This space may be adjusted depending on the length of the letter. The inside address usually contains a courtesy title (such as Mr. or Ms.).

4. **Salutation.** Begin the salutation a double-space below the inside address. The salutation usually begins with *Dear* and gives the courtesy title or professional title and the addressee's last name. (The addressee is the person receiving the letter.) If you are on a first-name basis with the addressee, you may use the first name. If you are writing to a company and the person's name is not known, use *Ladies and Gentlemen* for the salutation. For standard punctuation, key a colon after the salutation.

5. **Body.** Begin the body of the letter a double-space below the salutation. The body is usually single-spaced, with a double-space between paragraphs. In block style, paragraphs are not indented.

6. **Closing.** Key the closing a double-space below the body. In standard punctuation, key a comma after the closing.

7. **Signature Block.** Key the name of the person writing the letter four lines below the closing to allow space for the handwritten signature. A woman may indicate the courtesy title that she   prefers with her keyed name. A man does not, however, include *Mr.* with his keyed name. Professional titles may be included with the keyed name.

Galaxy Gazette

You need to practice your newly acquired word-processing skills in preparing an article for the *Galaxy Gazette*.

1. Key the following article in the *Galaxy Gazette*. Punctuate and capitalize as needed. Correct keying errors as you enter the paragraph.
2. Use 1½-inch side margins and a 1-inch margin at the top and bottom.
3. Double-space the copy, which means leave one blank line between each line of the document. To automatically double-space a document, access the format pulldown menu by pressing Alt-D (⌘-D). Move the cursor to the line spacing setting. Press the right arrow key one time to change to double-spacing. Press Enter.

```
the moon is responsible for occurrences
called eclipses that affect the earth.  lunar
and solar are two types of eclipses.  a lunar
eclipse occurs when the earth which revolves
around the sun lies directly between the moon
and the sun.  the result is the sun is
completely within the earths shadow.

in a solar eclipse the moon lies directly
between the sun and the earth.  the moons
shadow is cast over part of the earth.  the
moon much smaller than the earth in size cannot
block all of the suns light projecting down to
earth.  people within the range of the moons
shadow see the total effect of the eclipse but
others may see only a partial eclipse or none
at all.
```

4. Proofread the complete document on the screen and correct any additional errors.
5. Select Alt-P (⌘-P) to print a copy. Press Alt-S (⌘-S) to save the document. Name it "Moon." Proofread the printed copy; mark all undetected errors on the printout. Exchange papers with a classmate who will be your Universal Editor. You will be

Minimum speed goal:
26 wam
Maximum errors allowed:
6

Mission Assessment

Take two 2-minute timings on the following paragraphs. Study the material; then following the copy in your book, key the lines on the computer or your typewriter.

1   A personal business letter is

2 more formal than the personal letter.

3 This type of letter is used when you

4 wish to write about a business-related

5 subject.

6   Personal business letters can be

7 keyed in several different styles.

8 One of the most popular today is the

9 block style. This style is easy to

10 key because all lines begin at the

11 left margin.

12   You will find it helpful to be

13 able to key personal business letters.

14 There will be times when you will need

15 to write to a company or a college to

16 inquire for information. You will

17 also need to know how to write letters

18 of application when you are ready to

19 apply for a job or college. This unit

20 will be very helpful to you.

| 1 | 2 | 3 | 4 | 5 | 6 | 7 | 8 |

Destination—Learn Personal Business Letters in Block Style

Personal business letters are similar to personal letters but have additional letter parts. Study the model personal business letter in block style on page 222. Look carefully at the formatting directions and how the document appears on the page. The letter should be centered on the page with equal margins on the left and right sides and on the top and bottom.

Universal Editor for one of your classmates. Your Universal Editor will edit your article and return it to you for additional corrections.

6. Press the home key to position the cursor at the top of the document, and press Alt-D (⌘-D). Change the side margins to 2 inches and the top margin to 2 inches.

7. Correct any errors you found in your proofreading and those indicated by the Universal Editor.

8. Press Alt-G (⌘-G) to have UKey2 check your work. Highlight *Galaxy Gazette* Score and press Enter. UKey2 now will check your document to see how well you and your Universal Editor completed your task. After you read your score and status, press Enter to save the document. Next select yes to print a copy. Write the name of your Universal Editor underneath your name on the printout.

9. Press Alt-Q (⌘-Q) to exit.

Mission accomplished! Your article has been transmitted to your home office on Earth.

LESSON 39 Learning to Underline Copy

Computers—use default margins for all drills unless otherwise indicated.
Typewriters—use these margins unless otherwise indicated: 10 Pitch 2", 12 pitch 2½".
Single-spacing unless otherwise indicated.

Countdown—Get Ready for Blast-off

Review the countdown procedures.

Launch Review

Key each line two times before moving on to key the next line.

1 Joy said, "Please meet me at 5:30 p.m."

2 The item cost @ $3.98 seemed excessive.

3 Please order #3, #2, & #7 for delivery.

4 See table 1298* for a listing of terms.

5 Practice will refine your keying skill.

In this mission you will:
1. Review comma usage.
2. Underline copy.

Strike the keys quickly.

Keep your eyes on the copy.

LESSON

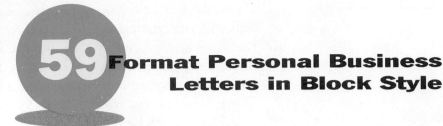

59 Format Personal Business Letters in Block Style

Computers—use default margins for all drills unless otherwise indicated.
Typewriters—use these margins unless otherwise indicated: 10 Pitch 2", 12 pitch 2½".
Single-spacing unless otherwise indicated.

MISSION BRIEFING

In this mission, you will:
1. Improve free-writing skills.
2. Format personal business letters in block style.

Strike the keys quickly.

Keep your eyes on the copy.

Countdown—Get Ready for Blast-off

Review the countdown procedures.

Launch Review

Key each line two times.

1 Were the 986 items for a price of $935?

2 The expert witness was qualified to win.

3 We bought 84 @ $88.93 and 192 @ $137.25.

4 Ask Katrina if she would like to go too.

Mission Report—Free Writing

Using the word processor, write your journal entry. Write about one of the dumbest things you have ever done. Some suggestions include to tell why you did it and how you felt afterward. Did you get in trouble? Would you do the same thing again? Double-space the copy. Print and save a copy. Name it "Jour59."

Galaxy Gazette—Build Word-Processing Skills

Punctuation Review—Comma

Study the following rules.

Use a comma after an introductory infinitive, a participial phrase, or a prepositional phrase. An **introductory infinitive** is a verb preceded by *to*. A **participial phrase** is a verb form used as an adjective. A **prepositional phrase** is a group of words containing a preposition and an object.

From the main menu, select Mission Report and *Galaxy Gazette*. Study and key these example sentences.

Infinitive →

1 To make a decision about the middle school talent
  show, the student council will meet Tuesday
  afternoon.

Participial →

2 Hoping to win the game, the team practiced every
  afternoon.

Prepositional →

3 During the student council meeting, the students
  decided to have a talent show.

Key each sentence once, punctuating as necessary.

1 Forced onto the sidelines by an injury Tom was in a
  lot of pain.

2 Upon receiving his report card Jose expressed a lot
  of excitement.

3 To do well in school Lynn found it necessary to
  study every afternoon.

1. When you are finished, proofread your text on the screen and then press Alt-P (⌘-P) to print a copy. Press Alt-S (⌘-S) to save a copy and name it "Lesson39."
2. Proofread your printed copy and then make any needed corrections on the computer.
3. When you are satisfied with your work, press Alt-G (⌘-G) to have UKey2 check your work. Press Enter to save your work and select yes to print a final copy. Exit the *Galaxy Gazette*.

Using the word processor, write a personal letter to a friend. Tell your friend all about your experiences on the space station. Draft, edit, and print final copy. Name the letter "Perlet3."

Great work.

2"
↓

682 Worthy Lane
Frederick, MD 21701
June 17, 2010

1" →

Hi Bill,

School just got out last week. Finals were hard, but I think I did all right.

I just landed a great summer job. I'll be working as a word processor at a local newspaper, <u>The Galaxy Gazette</u>. That way I'll have a chance to find out if I really do want to be an editor. The people there seem pretty friendly—and the pay isn't so bad either.

← 1"

At my interview, I told them about the trip to see you in August; and they agreed to let me take the time off. My first job and I'll be spoiled! I can't wait to see you. Write soon.

Your friend,

Minimum speed goal:
21 wam
Maximum errors allowed:
6

Take two 2-minute timings on the following paragraphs. Following the copy in your book, key the lines on the computer or your typewriter.

1   Michael Jordan is a professional

2 basketball star with the Chicago Bulls.

3 He is a native of North Carolina and

4 played basketball for the University of

5 North Carolina. In 1982, he led his

6 school to its first national

7 championship in 25 years. He was the

8 captain of the U.S. Olympic basketball

9 team that won the gold medal.

10   Jordan is an excellent role model.

11 He gives unselfishly of his time to

12 many youth groups and charities. He

13 feels that a good part of being famous

14 is being able to help other people.

| 1 | 2 | 3 | 4 | 5 | 6 | 7 | 8 |

Destination—Learn to Underline

Key the following exercises in the open screen option. Follow these directions to underline text on DOS computers.

1. Key the text to be underlined.
2. Use the arrow keys to move the cursor directly under the character where you wish the underline to begin.
3. Select Alt-E to access the edit menu and choose highlight.
4. On the text screen, move the cursor with the right arrow key to highlight all of the text you wish to underline.
5. Press Alt-E. Move the cursor to the underline option and press Enter.
6. On the text screen, follow the message at the bottom of the screen to press Enter to underline text. Notice that the text on the screen does not appear with the underline. The brackets ([ ]), however, indicate that the text will be underlined when printed.

TYPEWRITER TIP

Key the words to be underlined, then backspace to the first character to be underlined. Underline the desired text using the underline key (the shift of the hyphen).

LESSON

58 Review and Compose Personal Letters

MISSION BRIEFING

In this mission, you will:
1. Improve free-writing skills.
2. Review and compose personal letters.

Strike the keys quickly.

Keep your eyes on the copy.

Computers—use default margins for all drills unless otherwise indicated.
Typewriters—use these margins unless otherwise indicated: 10 Pitch 2", 12 pitch 2½".
Single-spacing unless otherwise indicated.

Countdown—Get Ready for Blast-off

Review the countdown procedures.

Launch Review

Key each line two times.

1 Would 54 shares net a profit of $1,689?

2 How did the ball team do in the league?

3 Those were Ana's highest/lowest grades?

4 Going to the water parks will be great.

Mission Report—Free Writing

Using the word processor, write your journal entry. Think about one of the best days you have had recently. Tell about what made this day special. Try to use words that will help the reader understand your special feelings about the day. Be as descriptive as possible in your word choices. Double-space the copy. Print and save a copy. Name it "Jour58."

Galaxy Gazette—Review an Unarranged Personal Letter

1. Use the *Galaxy Gazette* to key and correctly format the personal letter on the next page. Use the default side margins. Set tabs five spaces from the left margin and at the center of the line.
2. Proofread your document on the screen. Correct any keying or format errors.
3. Select Alt-P (⌂-P) to print a copy. Press Alt-S (⌂-S) to save the document. Name it "Perlet2." Proofread the printed copy; mark all undetected errors on the printout. Correct any errors you found in your proofreading.
4. Select Alt-G (⌂-G) and UKey2 will check your document to see how well you completed your task. After you read your score and status, press Enter to save the document. Next, select yes to print a final copy.

On Macintosh computers, follow these steps.

1. Key the text to be underlined.
2. Using the mouse, position the cursor at the beginning of the text to be underlined. Click and drag the mouse to highlight the desired text.
3. Use the mouse to access the edit menu. Click on underline. The text will appear underlined.
4. Click the mouse anywhere on the text screen to remove the highlighting feature.

Exercise

1. Practice keying the following sentences, underlining as indicated.

1 Have you read <u>Fifteen</u> by Beverly Cleary?

2 I enjoyed reading <u>The Black Pearl</u> during the summer.

3 The book, <u>Where the Red Fern Grows</u>, is a popular one with my friends.

4 Have you noticed that many students often misspell the word <u>convenience</u>?

5 <u>Teen</u> magazine has a large circulation among high school students.

2. Select Alt-P (⌘-P) to print a copy. Is the indicated text underlined? If not, consult your instructor and try the exercise again.
3. Select Alt-N (⌘-N) to save the file. Name it "Under."

Shortcut Method

You can underline copy directly from the text screen by using the shortcut keys.

1. Key each sentence and position the cursor at the first character where underlining is to begin.
2. Key Alt-H (use mouse) for highlighting and highlight the text to be underlined.
3. Key Alt-U (⌘-U) to indicate underline.
4. Follow the directions at the bottom of the screen to press Enter to underline text.
5. Select Alt-P (⌘-P) to print a copy.
6. Select Alt-S (⌘-S) to save the copy. Name this one "Undersc" (for underline shortcut).
7. Exit the word processor by selecting Alt-Q (⌘-Q).

Discuss with students the reasons text material is underlined.

Review with students the method for underlining by using the pulldown menus and the shortcut method.

REENTRY
BRIEFING

You're making progress.

2"
↓

Begin at Center
on Line 13
↓

17 Star Zone ← **Return Address**
Mars Outpost
August 5, 2019 ← **Date**

4 lines

Salutation → Dear Jenny,

double-space

I wish you were here at the space camp with me. It is great, and the flight teachers are very friendly and helpful. The food is pretty good—but there's not enough pizza.

double-space

We have 12 girls in my cabin. They come from all over the Earth. We even have 2 girls who grew up on the outpost camp. I have made many new friends, and I know I will have some pen pals after camp.

1" → double-space **← 1"**

We have many fun activities every day. After our flight and science classes, we can spend time in the weightlessness room where we play "keep away"; or we can play video games. Some of the crew members design their own computer games and for fun they make one of us a character in the game.

Body double-space

Every Friday night we have a dance. We all enjoy that a lot!

double-space

Write me as soon as you get my letter, and let me know what you have been doing. I'll be back to the space station in two weeks and have loads of things to tell you about! See you then.

double-space

Begin at Center → Your friend, ← **Closing**

Samantha ← **Signature**

LESSON

40 Learning to Bold Copy

In this mission you will:
1. Review comma usage.
2. Bold copy.

Strike the keys quickly.

Keep your eyes on the copy.

Computers—use default margins for all drills unless otherwise indicated.
Typewriters—use these margins unless otherwise indicated: 10 Pitch 2", 12 pitch 2½".
Single-spacing unless otherwise indicated.

Countdown—Get Ready for Blast-off

Review the countdown procedures.

Launch Review

Key each line two times.

1 Keying skill can help with school work.

2 Many students use computers in writing.

3 Computer programming should be perfect.

4 Jupiter is a giant in our Solar System.

5 They quickly learned the zany exercise.

Galaxy Gazette—Build Word-Processing Skills

Punctuation Review—Comma

Study the following rule.

   Use commas to set off an appositive or appositive phrase from the rest of the sentence. An **appositive** is a word or phrase that renames or explains previously mentioned nouns or pronouns.

From the main menu, select Mission Report and *Galaxy Gazette*. Study and key each sentence.

1 Have you ever been to North Carolina, the Tarheel

  State?

2 The Amazon, one of the largest rivers in the world,

  is in South America.

3 Beverly Cleary, an author of children's books, is a

  very popular writer.

Key each sentence once, punctuating as necessary.

1 All of the students had appointments with Ms.

  Abernathy our principal.

3. Begin the return address at the center of the line leaving two inches blank at the top of the page. Set the top margin. Leave four lines below the return address, so press Enter five times after you key the date. Press Enter after the short lines, but use wordwrap on the paragraph copy.

4. Proofread your document on the screen. Correct any keying or format errors.

5. Select Alt-P (⌘-P) to print a copy. Press Alt-S (⌘-S) to save the document. Name it "Perlet1." Proofread the printed copy; mark all undetected errors on the printout. Correct any errors you found in your proofreading.

6. Select Alt-G (⌘-G) and UKey2 will check your document to see how well you completed your task. After you read your score and status, press Enter to save the document. Next, select yes to print a copy.

Good job!

2 Pluto the smallest of the planets takes 250 years to

make one trip around the Sun.

3 The Big Dipper part of the Great Bear constellation

is the best known star group.

1. When you are finished, proofread your text on the screen and then press Alt-P (⌘-P) to print a copy. Press Alt-S (⌘-S) to save a copy and name it "Lesson40."
2. Proofread your printed copy and then make any needed corrections.
3. When you are satisfied with your work, press Alt-G (⌘-G) to have UKey2 check your work. Press Enter to save your work and select yes to print a final copy. Exit the *Galaxy Gazette*.

Mission Assessment

Take two 2-minute timings on the following paragraphs. Following the copy in your book, key the lines on the computer or your typewriter.

<table>
<tr><td>Minimum speed goal:
22 wam
Maximum errors allowed:
6</td></tr>
</table>

1   Between the Mississippi River and

2 the Rocky Mountains is an area of the

3 United States known as the Great Plains.

4 Lewis and Clark, the explorers, told

5 about the lifestyle of the Native

6 Americans living on the Great Plains.

7 Their way of life was different from the

8 Native Americans living on the East

9 Coast. The Great Plains tribes were

10 divided into groups of 300 to 500

11 people. Every group had a chief.

12   Some of these tribes lived in

13 villages and grew crops. Most of the

14 Native Americans, however, were nomads

15 or wanderers. They followed and hunted

16 the buffalo in order to have food,

17 shelter, and clothing.

| 1 | 2 | 3 | 4 | 5 | 6 | 7 | 8 |

bottom margins. Start the return address at the approximate center of the line. The address of the writer is placed on two lines. The street address is on the first line and the city, state, and zip code on the second. Space one time between the state and the zip code. Two-letter state abbreviations can be used even in a personal letter.   Do not use any punctuation at the ends of these lines.

2. **Date.** The current date is keyed on the line below the return address and in line with it.

3. **Salutation.** The salutation is the name of the person who will receive the letter. The salutation begins at the left margin and is placed four to eight lines below the return address. The amount of space to be left depends on the length of the letter. In a personal letter, the salutation is followed by a comma.

4. **Body.** The body of a personal letter is the message. It begins a double-space below the salutation. Paragraphs may begin at the left margin or be indented five spaces. If the first paragraph is indented, all of them must be indented. Double-space between each paragraph.

5. **Closing.** The closing for a personal letter should be appropriate for a letter to a friend. Some examples are *Sincerely, Sincerely yours,* or *Your friend.* Begin the closing a double-space below the body and align it with the return address. The closing is followed by a comma. Only the first word of the closing begins with a capital letter.

6. **Signature.** You only need to use your first name in the signature in a personal letter. Center it under the closing. Always write the signature by hand, even if you have keyed the letter.

Exercise

1. In the *Galaxy Gazette,* key the model personal letter on page 215. Follow the steps outlined above. Use the default side margins. Use single-spacing.

2. Indent each paragraph by pressing the tab key. Set a tab at the center of the line.   To set a tab, press Alt-R (use the mouse) to access the pulldown format menu. Highlight tabs and press Enter. Choose the number of tabs you want to set.   In this case, you want to set two: one for the paragraph indent and one for the center. Use the arrow keys to change the number and press Enter. This will give you the tab format chart that allows you to set tabs where you want. In 10 pitch, tabs can be set from 1 to 85. Setting a tab at 1 would place your first character on the very left edge of the paper. When you are using the default margin of 10 characters, your first tab must be set at a number higher than 10.

   When you see the tab format screen, set your first tab at 15. This gives you the 10 characters you need for the left margin plus the 5 characters for the paragraph indent. Set your center tab at 42 characters (the center of the page with 10 pitch). Press Enter and your tabs are set.

Shortcut Method
Press Alt-T (⌂-T) to access the tab menu.

Destination—Learn to Bold

On your computer, use Mission Report and the open screen option to complete this exercise. Follow these directions to bold text.

1. Key the text to be bolded.
2. Use the arrow keys to place the cursor where you wish bold to begin.
3. Select Alt-E to access the edit menu and choose highlight.
4. Use the cursor to highlight the text to be bolded.
5. Select Alt-E and the bold option and press Enter.
6. On the text screen, follow the message at the bottom of the screen to press Enter to bold text. The tilde (~) indicates the bold.

On Macintosh computers, follow these steps.

1. Key the text to be bolded.
2. Using the mouse, position the cursor at the beginning of the text to be bolded. Click and drag the mouse to highlight the desired text.
3. Use the mouse to access the edit menu. Click on bold and the text will appear bolded.
4. Click the mouse anywhere on the text screen to remove the highlighting feature.

Exercise

1. Practice keying these sentences, using bold as indicated.

Instead of stars, navigators can now rely on the U.S. Defense Department's Global Positioning System **GPS**. **GPS** is a network of 24 spacecraft orbiting the Earth at an altitude of 11,000 miles.

This new **space navigation system** has receivers that communicate with satellites and show the receiver's position.

The cheapest units (which weigh 2 pounds and cost $1,500) can correctly tell their position to within 15 meters. More advanced units work to within 1 centimeter. Each satellite broadcasts the same radio signal in the same code at exactly the same time--**exact means better than nanosecond (0.000000001 second) accuracy**.

2. Select Alt-P (⌘-P) to print a copy. Is the indicated text in bold print? If not, consult your instructor and try the exercise again.
3. Select Alt-N (⌘-N) to save the file. Name it "Bold."

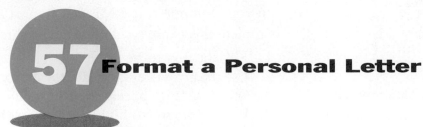

LESSON 57 Format a Personal Letter

MISSION BRIEFING

In this mission, you will:
1. Improve free-writing skills.
2. Format a personal letter.

Strike the keys quickly.

Keep your eyes on the copy.

Computers—use default margins for all drills unless otherwise indicated.
Typewriters—use these margins unless otherwise indicated: 10 Pitch 2", 12 pitch 2½".
Single-spacing unless otherwise indicated.

Countdown—Get Ready for Blast-off

Review the countdown procedures.

Launch Review

Key each line two times.

1 The new computer lab will be 95 sq. ft.

2 Lena's expensive jewelry was misplaced.

3 Nhuan and Trani excel in English class.

4 Your school band will be in a festival.

Mission Report—Free Writing

Using the word processor, write your journal entry. A suggested topic is music. What type of music do you like? Do you like to play, sing, or listen to music? Try to describe the music you like to the reader so that the reader could almost hear it, too. Double-space your copy. Print and save a copy. Name it "Jour57."

Galaxy Gazette—Learn to Format Personal Letters

In a personal letter, you write about things that interest you and the person to whom you are writing. Now that you can key by touch, you can prepare your letters on a typewriter or computer. They will be much easier to read, and you will gain extra keyboarding practice.

Study the model personal letter on page 215. Look carefully at the formatting directions and how the document is arranged on the page. The letter should be centered on the page with equal margins on the left and right sides and on the top and bottom.

Parts of a Personal Letter

1. **Return address.** The return address is the address of the writer of the letter. Begin the return address leaving about two inches (12 lines) in the top margin. For longer letters, you may need to leave a smaller margin. For shorter letters you may need a bigger top margin. Remember that the letter should have equal top and

Shortcut Method

You can bold copy directly from the text screen by using the shortcut keys. Key the paragraphs on the previous page and this time use the shortcut method to bold.

1. Key the sentences and place the cursor on the first character where bold is to begin.
2. Key Alt-H for highlight (use the mouse) and highlight the text to be bolded.
3. Key Alt-B (⌘-B) to indicate bold. Follow the on-screen directions and press Enter to bold text.
4. Select Alt-P (⌘-P) to print a copy.
5. Select Alt-S (⌘-S) to save the copy. Name this file "Boldsc" (for bold shortcut).
6. Exit the word processor by selecting Alt-Q. For Macintosh computers, access the file menu and select quit.

Great flight!

41 Learning to Center Copy

Computers—use default margins for all drills unless otherwise indicated.
Typewriters—use these margins unless otherwise indicated: 10 Pitch 2", 12 pitch 2½".
Single-spacing unless otherwise indicated.

Countdown—Get Ready for Blast-off

Review the countdown procedures.

Launch Review

Key each line two times before moving on to key the next line.

1 On the job, he must function precisely.

2 In business, people have job deadlines.

3 I am interested in your computer class.

4 Voice mail records all electronic mail.

5 Earth is about 8,000 miles in diameter.

2"
↓

LIST OF REFERENCES ← Centered on Line 13

double-space

Billings, Henry F. Introduction to Economics. St.
     Paul, MN: EMC Publishing, 1991.

double-space

Canby, Thomas Y. "After the Storm." National
     Geographic. August 1991. Vol. 180, No. 2, 2-32.

double-space

Fruehling, Rosemary T. and Constance K. Weaver.
     Today's Electronic Office 2nd Edition. St. Paul,
     MN: EMC Publishing, 1992.

double-space

Fruehling, Rosemary T.; Neild B. Oldham; and
     Charlotte Montanus. Microcomputer Applications.
     Eden Prairie, MN: Paradigm Publishing
     International, 1991.

double-space

Lyons, Art and Patricia Seraydarian. The Paradigm
     Reference Manual. Eden Prairie, MN: Paradigm
     Publishing International, 1993.

double-space

Lininger, Skye. "Bar Codes: They're Everywhere."
     Personal Publishing. June 1991, 15-20.

double-space

Smolowe, Jill. "A Game of Chances." Time. 19
     August 1991, 26-30.

double-space

"Thomas Jefferson." The New Encyclopedia Britannica.
     15th Ed. Vol.10, Chicago: Encyclopedia
     Britannica, Inc., 1989.

1" →   ← 1"

↑
1"

Galaxy Gazette—Build Word-Processing Skills

Punctuation Review—Comma

Study the following rules.

Use commas to set off interrupters, parenthetical expressions, or words of direct address from the rest of the sentence. An **interrupter** is a word or words that breaks the flow of a sentence. A **parenthetical expression** is usually a group of words that depart from the theme of the sentence. A **direct address** is using a proper noun, noun, or pronoun to name the person or thing spoken to.

From the main menu, select Mission Report and *Galaxy Gazette*. Study and key each example sentence. Press Enter at the end of each line to divide the sentences as shown.

Interrupter →

1 Yes, I will go with you to the movie.

Parenthetical Expression →

2 He will, of course, be permitted to leave school at noon.

Direct Address →

3 Would you like to go to France for the study program, Jackie?

4 Can you tell us, Tim, what date school will break for vacation?

Key each sentence once, punctuating as necessary.

1 Elizabeth will you be able to complete the science quiz on time?

2 Our strategy of course was to leave as early as possible.

3 Well it's time to run laps again to get ready for tryouts.

4 OK we can all go to the concert.

1. When you are finished, proofread your text on the screen and then press Alt-P (⌃-P) to print a copy. Press Alt-S (⌃-S) to save a copy and name it "Lesson41."
2. Proofread your printed copy and then make any needed corrections on the computer.
3. When you are satisfied with your work, press Alt-G (⌃-G) to have UKey2 check your work. Press Enter to save your work and select yes to print a final copy. Exit the *Galaxy Gazette*.

4. If only specific parts of a reference were used, include the page numbers.
5. The reference page is numbered at the bottom. In a finished report, it would be the last page. In your document for this lesson, you can leave it as page number one.

Exercise

1. Key the list of references on page 211 in *Galaxy Gazette*.
2. Use the default side margins. Do not set a top margin; use the Enter/Return key.
3. The wordwrap feature will not work for this exercise. Press Enter at the end of each line. Press the tab key to indent the second and third lines.
4. Proofread your document on the screen. Correct any keying or format errors.
5. Select Alt-P (⌂-P) to print a copy. Press Alt-S (⌂-S) to save the document. Name it "Refer." Proofread the printed copy; mark all undetected errors on the printout. Correct any errors you found in your proofreading.
6. Select Alt-G (⌂-G) and UKey2 will check your document to see how well you completed your task. After you read your score and status, press Enter to save the document. Next, select yes to print a final copy.

Nice job.

Mission Assessment

Take two 2-minute timings on the following paragraphs. Following the copy in your book, key the lines on the computer or your typewriter.

1   The United Nations was formed to

2 maintain world peace and security. It

3 was formed in 1945 after World War II.

4 The United Nations is made up of

5 nations of the world. A country's

6 membership shows that it is committed

7 to finding peaceful answers to existing

8 or possible problems. Membership is

9 open to all countries.

10   The role of the United Nations as a

11 peacekeeping force has expanded in the

12 last several decades. Worldwide

13 tensions have created a greater need for

14 an organization that can help maintain

15 peace. Hopefully with the leadership of

16 the United Nations, we will see people

17 from all countries living in harmony

18 with one another.

| 1 | 2 | 3 | 4 | 5 | 6 | 7 | 8 | |

Destination—Learn Manual Horizontal Centering on a Typewriter

Sometimes it is desirable to center lines of type on the page. Study the following steps to learn the manual method of horizontal centering.

1. Decide what is the horizontal center of a line of type. The center of a standard size, 8½- by 11-inch, sheet of paper is 42 for 10 pitch and 51 for 12 pitch. (See the Introduction for review.)
2. On the typewriter, space to the center of a line of type. That would be 42 or 51, depending on the pitch you are using.
3. Use the backspace key to move the typing element to the left one time for each two characters or spaces in the material to be

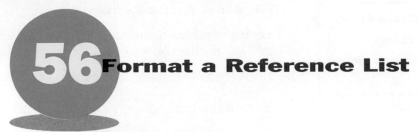

56 Format a Reference List

BRIEFING

In this mission, you will:
1. **Improve free-writing skills.**
2. **Format a reference list.**

Strike the keys quickly.

Keep your eyes on the copy.

Computers—use default margins for all drills unless otherwise indicated.
Typewriters—use these margins unless otherwise indicated: 10 Pitch 2", 12 pitch 2½".
Single-spacing unless otherwise indicated.

Countdown—Get Ready for Blast-off

Review the countdown procedures.

Launch Review

Key each line two times.

1 We needed 35 missions to make the trip.

2 Zar visited a quaint village yesterday.

3 Please call us in time for the speech.*

4 We should do all we can for each other.

Mission Report—Free Writing

Using the word processor, write your journal entry. Think about a product your really like. This could be something you eat or wear. Write an ad for the product. Describe it in such a way that the reader will want it. Double-space the copy. Print and save a copy. Name it "Jour56."

Galaxy Gazette—Learn to Format a List of References

A list of references used for a report should be included as the last page of the report. Any source that is referred to as well as any material that is directly quoted in the report should be included. Consult a style manual for the formats to use in listing the references. One standard format for listing references is illustrated in this lesson.

1. List the items alphabetically by authors' last names. If an author is unknown, alphabetize the reference entry by title.
2. Center the heading *List of References* in all capital letters leaving two inches blank at the top edge of the paper. Double-space between the heading and the first reference.
3. Single-space each reference but double-space between references. That means in the word processor, set the document on single-space and press Enter twice between references. If a reference requires more than one line, indent the second and succeeding lines five spaces by pressing the tab key.

centered. For example, if you were going to center the word *homecoming*, you would backspace five times. If there is a single character left over at the end, do not move the typing element back for that character.

4. Key the text beginning at that point. The text should be centered on the page.

Exercise

Follow these steps now to center the words *Microcomputer Keyboarding*.

Microcomputer Keyboarding

1. Space to the center of the line of type (42 for 10 pitch and 51 for 12 pitch). Key the words. They should be centered on the page.

Say *Mi* and backspace one time.

Say *cr* and backspace one time.

Say *oc* and backspace one time.

Say *om* and backspace one time.

Say *pu* and backspace one time.

Say *te* and backspace one time.

Say *r space* and backspace one time.

Say *Ke* and backspace one time.

Say *yb* and backspace one time.

Say *oa* and backspace one time.

Say *rd* and backspace one time.

Say *in* and backspace one time.

Do not backspace for the single character *g*.

2. For additional practice, center the following. (Remember to not backspace for a single character left over at the end of a line.)

Horizontal Centering

Word Processing Software

Writing on a Computer Can Be Easy and Fun

It's Easy to Compose with a Computer

Destination—Learn Automatic Centering on a Computer

Most microcomputer word-processing software programs have an automatic centering feature. In this program, follow these steps to activate the automatic centering feature. Use the Mission Report and open screen option to complete this exercise.

Microcomputer Keyboarding

PRESIDENCY   ← Line 18

(Insert your name)   ← Line 32
double-space
(Insert your school name)
double-space
Social Studies

(Insert today's date)   ← Line 50

1. Beginning at the left margin, key the text to be centered.
2. Move the cursor to the first character in the line to be centered.
3. Select Alt-E and choose highlight.
4. On the text screen, move the cursor with the right arrow key to highlight the text that you wish to center.
5. Select Alt-E and choose the center option.
6. On the text screen follow the message at the bottom of the screen to press Enter to center the text. To key other lines, move the cursor down to the next line.

On Macintosh computers, follow these steps.

1. Key the text to be centered.
2. Using the mouse, position the cursor at the beginning of the text to be centered. Click and drag the mouse to highlight the desired text.
3. Use the mouse to access the edit menu. Click on center and the text will appear centered.
4. Click the mouse anywhere on the text screen to remove the highlighting feature.

Exercise

1. Center the following lines:

```
Microcomputer Keyboarding

Horizontal Centering

Word Processing Software

Writing on a Computer Can Be Easy and Fun

It's Easy to Compose with a Computer
```

2. Select Alt-P (⌘-P) to print a copy. Is each line centered? If not, consult your instructor and try the exercise again.
3. Select Alt-S (⌘-S) to save the file. Name it "Center."

Shortcut Method

Use the following steps to key the lines above using the shortcut method to center.

1. Key the text.
   ```
   Microcomputer Keyboarding
   Horizontal Centering
   Word Processing Software
   Writing on a Computer Can Be Easy and Fun
   It's Easy to Compose with a Computer
   ```
2. Use the arrow keys to move the cursor to the first character of the line to be centered.
3. Key Alt-H (use mouse) to highlight.
4. Key Alt-Y (⌘-Y) to indicate center.
5. Follow the directions at the bottom of the screen to press Enter to center text for DOS computers. Center each of the lines using the shortcut method.

Mission Report—Learn to Format Cover Pages

Formal reports should have a cover page, which is keyed on a separate sheet of paper. Cover pages are not numbered. A cover page has the name of the report, the author's name (and the person's title, if appropriate), and the date of the report. Additional information, such as the school name, class name, or section number may be included, if needed. Center each line on the cover page.

Look at the example cover page on page 208 for the report keyed in Lesson 53. Use the following formatting instructions.

1. Center the title on line 18 from the top of the page. Key it in all capitals. You may make it bold, too, if you want.
2. Place the writer's name on line 32. Key additional information, such as school or course name, double-spaced below the writer's name.
3. Key the date on line 50.

Exercise 1

1. From the main menu, choose Mission Report and the open screen option. Key a copy of the cover page for "Presidency" in the word processor. Center each line. Proofread on the screen and correct any errors.
2. Press Alt-R to get the format options in the word processor. On Macintosh, use the mouse to access the format menu. Move the highlight bar down to *Number Pages* and press the arrow key to change the option to no.
3. Select Alt-P (⌘-P) to print a copy. Press Alt-S (⌘-S) to save the document. Name it "Prescov." Proofread the printed copy; mark all undetected errors on the printout. Correct any errors you found in your proofreading.
4. If needed, print a final copy.

Exercise 2

1. Follow the directions above and key a cover page for the report in Lesson 54. The title of the report is "Indiana."
2. Insert your name, school name, and a class name. Indicate the report was prepared for one of your classes.
3. Proofread, print, and save a copy. Name it "Indcov."

Great job!

6. Select Alt-P (⌘-P) to print a copy, and select Alt-N (⌘-N) to save a document. When asked if you want to save this document, press Enter to accept yes. Name the document "Centersc" (for center shortcut).

Extended Activity

1. In the open screen, key the following announcement. Double-space the copy.

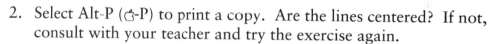

THE STUDENT GOVERNMENT ASSOCIATION
of
KENT MIDDLE SCHOOL
Cordially invites you to attend
the
ANNUAL SPRING BANQUET
on
April 20, 1999
at 7:30 p.m.

2. Select Alt-P (⌘-P) to print a copy. Are the lines centered? If not, consult with your teacher and try the exercise again.
3. Select Alt-S (⌘-S) to save the document. Name it "Announce."
4. Exit the word processor by selecting Alt-Q (⌘-Q).

Great job! You have completed this mission!

your papers, keep them in a journal file for future reference.
Double-space the copy. Print and save a copy. Name it "Jour55."

Mission Assessment

Take two 2-minute timings on the following paragraphs. Study the material; then following the copy in your book, key the lines on the computer or your typewriter.

1   Because of so much traffic in

2 major cities in this country, high-

3 speed trains are being considered.

4 Japan and Europe have successfully used

5 these trains for years.

6   These super trains may reach

7 speeds of 310 miles per hour. One of

8 these super trains is proposed for a

9 Dallas to Houston route. This

10 straight, flat area makes it a good

11 prospect for the super train. This

12 super train would be like a regular

13 train, but changed for high-speed

14 travel.

15   Another type of high-speed train

16 is being proposed for the Orlando,

17 Florida, area. This train will run on

18 magnets, the first in the world. It

19 will take visitors from the airport to

20 Walt Disney World in 6.5 minutes.

21   If these projects are successful,

22 look for other major urban areas to

23 consider similar super trains.

| 1 | 2 | 3 | 4 | 5 | 6 | 7 | 8 |

LESSON

42 Review Format Changes

MISSION BRIEFING

In this lesson you will:
1. Review comma usage.
2. Review format changes.

Strike the keys quickly.

Keep your eyes on the copy.

Countdown—Get Ready for Blast-off

Review the countdown procedures.

Launch Review

Key each line two times before moving on to key the next line.

1 and but for the are you the her met oar

2 He clocked me at 64 MPH, but it was 59.

3 A world goal is to negate nuclear arms.

4 We must learn to cope with fast change.

5 Her new book is nominated for an award.

Mission Report—Build Word-Processing Skills

Punctuation Review—Comma

Study the following rules.

Use commas to separate items in dates and addresses.

From the main menu, choose the Mission Report and open screen option. Study and key each sentence.

1 Our class will go to Washington on April 17, 1995.

2 The school year will end on May 28, 1997, for all schools.

3 My best friend moved to 4982 Elm Place, Chicago, Illinois.

Key each sentence once, punctuating as necessary. Press Enter at the end of each line to break the sentences as shown.

1 Her birthday was February 29 1984 so she didn't know when to celebrate it.

LESSON

55 Format Report Cover Pages

Computers—use default margins for all drills unless otherwise indicated.
Typewriters—use these margins unless otherwise indicated: 10 Pitch 2", 12 pitch 2½".
Single-spacing unless otherwise indicated.

Countdown—Get Ready for Blast-off

Review the countdown procedures.

Launch Review

Key each line two times.

1 Is the correct total for the order $49?

2 A new hero exhibited exceptional valor.

3 How many #2 pencils did Ed order today?

4 The new student was glad to be greeted.

Mission Report—Free Writing

Beginning in this lesson, you are encouraged to include a free-writing exercise as part of each lesson. For this activity your instructor will allow a specific time (three to five minutes). During this time, you are to use the word processor to write without stopping. Do not worry about the correctness of the copy. Just try to let your thoughts flow freely and get as much information keyed as possible.

Your assignment for the free-writing exercises will be to keep a journal. You may include anything you wish in your journal—your thoughts, feelings, activities. Just remember that someone else may read your journal. Some lessons will include suggested topics to help you make your writing easier and more creative.

Journal Entry

In this lesson select an activity that you participated in yesterday. Write as much as you can about that activity in the time allowed. Describe the activity and tell how you felt at the time. Some suggestions include a sport, a test or class, a chore at home, a discussion with your teacher or parents. Do not stop—just write, write, write. Remember, do not worry about correctness at this time.

Some of your journal entries may serve as a basis for a future paper either in this class or other classes. Once your teacher has reviewed

MISSION BRIEFING

In this mission, you will:
1. **Learn free-writing techniques.**
2. **Format report cover pages.**

Strike the keys quickly.

Keep your eyes on the copy.

2 Does it seem possible that it was the week of
December 21-27 1968 that Americans first orbited the
Moon?

3 The address for the Science Museum is 4302 Beacon
Street Los Angeles CA.

When you have finished and proofread your work on the screen, press Alt-P (⌘-P) to print. Press Alt-S (⌘-S) to save your document. Name it "Lesson42." Exit the word processor.

Mission Assessment

Take two 2-minute timings on the following paragraphs. Following the copy in your book, key the lines on the computer or your typewriter.

1   Angel Cordero is a professional

2 jockey. He grew up in San Juan, Puerto

3 Rico, where his father was also a

4 professional jockey. His father trained

5 him to ride horses and taught him to be

6 a fearless rider.

7   In 1962, he came to the United

8 States. Because of his lack of language

9 skills in English, he was unsuccessful.

10 He returned home to improve his language

11 skills and came back to the United

12 States in 1965. He became one of the

13 best jockeys in the world.

14   He is noted for riding every race

15 with skill and possessing a drive for

16 winning. Angel loves horses and plans

17 to train them when he retires as a

18 jockey.

| 1 | 2 | 3 | 4 | 5 | 6 | 7 | 8 |

<u>Interesting Facts</u>

There are several interesting facts about Indiana. Did you know the first professional baseball game was played in Fort Wayne, Indiana, on May 4, 1871? The huggable, lovable, button-eyed Raggedy [Andy] and [Ann] dolls were created in Indiana in 1914 by Marcella Gruelle. The story goes that Marcella found one of her grandmother's old dolls. It was worn and battered. She took it to her father, John, who was a cartoonist. He made a new face for the doll and added two buttons for eyes. He began making up stories for his daughter.

In 1852, a town was named Santa Claus. Now, during the Christmas season, the Santa Claus post office receives more than half a million packages, letters, and cards for remailing with the famous postmark Santa Claus, Indiana.

<u>A Famous Event</u>

Indiana's most famous event, the Indianapolis 500 auto race, is held every year on memorial day weekend. The Indianapolis Motor Speedway is located in Speedway, Indiana. About 300,000 people attend the race.

2

Galaxy Gazette

As a reporter for the *Galaxy Gazette*, you will be required to write many reports using your newly acquired word-processing skills. Practice making format changes to documents by keying the following exercise in the *Galaxy Gazette*. You also must learn to proofread documents carefully if you wish them to be acceptable for publication.

1. Key the following biology article for the paper's science column. Correct keying errors as you enter the text.
2. Use 1½-inch side margins, a 2-inch top margin, and a 1-inch bottom margin.
3. Double-space the copy.
4. Key the title in all capital letters. Center the title and strike the Enter key once after it.
5. Insert commas in the copy as needed.
6. Proofread the copy on the screen and correct any additional errors.
7. Select Alt-P (⌘-P) to print a copy and Alt-S (⌘-S) to save the document. Name it "Skin."
8. Proofread the printed copy and circle any uncorrected errors.
9. Correct your copy on screen. When you are satisfied with your work, select Alt-G (⌘-G) to have UKey2 check your document. UKey2 will see how well you have completed this assignment. After you have viewed your score, press Enter to save the document and select yes to print it.
10. Press Esc to exit the *Galaxy Gazette*.

INDIANA

Indiana is the smallest state in the midwest. It has fertile ground and is a leading farm state, with corn as the chief product. Indiana is one of the nation's top manufacturers of oil refinement and steel. Indianapolis is the capitol and largest city.

The Hoosier State

Indiana is known as the Hoosier State and residents are called Hoosiers. No one knows how the state got this nickname, but there are several ideas. One idea states that the name was taken from a contractor named Samuel Hoosier who liked to hire people from Indiana. Many people believe that the word is a slang expression such as "husher" for a person who could stop a fight or "hoozer" meaning "hill." Some famous Hoosiers include Benjamin Harrison, twenty-third president of the United States; Michael Jackson, a rock star; Larry Bird, a professional basketball player; and Jim Davis, creator of the comic strip "Garfield."

1" →   ← 1"

↑
1"

SKIN

Skin is considered the largest organ of the body. Skin is made up of two layers--the dermis and the epidermis. The epidermis is the outer layer and the dermis is the inner layer. The dermis is thicker and rich in blood vessels and connective tissue. The dermis does not drop away and shed. The epidermis produces the cells of the skin that die and shed and are constantly being replaced.

In addition to connective tissue and blood vessels the skin creates hair nails sweat and oils. The skin is called an excretory because it helps the body get rid of excess water salts and other body waste. Oil glands keep the skin soft and prevent too much shedding of skin cells.

1½" →

← 1½"

↑
1"

LESSON

54 Format a Rough Draft Report

MISSION BRIEFING

In this mission, you will:
1. Format a rough draft report.

Strike the keys quickly.

Keep your eyes on the copy.

Computers—use default margins for all drills unless otherwise indicated.
Typewriters—use these margins unless otherwise indicated: 10 Pitch 2", 12 pitch 2½".
Single-spacing unless otherwise indicated.

Countdown—Get Ready for Blast-off

Review the countdown procedures.

Launch Review

Key each line two times.

1 The car route you take covers 24 miles.

2 The officials were in a quota quandary.

3 We need to allow for a discount on eel.

4 Ken wanted to win a medal for the team.

Galaxy Gazette—Keying a Rough Draft Report

1. Key the following report on page 203 in the *Galaxy Gazette* according to the report formatting instructions. This time, do not set the top margin, but instead press the Enter key.
2. Make the changes indicated by proofreader's marks.
3. Proofread your document on the screen. Correct any keying or format errors.
4. Select Alt-P (⌘-P) to print a copy. Press Alt-S (⌘-S) to save the document. Name it "Indiana." Proofread the printed copy; mark all undetected errors on the printout. Correct any errors you found in your proofreading.
5. Select Alt-G (⌘-G) and UKey2 will check your document to see how well you completed your task. After you read your score and status, press Enter to save the document. Next, select yes to print a copy.

REENTRY BRIEFING

Terrific effort.

LESSON

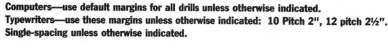

43 Learning Proofreader's Marks and to Move Text

Computers—use default margins for all drills unless otherwise indicated.
Typewriters—use these margins unless otherwise indicated: 10 Pitch 2", 12 pitch 2½".
Single-spacing unless otherwise indicated.

Countdown—Get Ready for Blast-off

Review the countdown procedures.

Launch Review

Key each line two times before moving on to key the next line.

1 seed clip away vats kiln vast blew mast

2 zany avid daze quad swap warp okra your

3 Use Bill's best beaten batter in bread.

4 That shirt company number was 873-3891.

5 His plan for the track has my approval.

Galaxy Gazette—Build Word-Processing Skills

Punctuation Review—Semicolon

Study the following rules.

Use a semicolon between **independent clauses** (clauses that may stand alone) in a sentence if they are not joined by a **coordinating conjunction** (and, but, or, nor, for, yet).

From the main menu, select Mission Report and *Galaxy Gazette*. Study and key each of these examples.

1 We went to the ball game; they chose to go to the
  movies.

2 I wanted to go to Disney World; my parents were not
  interested.

Very short independent clauses without conjunctions may be separated by commas.

The clouds darkened, the rain poured, the winds
blew.

MISSION BRIEFING

In this mission you will:
1. Review semicolon usage.
2. Learn proofreader's marks.
3. Move text.

Strike the keys quickly.

Keep your eyes on the copy.

---

their message to the people. The candidates will be

spotlighted on television and radio. The cost of a

campaign is very expensive, usually costing millions

of dollars.

Election day is the first Tuesday after November

1. This is the day the citizens of the United States

go to the polls to vote for the candidate of their

choice. January 20 is inauguration day. During the

ceremony the elected candidate takes an oath to

"preserve, protect, and defend the Constitution of

1" → the United States."   ← 1"

Key each sentence punctuating as necessary. Key each sentence once.

1 Mars has an extinct volcano called Olympus Mons it is three times larger than Mount Everest.

2 Jupiter is a gigantic planet that is over 10 times larger than Earth.

3 Saturn's rings are over 65 thousand kilometers wide and only a few kilometers thick.

4 Pluto is the smallest of all planets it takes 248 years to make one trip around the Sun.

5 The Milky Way is made up of billions of stars that are very close together our Sun is just one of those stars.

6 The Sun is large it is very bright it has great heat.

1. When you are finished, proofread your text on the screen and then press Alt-P (⌘-P) to print a copy. Press Alt-S (⌘-S) to save a copy and name it "Lesson43."
2. Proofread your printed copy and then make any needed corrections on the computer.
3. When you are satisfied with your work, press Alt-G (⌘-G) to have UKey2 check your work. Press Enter to save your work and select yes to print a final copy. Exit the *Galaxy Gazette.*

2"
↓

PRESIDENCY ← Centered on Line 13

Have you ever thought "I'll run for president when I get older"? In order to run for the presidency a person must meet several conditions that are stated in the Constitution of the United States. First, the person must have been born in the United States. Also, the individual has to be at least 35 years old. Last, the person must have lived in the United States for at least 14 years.

Political parties nominate presidential candidates. They do so at a national convention. The national convention is held two to three months before election day. It serves to draw public attention to the party, raise money for the campaign, and unite party members. The final outcome of the convention is the nomination of the people who will be party candidates for the office of president and vice president of the United States.

Once nominated, the candidates for each party are off to campaign for the election. The candidates hire a staff and travel around the country to deliver

1" →
← 1"

1"
1 ← page number

Minimum speed goal:
23 wam
Maximum errors allowed:
6

Mission Assessment

Take two 2-minute timings on the following paragraphs. Following the copy in your book, key the lines on the computer or your typewriter.

1   We must protect our marshes and

2   wetlands from development if we are to

3   save our plant and animal life. These

4   wetlands are home to a lot of animals.

5   Herons, egrets, and other birds live

6   here. Scallops, oysters, crabs, and

7   shrimp also live in these marshes.

8   Building businesses and homes along

9   many of these marshes can ruin the

10   delicate balance of life. The grass

11   that grows in the marshes is a great

12   source of food for the animal life.

13   Rivers that flow in the wetlands carry

14   food, too. Pollution carried by the

15   rivers into the wetlands can destroy the

16   food the marine life eats. This

17   pollution also can be harmful to the

18   animals that live there. It is not too

19   late to protect these natural lands and

20   help save the animals that live there.

| 1 | 2 | 3 | 4 | 5 | 6 | 7 | 8 |

Destination—Learn Proofreader's Marks

Authors, reporters, editors, and proofreaders use a standard set of marks to indicate desired changes in printed copy. To advance in your work on the *Galaxy Gazette* and prepare quality copy to transmit to your coworkers on Earth, you need to understand proofreader's marks. During the next several lessons, you will be instructed on the use of this set of standard proofreader's marks. In this lesson, you need to learn the following marks:

4. If subheads are used, key them at the left margin. Do not indent them. They should be underlined. Double-space before and after subheads.

5. Number each page. In this software, the page number will be centered at the bottom on the page. To turn on the page numbers, press Alt-D (⌂-D) for the format menu. Move the highlight bar to the correct space and set the software to number the pages.

6. Beginning with page 2, leave a one-inch top margin. Unless you change the default top margin, the software will automatically leave the one-inch top margin.

7. Leave one-inch side margins, which is how the software is set. (For 10 pitch on typewriters, set margins at 10 and 75. For 12 pitch on typewriters, set the margins at 12 and 90.)

8. Leave at least a one-inch bottom margin. That is the default margin in this software (six blank lines). Your software will automatically leave a one-inch margin if you do not change the bottom margin setting. Do not key below line 60.

9. Leave at least two lines of a paragraph at the bottom of a page if you need to divide a paragraph. Carry at least two lines of a paragraph to the top of the next page. You may need to manually divide the paragraph by pressing the Enter key an extra time. (One line of a paragraph left at the bottom or the top of a page is called a **widow.**)

Exercise

1. Key a copy of the "Presidency" report in the *Galaxy Gazette.* Proofread the copy on the screen. Make any corrections using the editing keys.

2. Select Alt-P (⌂-P) to print a copy. Press Alt-S (⌂-S) to save the document. Name it "Pres." Proofread the printed copy; mark all undetected errors on the printout. Correct any errors you found in your proofreading.

3. Select Alt-G (⌂-G) and UKey2 will check your document to see how well you completed your task. After you read your score and status, press Enter to save the document. Next, select yes to print a copy.

BRIEFING

Wonderful.

	Example	**Revised Copy**
Transpose	The outside layer of the Earth is called the crust. It is made of iron ore, gas, oil, water, and other materials	The outside layer of the Earth is called the crust. It is made of iron ore, oil, gas, water, and other materials.
Move as shown 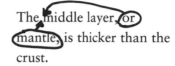	The middle layer, or mantle, is thicker than the crust.	The mantle, or middle layer, is thicker than the crust.
Insert ∧ ∨	In the center is the core. *of the Earth*	In the center of the Earth is the core.

Exercise

Choose Mission Report on the main menu and then select the open screen option. Key the three example sentences.

Cross section of the Earth

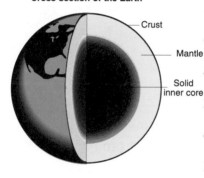

— Crust

— Mantle

— Solid inner core

1. The outside layer of the earth is called the crust. It is made up of iron ore, gas, oil, water, and some other materials.

2. The middle layer, or mantle, is thicker than the crust.

3. In the center is the core.

Correct each sentence using the following steps.

Sentence 1

1. Place the cursor directly under the *o* in oil.
2. Select Alt-H (the mouse) to highlight the word *oil* (include the comma and space following it).
3. Select Alt-X (⌘-X) to indicate you want to **cut** the copy from the sentence. The word *oil* temporarily leaves the screen.
4. Place the cursor directly under the *g* in gas. Select Alt-V (⌘-V) to paste the word back in correct position in the sentence.

Sentence 2

1. Place the cursor in the space before the *m* in *mantle*.
2. Select Alt-H (the mouse) to highlight the space, the word *mantle*, and the comma following it.
3. Select Alt-X (⌘-X) to indicate that you want to cut the copy from the sentence. The word *mantle* temporarily leaves the screen.
4. Place the cursor directly in the space before the *m* in middle. Select Alt-V (⌘-V) to paste the word back in correct position in the

LESSON

53 Format a Report

Computers—use default margins for all drills unless otherwise indicated.
Typewriters—use these margins unless otherwise indicated: 10 Pitch 2", 12 pitch 2½".
Single-spacing unless otherwise indicated.

MISSION
BRIEFING

In this mission, you will:
1. Format a report.

Strike the keys quickly.

Keep your eyes on the copy.

Countdown—Get Ready for Blast-off

Review the countdown procedures.

Launch Review

Key each line two times.

1 Where are 247-44-0742 and 364-659-0321?

2 An icy zone made all the drivers weary.

3 Please bring me Hiteo's book, Adrianne.

4 Are you able to go with me to the game?

Galaxy Gazette—Learn to Format Reports

A **report** sums up an activity or presents facts and information on a specific topic. A report needs to be concise. Report format may be used for book summaries, minutes of meetings, research reports, and class projects and assignments.

A report usually includes a cover page, the text, and, if needed, a reference list. More formal reports may include additional parts.

The format for reports may vary depending on the style manual you are using. Always consult your manual before keying a report. Your textbook uses a standard report format.

Format for Unbound Reports

Study the model report on page 200 and read the following information:

1. For most reports, double-space the body. (Some reports, such as minutes of meetings, may be single-spaced.)
2. Center the title of the report in all capital letters on the first page. The title may be in bold for emphasis. Leave a two-inch top margin on page 1 and begin keying the title on line 13. Pressing the Enter key three times will place your cursor on line 13, and you will not need to change the top margin. Double-space after the title.
3. Indent all paragraphs five spaces.

sentence. Because you also moved the space before *mantle*, you will notice that the spacing between *mantle,* and *middle* is correct.

5. Move the cursor to the space before the *m* in *middle*. Select Alt-H (the mouse) to highlight *middle layer,* (include the comma after it). Select Alt-X (⌘-X) to cut the space, words, and comma from sentence. Move the cursor to the space before the *i* in is. Select Alt-V (⌘-V) to paste the word back in correct place in the sentence.

Sentence 3

1. Place the cursor directly under the *i* in *is*.
2. Key the words *of the Earth* and a space.

After you have keyed the three sentences and made the corrections, proofread your work. You may need to make minor corrections to the spacing of the copy after you have moved text. With practice, however, you will become proficient in moving copy in text.

When you are satisfied with your work, select Alt-P (⌘-P) to print your document. Select Alt-S (⌘-S) to save your document. Call it "Proof1." Proofread your printed document and make any corrections needed. Save your document again if you made changes. Press Alt-Q (⌘-Q) to exit the word processor.

You have completed your transmission!

44 Review Moving Text

Computers—use default margins for all drills unless otherwise indicated.
Typewriters—use these margins unless otherwise indicated: 10 Pitch 2", 12 pitch 2½".
Single-spacing unless otherwise indicated.

Countdown—Get Ready for Blast-off

Review the countdown procedures.

Launch Review

Key each line two times.

In this mission you will:
1. Review semicolon usage.
2. Review moving text.

Strike the keys quickly.

Keep your eyes on the copy.

```
1 try that fable alone verse plaza crease

2 Do worried citizens carry credit cards?

3 The sale of the cats totaled $1,598.31.

4 How do the zany, crazy zebras have fun?

5 Everyone needs to understand the files.
```

Skill Exploration

Take two 30-second timings on the following drill. Try to reach a new speed goal.

1 Traveling can be a fabulous experience.

2 You have the chance to meet new people.

3 Plan your trip so everything works out.

Mission Assessment

Take two 2-minute timings on the following paragraphs. Study the material; then following the copy in your book, key the lines on the computer or your typewriter.

1   Now that you are skilled at

2 keying, you need to give attention to

3 arranging your reports in a standard

4 report format. The way you present

5 your writing depends on what you have

6 written.

7   Many of your assignments are

8 creative writings. These pieces may

9 best be presented with artwork or

10 designs. There are many desktop

11 publishing programs you can use.

12   Formal writing such as research

13 reports, class projects, and minutes

14 of meetings requires different

15 presentation. Formats for these

16 reports will be presented in the next

17 lessons.

| 1 | 2 | 3 | 4 | 5 | 6 | 7 | 8 |

REENTRY BRIEFING

Keep up the good work!

Galaxy Gazette—Build Word-Processing Skills

Punctuation Review—Semicolon

Study the following rules.

Use a semicolon between two independent clauses (complete thoughts) separated by a transitional expression. Use a comma after the transitional expression. A **transitional expression** is a word that shows a change in thought. Some frequently used transitional expressions are *accordingly, consequently, furthermore, however, nevertheless, otherwise, so, therefore, yet.*

From the main menu, select the Mission Report and *Galaxy Gazette.* Study and key each example sentence.

1 New textbooks will be issued this fall; therefore, all students will be assigned homework.

2 I wanted to go to the football game; however, Dad asked me to babysit.

Key each sentence once, punctuating as necessary.

1 The Milky Way is over 15 billion years old however it still contains enough bright stars to create a band of light across the sky.

2 An ordinary star like the Sun lives about 10 billion years but some stars die much quicker.

3 The spacecraft landed at daybreak all the astronauts were relieved to be back on Earth.

4 A black hole in space is a place where gravity is a hundred thousand times more powerful than on Earth so anything that gets too close may be sucked up and disappear from our universe.

1. When you are finished, proofread your text on the screen and then press Alt-P (⌥-P) to print a copy. Press Alt-S (⌥-S) to save a copy and name it "Lesson44."
2. Proofread your printed copy and then make any needed corrections on the computer.
3. When you are satisfied with your work, press Alt-G (⌥-G) to have UKey2 check your work. Press Enter to save your work and select yes to print a final copy. Exit the *Galaxy Gazette.*

LESSON

52 Review and Skill Building

Computers—use default margins for all drills unless otherwise indicated.
Typewriters—use these margins unless otherwise indicated: 10 Pitch 2", 12 pitch 2½".
Single-spacing unless otherwise indicated.

BRIEFING

In this mission, you will:
1. **Improve straight-copy skill building.**

Strike the keys quickly.

Keep your eyes on the copy.

Strike the space bar quickly.

Remember the number reading rules.

Countdown—Get Ready for Blast-off

Review the countdown procedures.

Launch Review

Key each line two times.

1 Why was Fawzia charged $89.95 for that?

2 Try to stop me from sneezing, Sung Won.

3 I'll take Marge Lind's book back today.

4 Do you know why everyone left the mall?

Landing Practice—Skill Review

Key each drill line two times. Try to increase your speed on the second try. After completing all of the drill lines for speed and if time permits, key each line again until it can be keyed with no more than one error.

Improve Stroking Practice (Part A)

Press the tab key between words. Key the drill two times.

1 it is on an me by to as we on no pa pup

2 and for but the wig max two nor oar man

3 much them land game heap leap team poet

4 mum poi are was vet wax car jip lip far

5 get mop vat rat wet cat hip sad fad sip

Improve Tabulation Skills and Number Skills

Press the tab key to put the numbers in columns. Key the numbers across the columns by pressing the tab key between groups and pressing Enter at the end of the line. Key the drill two times.

1 1083	2904	9845	9834	90743
2 8942	8943	8936	0931	98745
3 4983	0959	6302	8309	34592
4 4290	8934	8903	8942	63021

Mission Assessment

Take two 2-minute timings on the following paragraphs. Following the copy in your book, key the lines on the computer or your typewriter.

1   Hummingbirds can give a family many

2 hours of pleasure. You may not even be

3 aware that these little birds live near

4 your house. Place a feeder with the

5 correct mixture of sugar and water

6 nearby, and soon these little birds will

7 be visiting. They will begin to dart and

8 swoop all around the feeder. Be sure to

9 refill the feeder promptly and keep it

10 clean. You wouldn't want these little

11 birds to get a disease from the germs

12 that form on dirty feeders.

13   The antics of the hummingbirds as

14 they fly all around are fun to watch.

15 They appear suddenly at the feeder and

16 then dart off. Their bright colors and

17 flying skills will brighten your day.

| 1 | 2 | 3 | 4 | 5 | 6 | 7 | 8 |

Landing Practice—Review Moving Text

During the editing stage of word-processed documents, you may decide to move text to a different location. As you learned in the last lesson, your word-processing software has a move feature. Moving text is done by highlighting the text to be moved and then following the steps to move the text to the new location.

1. Use the arrow keys to place the cursor directly into the space before the first character of the text to be moved.
2. Select Alt-H (the mouse) to highlight the text to be moved.
3. Select Alt-X (⌘-X) to cut the text from the page. The text leaves the screen and is held in the computer's memory.

TYPEWRITER TIP

You will not be able to use the move feature. You must key the document, edit it, and then key it again if the corrections cannot be made with correction techniques.

Skill Exploration

Take two 30-second timings on the following drill. Try to reach a new speed goal.

1 Do you like to travel? It's great fun.

2 Many interesting places could be close.

3 Why not investigate your own home town?

Mission Assessment

Take two 2-minute timings on the following paragraphs. Study the material; then following the copy in your book, key the lines on the computer or your typewriter.

1   Dating is a chance for young men

2 and women to get to know each other.

3 That has always been the case, but

4 dating patterns have changed.

5   In the 1950s, couples went to

6 dances held in the school gym. These

7 dances were called sock hops, because

8 everyone took off their shoes to dance

9 on the gym floors.

10   Throughout the 1960s and 1970s,

11 teens began going out on "dates" with

12 groups of friends. This included

13 spending time at local hangouts, such

14 as restaurants, theaters, the mall, or

15 a friend's house. Sometimes teens

16 would have parties.

17   Today, dates seem to combine

18 these previous styles. Teens enjoy

19 spending time together in their

20 parents' homes, going to school events

21 together, and having fun with friends.

| 1 | 2 | 3 | 4 | 5 | 6 | 7 | 8 |

REENTRY
BRIEFING

Good job!

4. Use the arrow keys to place the cursor to the position where you wish to insert the text. Select Alt-V (⌘-V) to paste the text back in the document. The text will be inserted in the document at the cursor position. Make any needed spacing additions or deletions.

Exercise

1. In the open screen of the word processor, retrieve the document "Skin" by selecting Alt-O (⌘-O). When you see your documents listed, move the cursor to highlight "Skin."
2. Press Enter to bring the document to the screen. Follow the steps to make the editing revisions to the document.
3. Proofread the document on the screen and correct any additional errors. Select Alt-P (⌘-P) to print a copy. Select Alt-S (⌘-S) to save the file. When asked if you want to replace the document "Skin," select no. Name this revised document "Skin44."

Mission completed.

SKIN

Skin is considered the largest organ of the body. Skin is made up of two layers--the dermis and the epidermis. The epidermis is the outer layer, and the dermis is the inner layer. The dermis is thicker and rich in blood vessels and connective tissue. The dermis does not drop away and shed. The epidermis produces the outer cells of the skin that die and shed and are constantly being replaced.

In addition to connective tissue and blood vessels, the skin creates hair, nails, sweat, and oils. The skin is called an excretory because it helps the body eliminate excess water, salts, and other body wastes. Oil glands keep the skin soft and prevent the excessive shedding of skin cells.

51 Review and Skill Building

Computers—use default margins for all drills unless otherwise indicated.
Typewriters—use these margins unless otherwise indicated: 10 Pitch 2", 12 pitch 2½".
Single-spacing unless otherwise indicated.

Countdown—Get Ready for Blast-off

Review the countdown procedures.

Launch Review

In this mission, you will:
1. Improve straight-copy skill building.

Press tab between each word.

Strike the keys quickly.

Keep your eyes on the copy.

Key each line two times. Press tab between each word in line three.

1 Trade 100 shares of Biomed; buy Medtro.

2 The young reporter had a zest for life.

3 for   the   and   buy   fix   cut   six   quo

4 A new coat is just what Roberto needed.

Landing Practice—Skill Review

Key each drill line two times. Try to increase your speed on the second try. After completing all of the drill lines for speed and if time permits, key each line again until it can be keyed with no more than one error.

Letter Combinations

1 bar barber barge barbecue baste baskets

2 bat batter battle batted bath bear bead

3 bed bedding bedlam began begged berries

4 cab cables cabaret cabbage cache cactus

5 car caret carrots carry case cask caste

6 cave caviar cavity certain certify crab

7 dark darken dare darts deaf dear deaths

8 dew deal decrease deduce deface defeats

9 detach demur deter device devote devise

LESSON

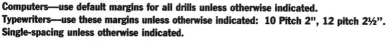

mission
BRIEFING

In this mission you will:
1. Review semicolon usage.
2. Learn proofreader's marks.

Strike the keys quickly.

Keep your eyes on the copy.

TOP-NOTCH
TRAINING TIP

Computers—use default margins for all drills unless otherwise indicated.
Typewriters—use these margins unless otherwise indicated: 10 Pitch 2", 12 pitch 2½".
Single-spacing unless otherwise indicated.

Countdown—Get Ready for Blast-off

Review the countdown procedures.

Launch Review

Key each line two times before moving on to key the next line.

1 pro jump sump lump jolly milk yolk silk

2 beat wade area feat seat brag best stew

3 ford also lake name disk gala dish make

4 Disdain saddened the despot in control.

5 Bring all 2,895 tickets to my 64 desks.

Galaxy Gazette—Build Word-Processing Skills

Punctuation Review—Semicolon

Study the following rules.

   Independent clauses are normally linked by a comma and coordinating conjunction (and, but, for, or). If either or both clauses contain one or more commas, they should be separated by a semicolon.

From the main menu, select Mission Report and *Galaxy Gazette*. Study and key each example sentence.

1 Several new classes were added for the summer session; and Mrs. Browning, our principal, reported that the response to them was wonderful.

2 Several classes visited San Francisco, Oakland, and Sacramento; but they were unable to visit Los Angeles.

3 You, of course, do not need to attend the SGA meeting; but I believe, John, you will find the information helpful.

Fourth-Finger Reaches

1 spa fad map lap sea cab ail pay tap cab

2 pane buzz panic azure equal quart topaz

3 plough azalea quartz stanza zapped quiz

Skill Exploration

Take two 30-second timings on the following drill. Try to reach a new speed goal.

1 A picnic in the creek area is relaxing.

2 It is pretty and the birds are singing.

3 I had chicken, cheese, salad, and cake.

Mission Assessment

Take two 2-minute timings on the following paragraphs. Study the material; then following the copy in your book, key the lines on the computer or your typewriter.

1   Recent fossil discoveries have

2 caused different opinions about the

3 origin of birds. There is a debate

4 among scientists about whether birds

5 evolved from dinosaurs. Some believe

6 that is the case. Another belief is

7 that birds and dinosaurs evolved from

8 a common ancestry. Others discount

9 these two theories altogether. They

10 say there is no link between the two.

11   Many of the top scientists in the

12 world have become involved in this

13 conflict. All of them, of course,

14 believe their evidence. It will be

15 interesting to see what the final

16 outcome of the debate will be.

| 1 | 2 | 3 | 4 | 5 | 6 | 7 | 8 |

REENTRY
BRIEFING

You have completed this mission!

4 Ms. Jarvis, our gym teacher, made us run a mile on Tuesday; but some of the girls could not finish.

Key each sentence once, punctuating as necessary.

1 Many new inventions such as laser technology can be used for space exploration and mining minerals on other planets.

2 About every 77 years Halley's Comet is visible from Earth and it is interesting to note that Mark Twain a famous novelist was born and died on its anniversary.

3 Many space destinations will take years to reach consequently it is possible that several generations could be born during a space flight.

4 There are possibly many new forms of life that may be found as we explore space some could be more intelligent than life on Earth.

5 Some astronomers do not think that we will explore beyond our Solar System but as new forms of space travel are invented the speed of travel may be increased to a point where other solar systems could be reached.

1. When you are finished, proofread your text on the screen and then press Alt-P (⌘-P) to print a copy. Press Alt-S (⌘-S) to save a copy and name it "Lesson45."
2. Proofread your printed copy and then make any needed corrections on the computer.
3. When you are satisfied with your work, press Alt-G (⌘-G) to have UKey2 check your work. Press Enter to save your work and select yes to print a final copy. Exit the *Galaxy Gazette*.

LESSON

50 Review and Skill Building

MISSION
BRIEFING

In this mission, you will:
1. Improve straight-copy skill building.

Strike the keys quickly.

Keep your eyes on the copy.

Computers—use default margins for all drills unless otherwise indicated.
Typewriters—use these margins unless otherwise indicated: 10 Pitch 2", 12 pitch 2½".
Single-spacing unless otherwise indicated.

Countdown—Get Ready for Blast-off

Review the countdown procedures.

Launch Review

Key each line two times.

1 The checks were paid for $289 and $149.

2 The quirky quartet sang many sad songs.

3 Al plans to be at the mall at 1:30 p.m.

4 Will you go to the dance with me, Tony?

Landing Practice—Skill Review

Key each drill line two times. Try to increase your speed on the second try. After completing all of the drill lines for speed and if time permits, key each line again until it can be keyed with no more than one error.

First-Finger Reaches

1 tug nut mum hum bug hub tub but fun mug

2 tutu turn hurt thug ruby hymn humb burn

3 hug thumb brown gruff rascal trend have

Second-Finger Reaches

1 her mid lid ink kit eve cod den vie fee

2 kind keen hike nice week feel tide bide

3 pike picnic recite ticket wedged melons

Third-Finger Reaches

1 to too lot bow sob woo ill owe sly sold

2 know toll slaw soil sole boss will swap

3 swan swollen poodle wallop lesson moose

Mission Assessment

Take two 2-minute timings on the following paragraphs. Following the copy in your book, key the lines on the computer or your typewriter.

1   The discovery of caves in Arizona

2 containing Native American artifacts has

3 been called an important discovery.

4 Artifacts are tools and other objects of

5 ancient civilizations. The most

6 distinctive features found include a

7 large room about 50 feet square and 10

8 feet high. This room had a special

9 entry, benches along each of the walls,

10 and a large firepit in the center. The

11 room was used for religious ceremonies.

12   Nearby is a large building called a

13 pueblo that once contained at least 58

14 rooms. The pueblo provided housing for

15 many families, with one family in each

16 room.

17   This discovery is very important

18 because there is not a lot of

19 information about how these cultures

20 lived. This discovery will provide new

21 facts about life in the Southwest during

22 this time.

| 1 | 2 | 3 | 4 | 5 | 6 | 7 | 8 |

UNIT 4

FORMATTING REPORTS, CORRESPONDENCE, AND TABLES

In this unit, you will realize that there are a variety of ways to use your word-processing skills. You will learn the proper method of formatting reports, correspondence, and tables. You will have the opportunity to apply your knowledge of proofreader's marks to key and format rough draft documents.

This unit begins with several skill building lessons. Use them to concentrate on building your speed and improving your accuracy. By the end of this unit, you should build your straight-copy keying rate to a minimum of 27 words per minute for two minutes with no more than six errors.

You also will have the opportunity in this unit to keep a journal. These activities will help you learn how valuable a tool the computer is for composing and writing. Exercise your imagination and creativity and learn that writing on the computer can be fun and exciting.

Destination—Learn Proofreader's Marks

You already have learned some proofreader's marks. Now you can build your editing skills by learning these new ones.

	Example	Revised Copy
Close up space ⌒	1. Keyboar⌒ding is fun.	1. Keyboarding is fun.
Add space # /	2. Good writing#skills are necessary.	2. Good writing skills are necessary.
Delete ♂ or ℓ	3. Word processors make writing ⟨very⟩ easy.	3. Word processors make writing easy.
Spell out ◯ sp	4. The ⟨U.S⟩ is a wonderful place to live.	4. The United States is a wonderful place to live.
Lowercase lc or /	5. Writing on the ¢omputer is fun.	5. Writing on the computer is fun.
Uppercase uc or ≡	6. c̲o̲me to the game after school.	6. Come to the game after school.
Move left ⊏	7. ⌐Playing sports is great fun.	7. Playing sports is great fun.
Move right ⊐	8. Homework is easier if you have a system.	8. Homework is easier if you have a system.

Exercise

1. Key the eight example sentences in the left column in the open screen of the Mission Report.
2. Correct each sentence using the following steps.

Sentence 1

Place the cursor on the *d* in *keyboarding*. Strike the backspace key.

Sentence 2

Place the cursor on the first *s* in *skills*. Strike the space bar.

Sentence 3

Place the cursor on the space following *very*. Strike the backspace key five times.

Exercise

1. Key the following article in the *Galaxy Gazette*. Make the corrections as indicated by the proofreader's marks as you key it.
2. Use 1½-inch side margins, a 2-inch top margin, and a 1-inch bottom margin.
3. Double-space the copy.
4. Center the title in all capitals. Include the *Gazette's* history expert byline as indicated. Strike the Enter key one time after the byline.
5. Insert punctuation in the copy as needed.
6. Proofread the copy on the screen and correct any additional errors.
7. Select Alt-G (⌘-G) and *Galaxy Gazette* Score. Save and print the document. Name it "Greek."
8. Proofread the printed copy and note any remaining errors, using proofreader's marks.

The Greek Golden Age

By Plato Pluto

The Greek Golden Age was from 500 to 338 B.C. The victories of Alexander the Great spread Greek culture to Egypt and other Near Eastern country. The period of the mixing of the other cultures with Greek culture was called the Hellenistic Age. It lasted from 323 B.C. of 133 B.C. After that time Roman influence became the major force in that part of the world.

Children of free parents received free elementary education. They studied reading writing literature and music. Higher education was private and costly. Secondary schools called The Gymnasium were for children of Greek descent. The students studied physical training philosophy reading writing rhetoric literature and music.

The Greeks believed in the development of the mind body and spirit. Education worked toward this Greek idea.

REENTRY
BRIEFING

You have completed this mission!

Sentence 4

Place the cursor on the period after *U* in *U.S.* Enter *nited*. Press the delete key to delete the period and strike the space bar. Move the cursor to the period after the *S*. Enter *tates*. Press the delete key to delete the period after *States*.

Sentence 5

Place the cursor on the *o* in *computer*. Strike the backspace key one time. Key the letter *c*.

Sentence 6

Place the cursor on the *o* in *come*. Strike the backspace key one time. Key the letter *C*.

Sentence 7

Place the cursor on the *P* in *playing*. Backspace to delete the spaces so the two lines align.

Sentence 8

Place the cursor on the *H* in *homework*. Strike the space bar until the two lines align.

After you have keyed the eight sentences and made the corrections, proofread your work. You may need to make minor corrections to the spacing of the copy after you have moved text. With practice, however, you will become proficient in moving copy in text.

When you are satisfied with your work, select Alt-P (⌘-P) to print your document. Select Alt-S (⌘-S) to save your document. Call it "Proof2." Press Alt-Q (⌘-Q) to exit the word processor.

REENTRY
BRIEFING

Great Job! Your editor at the *Galaxy Gazette* office on Earth is happy with your progress.

Balanced-Hand Reaches

Key each line two times before moving on to key the next line.

1 fox sit oak tie bus bid she pay the end

2 lake name lend lazy dock form foam city

3 bit usual brush rigid ivory cubic cycle

Mission Assessment

Take two 2-minute timings on the following paragraphs. Following the copy in your book, key the lines on the computer or your typewriter.

1   You are making excellent progress

2 in keyboarding development. You now

3 have a touch keying skill on all the

4 alphabet keys and top-row numbers. You

5 have learned the punctuation marks and

6 symbols.

7   In this unit, you learned to use

8 the word processor. Your word-

9 processing skills will be very helpful

10 to you as you prepare papers for all

11 your classes. Be sure to use your newly

12 developed skills at every opportunity

13 that you have. By using these skills

14 frequently, you skill level will

15 continue to grow. You can be proud of

16 your success.

| 1 | 2 | 3 | 4 | 5 | 6 | 7 | 8 |

Galaxy Gazette

In this assignment for the *Galaxy Gazette* you will review many of the skills you have learned in the word-processing unit. You should now be able to key documents in the word processor and make corrections with ease. In addition to articles for the *Galaxy Gazette*, you should begin to use the word processor for your own personal writing.

LESSON

46 Learning Proofreader's Marks and Reviewing Edited Copy

MISSION BRIEFING

In this mission you will:
1. Review colon usage.
2. Learn proofreader's marks.
3. Review edited copy.

Strike the keys quickly.

Keep your eyes on the copy.

Computers—use default margins for all drills unless otherwise indicated.
Typewriters—use these margins unless otherwise indicated: 10 Pitch 2", 12 pitch 2½".
Single-spacing unless otherwise indicated.

Countdown—Get Ready for Blast-off

Review the countdown procedures.

Launch Review

Key each line two times before moving on to key the next line.

1 The orders were for #3742, 8921, & 0421.

2 That referee decreed their new event OK.

3 Ask a quaint usher which exit has value.

4 Did you run into the house to get money?

5 We should make an effort to enjoy games.

Galaxy Gazette—Build Word-Processing Skills

Punctuation Review—Colon

Study the following rules.

Use a colon after an independent clause that introduces a listing of items. Don't forget that two spaces are used after a colon.

In the *Galaxy Gazette*, study and key each example sentence.

TOP-NOTCH TRAINING TIP

1 The principal ordered the following furniture and
equipment for the classroom: desks, chairs,
computers, and maps.

2 Be sure to bring the following equipment for
camping: sleeping bag, flashlight, and warm
clothing.

3 Observe these rules at an interview:

1. Arrive promptly.

2. Dress appropriately.

3. Speak courteously.

LESSON

49 Improving Straight-Copy Rate and Reviewing Word-Processing Skills

MISSION BRIEFING

In this lesson you will:
1. Improve straight-copy rate.
2. Review word-processing skills.

Strike the keys quickly.

Keep your eyes on the copy.

Computers—use default margins for all drills unless otherwise indicated.
Typewriters—use these margins unless otherwise indicated: 10 Pitch 2", 12 pitch 2½".
Single-spacing unless otherwise indicated.

Countdown—Get Ready for Blast-off

Review the countdown procedures.

Launch Review

Key each line two times before moving on to key the next line.

1 We asked to receive parts #1523 & 6789.

2 Hungry hikers harbor high hope for ham.

3 The feast included lasagna and papayas.

4 Once vacations are over, school begins.

5 I will be happy to practice slam dunks.

Landing Practice—Build Keying Skill

Vertical Reaches

Key each line two times before moving on to key the next line.

1 swap math name bravo zenith zippy bunny

2 mast vast mart favors amaze avid yokels

3 vocal color zeal daze tread bacon plaza

Right-Hand Reaches

Key each line two times before moving on to key the next line.

1 oily pupil pulp plunk kiln pomp popping

2 you joins lymph minimum million pumpkin

3 phony mummy loony hippos pulpit purpose

Left-Hand Reaches

Key each line two times before moving on to key the next line.

1 fever beast verse trade evade wave wade

2 bazaar brass crew asset cedar fast daze

3 adverse brass reverse batter stew farce

Now you try. Key each sentence once, punctuating as necessary.

1 Here is a list of the most commonly misspelled words consequently convenience accommodate knowledge and privilege.

2 All students should bring the following supplies to class markers graph paper binders and colored pencils.

3 These rules should be followed to prepare for a test

1. Pay attention in class.

2. Take complete notes.

3. Read and study all text material.

4. Ask questions when you do not understand the material.

1. When you are finished, proofread your text on the screen and then press Alt-P (⌘-P) to print a copy. Press Alt-S (⌘-S) to save a copy and name it "Lesson46."
2. Proofread your printed copy and then make any needed corrections on the computer.
3. When you are satisfied with your work, press Alt-G (⌘-G) to have UKey2 check your work. Press Enter to save your work and select yes to print a final copy. Exit the *Galaxy Gazette.*

Key an **r**, now key an **a**

Like a toy your fingers play.

Key a **p**, a **p**, and an **e**.

You'll spell this right

Now follow me.

Key an **r,** that's what we are

We just spelled **rapper**!

Now hit the space bar!

Chorus (repeat)

Let's end this rap,

It's time to go.

You're learning skills, don't you know.

They'll take you far,

They'll help you out,

Of this I surely have no doubt.

Chorus (repeat)

Now repeat this rap and build your skill,

If Hammer could key, he would love this drill.

You know you're cool; you're no one's fool.

Learn to key and stay in school.

Chorus (repeat)

Press Alt-P (⌂-P) to print your assignment. Press Alt-N (⌂-N) to save your document. When asked if you want to save your work, select yes and name it "Rapper." Press Alt-Q (⌂-Q) to exit the word processor.

You have completed this mission!

Minimum speed goal:
24 wam
Maximum errors allowed:
6

Mission Assessment

Take two 2-minute timings on the following paragraphs. Following the copy in your book, key the lines on the computer or your typewriter. Decide on a goal of increased speed or accuracy.

1   Thurgood Marshall was the first

2 person of African descent to serve on

3 the U.S. Supreme Court. He was born in

4 Baltimore, Maryland. His mother was a

5 school teacher; his father was a steward

6 at a country club.

7   After graduating from Howard

8 University Law School, Marshall

9 practiced law in Baltimore. He served

10 as chief legal counselor for the NAACP.

11 He won national attention for his

12 victory in Brown versus the Topeka Board

13 of Education. The case, argued before

14 the Supreme Court, ended segregation in

15 public schools.

16   Marshall was appointed to the

17 Supreme Court by President Lyndon

18 Johnson in 1967. He retired in 1991

19 after serving a distinguished career.

| 1 | 2 | 3 | 4 | 5 | 6 | 7 | 8 |

Destination—Learn Proofreader's Marks

	Example	Revised Copy
Let stand stet	1. What kind of new stet computer did you buy?	1. What kind of new computer did you buy?
New paragraph ¶	2. Proofreader's marks will help you edit copy.	2. Proofreader's marks will help you edit copy.
Underline	3. Have you read Tom Sawyer?	3. Have you read Tom Sawyer?

To copy text, you will need to key the material again.

Destination—Learn to Copy Text

The copy feature of the word-processing software works very much like the move feature. The only difference is that with the copy feature the text is duplicated in the document in another location. Move deletes text from one position and moves it to another location. Copy makes the text in both locations.

In this program, follow these steps to copy blocks of text from one location to another. Use the open screen option of the Mission Report for this exercise.

1. Use the arrow keys to place the cursor directly under the first character of the text to be copied.
2. Select Alt-H (the mouse) to highlight the text to be copied. Move the cursor with the right arrow until all text to be copied is highlighted (plus any needed punctuation marks and spaces).
3. Select Alt-C (⌘-C) to copy the text.
4. Use the arrow keys to place the cursor to the position where you wish to insert the text. Select Alt-V (⌘-V) to paste the text in the document at the new location. The text will be automatically inserted in the document at the cursor position. Make any needed spacing additions or deletions.

Exercise

Key the following exercise in the open screen of the word processor. Key the chorus the first time and then follow the steps above to copy the chorus after each verse.

```
Learning writing can be fun.

No mistakes, I say none.

Your fingers walk

Your fingers talk

The rapper's write has just begun.


(Chorus)

You know, you know, you know,

You have to learn this!

You know, you know, you know,

You have to practice!

You know, you know, you know,

You have to key this!

Now dance your fingers!
```

Bold 	4. The help wanted ad was titled word processor.	4. The help wanted ad was titled **word processor.**
Run in	5. Effective studying will improve your grades.	5. Effective studying will improve your grades.
Single-space **SS**	6. Work hard in school. You will be rewarded.	6. Work hard in school. You will be rewarded.
Double-space **DS**	7. Do you enjoy sports? Which one is your favorite?	7. Do you enjoy sports? Which one is your favorite?

Exercise

1. Select the open screen option and key the example sentences.
2. Correct each sentence using the following steps.

Sentence 1

No corrections needed.

Sentence 2

Place the cursor on the *P* in *Proofreader's* and strike the tab key.

Sentence 3

Highlight the name of the book using the Alt-H (⌘-H) keys and use the underline feature by pressing Alt-U (⌘-U).

Sentence 4

Highlight *word processor* using the Alt-H (⌘-H) keys and use the bold feature by pressing Alt-B (⌘-B).

Sentence 5

Place the cursor on the *y* in *your*. Strike the backspace key until the text moves to the previous line.

Sentence 6

Change the line spacing for the document to single-spacing by using the format menu (Alt-D or ⌘-D). Press Alt-P (⌘-P) to print the document and see single-spacing.

Sentence 7

Change the line spacing for the document to double-spacing. Press Alt-P (⌘-P) to print the document and see double-spacing.

After you have completed all the sentences and are satisfied with your work, press Alt-N (⌘-N) to save your work. Call it "Proof46." Press Alt-Q (⌘-Q) to exit the word processor.

REENTRY
BRIEFING

Good job!

Minimum speed goal:
24 wam
Maximum errors allowed:
6

Mission Assessment

Take two 2-minute timings on the following paragraphs. Following the copy in your book, key the lines on the computer.

1   Leontyne Price was known as the

2 queen of the opera. She worked very

3 hard to gain this reputation. After

4 graduating from high school, she decided

5 to become a teacher and earned a degree

6 from Central State College in Ohio.

7 During her senior year, Price was

8 encouraged to apply for a scholarship in

9 music at the Julliard School of Music in

10 New York.

11   Ira Gershwin heard Price sing and

12 gave her a role in "Porgy and Bess."

13 She was known as the girl with the

14 golden voice and sang at the opening of

15 the Metropolitan Opera House. In 1955,

16 she was given the title role in the

17 opera "Tosca" and performed on

18 television.

19   Price received numerous

20 international awards and is recognized

21 as a great opera star. She feels that

22 the key to her success is that she loves

23 to sing and perform.

| 1 | 2 | 3 | 4 | 5 | 6 | 7 | 8 |

LESSON 47 Review Editing Copy

MISSION BRIEFING

In this lesson you will:
1. Review colon usage.
2. Review edited copy.

Computers—use default margins for all drills unless otherwise indicated.
Typewriters—use these margins unless otherwise indicated: 10 Pitch 2", 12 pitch 2½".
Single-spacing unless otherwise indicated.

Countdown—Get Ready for Blast-off

Review the countdown procedures.

Launch Review

Key each line two times before moving on to key the next line.

1 Send Al two giant balloons @ $.58 each.

2 Can Sal afford a fourth frantic fencer?

3 The azure sky made quite an excitement.

4 Keep up the good work so target is met.

5 Keep trying to improve the skill level.

Mission Report—Build Word-Processing Skills

Punctuation Review—Colon

Study the following rule.

Use a colon after the salutation of a business letter and in expressions of time.

Select Mission Report and the open screen option to key each example.

1 Dear Arthur: Dear Mrs. Flanigan:

2 Ladies and Gentlemen:

3 She will arrive at 8:30 a.m. on Wednesday, April 15.

Key each sentence once, punctuating as necessary.

1 The train will leave the station at 1220 pm on

Tuesday February 20 1997.

2 Dear Joao

Thank you for your quick response to my letter. I

will meet you at 1030 am on January 5 1995.

When you are done, press Alt-P (⌘-P) to print your work. Press Alt-N (⌘-N) to save the document. Name it "Lesson47."

LESSON

48 Learning to Copy Text

MISSION
BRIEFING

In this mission, you will learn how to:
1. Copy text.

Strike the keys quickly.

Keep your eyes on the copy.

Computers—use default margins for all drills unless otherwise indicated.
Typewriters—use these margins unless otherwise indicated: 10 Pitch 2", 12 pitch 2½".
Single-spacing unless otherwise indicated.

Countdown—Get Ready for Blast-off

Review the countdown procedures.

Launch Review

Key each line two times before moving on to key the next line.

1 Your #76803 order was shipped 10/14/91.

2 Eggs and gravy for the gang gave glory.

3 Quin excelled in robust exhibit prizes.

4 Your new composition skills are useful.

5 You're going to be a very good student.

Galaxy Gazette—Build Word-Processing Skills

From the main menu, select Mission Report and *Galaxy Gazette.* Key this paragraph once, adding correct the punctuation. This exercise will help you review the punctuation rules you have learned in the previous chapters.

Dear Qian

I am planning to arrive on Jupiter on March 7 2022

and would like to meet with you however if that date

is not convenient for you I could reschedule.

Please Qian let me know your plans. I look forward

to meeting with you hope to hear from you soon.

1. When you are finished, proofread your text on the screen and then press Alt-P (⌘-P) to print a copy. Press Alt-S (⌘-S) to save a copy and name it "Lesson48."
2. Proofread your printed copy and then make any needed corrections on the computer.
3. When you are satisfied with your work, press Alt-G (⌘-G) to have UKey2 check your work. Press Enter to save your work and select yes to print a final copy. Exit the *Galaxy Gazette.*

Mission Assessment

Take two 2-minute timings on the following paragraphs. Following the copy in your book, key the lines on the computer or your typewriter.

1   In 1988, major league baseball

2 pitcher Orel Hershiser pitched 59

3 straight scoreless innings breaking a

4 20-year record. His team, the Los

5 Angeles Dodgers, won the World Series;

6 and he was named the Most Valuable

7 Player. In addition, he won the Cy

8 Young award for pitching.

9   In high school, Hershiser was cut

10 from the baseball team. He worked very

11 hard and was later a starting baseball

12 player for his school. After graduating

13 from school, he was drafted by the

14 Dodgers. His minor league career was

15 fairly poor, and he considered quitting

16 several times. Finally, however, he

17 moved up to the majors.

18   Within a short period, Hershiser

19 became a starting pitcher and went on to

20 achieve star status. He proves that

21 with hard work you can be a success even

22 though at times it may look impossible.

| 1 | 2 | 3 | 4 | 5 | 6 | 7 | 8 |

Galaxy Gazette

As part of your work as a reporter for the *Galaxy Gazette*, you have been asked to prepare the following report for final publication.

1. Key the following article in the *Galaxy Gazette*. Make the corrections as indicated by the proofreader's marks as you key it. As you enter the text, correct any keying errors you may make.
2. Use 1½-inch side margins, a 2-inch top margin, and a 1-inch bottom margin.
3. Double-space the copy.
4. Key the title in all capital letters and center it. Include a byline as a part of the title. A **byline** is where you list your name so readers will know you wrote the article. In this case, use the byline of the fashion editor. Insert her name as indicated. Strike the Enter key one time after the byline.
5. As you are keying, insert punctuation in the copy as needed.
6. Proofread the copy on the screen and correct any additional errors. Select Alt-G (⌂-G) and *Galaxy Gazette* Score. Your article will be checked by UKey2 to see if it is ready for publication. Save and print the document. Name it "Ornament."
7. Proofread the printed copy and note any remaining errors.

Ornaments

By Desiree Gilardo

The custom of wearing body ornaments such as necklaces may have started with creative people. Scientific discoveries of artifacts have revealed necklaces made from animal parts.

For instance scientists have found beads carved from a mammoth tusk a string of snail shells and a necklace made of the teeth of an animal.

The true purpose of the ornaments will never be known however they may have been used for making the wearer beautiful. Perhaps the tooth necklace stood for an individual's strength & success as a hunter and each tooth displayed a beast killed in a past hunt. Perhaps the necklaces warded off evil spirits. *it was believed that*

You have completed this mission!